THE MURDER CLUB

"Well, I do not like accidents," replied Mrs Mush. "there's no meaning in them: but," she added confidentially, "I dearly like a murder. Of course I do not wish for murders," she continued, in a tone of resigned virtue: "but when there is one, why, I like it. It is human nature."

(Julia Kavanagh, *Sybil's Second Love*, 1867)

THE MURDER CLUB

Guide to

SOUTH-WEST ENGLAND AND WALES

Devised and Edited by Brian Lane

HARRAP
London

ACKNOWLEDGEMENTS

Sincere thanks go primarily to Derek Johns, former Publishing Director of Harrap, whose imaginative response to the proposal for these *Guides* provided their initial impetus, and whose continued encouragement and practical support have ensured their realization. Thanks also to our editor, Roy Minton, whose knowledge and understanding has saved us from more than a few pitfalls; and to Tim Pearce, who helped turn our ideas into books.

On the Murder Club side there are people too numerous to mention whose contributions to our Archive of illustrations and texts have made the compilation of these books possible. In particular, credit must be given to Steve Wheatley, whose work on the overall concept of the *Murder Club Guides* was of immense value, as were his written contributions to Volume One. And to John Bevis whose creative application to the layout and overall appearance has helped make the concept a tangible reality.

For the kindness and generosity we have been shown in scores of libraries and museums, large and small, all over Britain, and for all those people who knew about things and were willing to share, we hope these books may represent our thanks.

First published in Great Britain 1989
by HARRAP Ltd
19-23 Ludgate Hill, London EC4M 7PD

ISBN 0 245 54686 3

Designed by Brian Lane and John Bevis

Printed by Biddles Limited,
Guildford and King's Lynn

THE MURDER CLUB
GUIDE TO SOUTH-WEST ENGLAND
AND WALES

CONTENTS

General Introduction

On Apologias

Madame Life's a piece in bloom
Death goes dogging everywhere;
She's the tenant of the room,
He's the ruffian on the stair.
(W.E. Henley, 1849-1903)

A disturbing by-product of the new fashionable 'humanism' and its inseparable partner 'attitude-baring' is that the individual is under constant pressure to apologize for his passions. And nothing needs an apologia quite as much as a fascination with the darker sides of humankind.

There can be few notions more difficult to promote than that an interest in, say, the ritual of Magic does not of itself lead to nocturnal harvesting of the parish graveyard; or that a diet of gangster movies results in St Valentine's Day madness. An interest in crime is viewed as decidedly sinister; but a fascination with the crime of Murder – be it as academic or aficionado – renders a person particularly vulnerable, particularly in need of an apologia.

And so, for all those members, and prospective members, and closet members of The Murder Club; for all those readers of these, its regional *Guides*, here are some excellent precedents for our common need to justify.

One of the earliest examples can be found in the first issue of what was to become a popular illustrated weekly paper for a number of years around the turn of the century. Though its name was *Famous Crimes Past and Present*, like so many similar magazines of the period "crime" meant "murder". Editor Harold Furniss wrote, "Down the vista of crime which stretches from the first transgression of our Father Adam to the last little boy punished for stealing a pennyworth of sweets, there stand at intervals landmarks – milestones, as it were – on the road of iniquity. These are the doings of great criminals, of men whose cunning, wicked-ness or brutality have thrown out their lives into relief against the sordid background of everyday transgressors. It is of these that we propose to write, and we do so with a two-fold purpose; firstly that those who are interested in criminology, and desirous of furthering the science by which the moral welfare of the country is preserved may have before them a reliable record of typical criminals; and secondly, that as the natural bent of man tends towards crime, we may provide him with reading matter, interesting and dramatic, which will afford him food for thought."[1]

That there was a lighter side to the "interest in criminology" even earlier is evidenced by David Jardine's *Criminal Trials* being published, in 1835, by The Society for the Diffusion of Useful Knowledge as part of its series 'The Library of Entertaining Knowledge'. Just why such material should be considered 'Entertaining' is spelt out by another chronicler of the Courts, Horace Wyndham: "Of course, the real truth is (as De Quincey, who was something of a connoisseur on such matters, has asserted) crime in itself is intrinsically interesting. We may protest to the contrary, but there is no getting over the fact that the traffic of the dock does make an appeal. An extended one, too. Still, there is abundant reason for this. After all, 'crime books' are concerned with human happenings, with real life, with the stir and fret and thrill of everyday occurrences. Again, crime is essentially dramatic, and touches the whole emotional gamut. Thus, there is tragedy; there is comedy; there is melodrama; and there is occasionally sheer farce. Even romance, too, at times. Anyway, plot and passion and swift moving incident from the rise to the fall of the curtain. Hence, not nearly so astonishing that such volumes are popular as that they are not still more popular."[2]

Other writers have sought to give equal stress to the 'Useful' and to the 'Entertaining' sides of the crime story. Few people have done more consistently to popularize the twilight world of the criminal than the much respected writer, broadcaster, and former barrister, Edgar Lustgarten: "The main aim of one approach is to probe psychology – and thereby to illuminate and instruct. The main aim of the other is to tell a story – and thereby to divert and entertain."[3] But whichever of these two caps Mr Lustgarten chooses to wear, he is clear on the moral foundation of his apologia, "Certainly the arrangement adopted in the construction of the book does not signify any departure by the author from the received opinion that murder is the wickedest and gravest of all crimes."[4]

A different approach is taken by Colin Wilson, whose prolific path has taken him through such dangerous territory as Black Magic, Extra-Terrestrialism, ESP, Assassination, and Murder. One of his contentions is that the study of murder is a necessity – indeed, an obligation – if one is to understand the counter-balance, which is man's great creative potential. We have to be very grateful to Wilson for much of our contemporary understanding of 'criminality', though it is an approach which has has led to accusations of pomposity – not much dispelled by his published feelings about some fellow-authors: "It will be observed that my references to certain other writers on murder – particularly Edmund Pearson, William Roughead and William Bolitho – are hardly complimentary. I dislike the 'murder for pleasure' approach. I consider this book, like the *Encyclopaedia of Murder*, as a tentative contribution to a subject that does not yet exist as a definite entity, a science that has not yet taken shape."[5] Wilson's co-author on the *Encyclopaedia of Murder* was Patricia Pitman, who took a rather less pedantic view of the task in hand, concluding that the fascination with murderers is that they are so utterly different from us, and that that fascination is perfectly natural. Further, she brings a refreshing down-to-earthness to it all by adding that, aside from psychological justifications, the *Encyclopaedia* can provide "...plots for novels, questions for quizes, and innocent entertainment for eerie winter evenings."[6]

But what of the "murder for pleasure" approach so despised by Wilson?

The late Edmund Pearson, tireless recorder of the classic American murders and controversial authority on the Lizzie Borden case

does, it is true, seem to take a wholesome relish in the retelling of a great murder story; England's own 'Brides in the Bath' killer, George Joseph Smith, he laments as a man "who only went to ruin because, like so many great artists, he could not resist one more farewell performance" [see *Murder Club Guide No.2*].[7] In the essay 'What Makes a Good Murder?', Pearson treats 'collectors' of murders with the respect that he feels due to a discerning cognoscente, noting that "...failure to recognise the elementary principle of an attractive murder is characteristic of many who should be better informed".[8]

Back on this side of the Atlantic, Pearson would recognize a soul-mate in Nigel Morland, who steers a course happily between detective fiction and criminology; he too is adamant about quality in a murder – "the critical eyes of aficionados recognise two distinct divisions of murder in the United States. There are the common-or-garden majority, whose ultimate destiny is the pages of popular magazines with lurid covers. The second, numerically minute, division is concerned with murders acceptable to the discerning taste, and here time has made certain classics".[9]

Edward Spencer Shew was one of the pioneers, with Wilson and Pitman, of the encyclopaedic approach to the recording of murder, and in the frank introduction to his indispensible *Second Companion to Murder*, Shew comes dangerously close to appearing to enjoy his subject: "Here the emphasis falls upon naked violence, raw and uncompromising, like the mallet strokes which destroyed Francis Mawson Rattenbury [see *Murder Club Guide No.6*], or the blows of the iron-stone brick with which Irene Munro was battered to death upon the sands of the Crumbles [see *Murder Club Guide No.2*]. Here murder wears its most savage face;[10] a face that Ivan Butler recognises: "it is in the strange vagaries of human behaviour that the persisting interest lies...the bizarre, the mysterious, the tragic, the gruesome, the just plain vicious".[11]

Two novel and distinguished vindications are advanced by Gordon Honeycombe in his introductory pages to *The Murders of the Black Museum* – "But the Black Museum made me realise what a policemen must endure in the course of of his duty; what sights he sees, what dangers he faces, what depraved and evil people he has to deal with so that others may live secure".[12] And later, "Murder is a very rare event in England. Its exceptional nature is in fact part of its fascination."

A counterpoint to this approach is provided by journalistic investigators, such as Paul Foot and Ludovic Kennedy. Their immediate motivation is the righting of a particular injustice, but they also have a wider purpose. As Kennedy writes in his introduction to 'Wicked Beyond Belief': "...once we start selecting those whom we think worthy or unworthy of Justice, we shall all in the end be diminished; for even if Justice is sometimes rough in practice, it is not for Cooper and McMahon alone that this book has been assembled; but for all those who, if Justice is allowed to go by default, may come to suffer in their time."[13] Kennedy's intention is to expose those attitudes and processes of the police, the courts, lawyers and judges which create an institutional tendency towards injustice.

A more academic, but no less absorbing, motive for the study of Murder derives from the fact that murder cases have tended to be so much better documented than the less notorious fields of human endeavour. The wealth of detailed information which can be gleaned from Court testimony and newspaper reports provides an eloquent picture of the everyday behaviour, social conditions, and moral attitudes of times past. We would, undoubtedly, be far more ignorant of conditions in London's East End in the 1880s if it were not for Jack the Ripper; the description of repressive middle-class life presented by the cases of Dr Crippen and Major Armstrong [see *Murder Club Guide No.4*] is, surely, as vivid as any novelist could invent; an examination of the predicament of Florence Maybrick [see *Murder Club Guide No.3*] or Edith Thompson provides a telling case study of the moral taboos of their time.

To be generous to the field, an example should be given of the "There but for the Grace of God..." argument. Take Tony Wilmot's introduction to *Murder and Mayhem*, "Why do we like reading crime stories, especially murder? For murder, that most heinous of crimes, both horrifies and fascinates at one and the same time...Could it be that deep down, we suspect that we are capable of committing murder, or other serious crimes, if we knew we could get away with it? That, perhaps, the only thing that holds us back is the fear of being caught and paying the price?"[14]

Probably not. But the one certainty is that there are as many reasons for a fascination with the "ruffian on the stair" as there are people to be fascinated by him.

References

[1] *Famous Crimes Past and Present*, Ed. Harold Furniss. Vol.1. No.1, 1903.
[2] *Famous Trials Retold*, Horace Wyndham. Hutchinson, London, 1925.
[3] *Illustrated Story of Crime*, Edgar Lustgarten. Weidenfeld and Nicolson, London, 1976.
[4] *Ibid.*
[5] *A Casebook of Murder*, Colin Wilson. Leslie Frewin, London, 1969.
[6] *Encyclopaedia of Murder*, Colin Wilson and Patricia Pitman. Arthur Barker, London, 1961.
[7] *Masterpieces of Murder*, Edmund Pearson.
Hutchinson, London, 1969.
[8] *Ibid.*
[9] *Background to Murder*, Nigel Morland. Werner Laurie, London, 1955.
[10] *Second Companion to Murder*, E. Spencer Shew. Cassell, London, 1961.
[11] *Murderers' London*, Ivan Butler. Hale, London, 1973.
[12] *Murders of the Black Museum 1870-1970*, Gordon Honeycmbe. Hutchinson, London, 1982.
[13] *The Luton Murder Case*, Ed. Ludovic Kennedy. Granada Publishing, London, 1980.
[14] *Murder and Mayhem*, Ed. Tony Wilmot. Harmsworth Publications, London, 1983.

Maps

The complexity of Britain's road system – particularly around the crowded inner-city areas – makes it impractical to provide a detailed road map to the regions covered in this series of *Guides*. Instead, individual cases are accompanied by a map of the immediate area, marked where possible with the nearest British Rail station as well as locational information relevant to the text.

To give an overview of the areas covered, each county is prefaced by a map on which the murder sites are numerically plotted and listed.

KEY TO MAPS

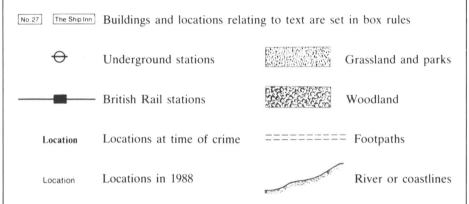

No.27 / The Ship Inn — Buildings and locations relating to text are set in box rules

⊖ — Underground stations

▬ — British Rail stations

Location — Locations at time of crime

Location — Locations in 1988

Grassland and parks

Woodland

========== Footpaths

River or coastlines

Location Photographs

In keeping with the status of this series of books as Guides, maps have been supplemented, where possible and appropriate, with photographs of buildings and locations relevant to the crime under discussion; in many cases, however, the precise spot on a landscape has been buried either by time or by the ubiquitous developer. Further research may unearth more precise information, and the compilers would be most grateful to receive it.

Public houses come quite naturally to the foreground in many of these cases, and provide a genuine excuse for refreshment in the amateur 'murder hunt'; but it should be remembered that those many private houses whose history has been blackened by dark deeds are not public monuments, and their present occupants' privacy should be respected.

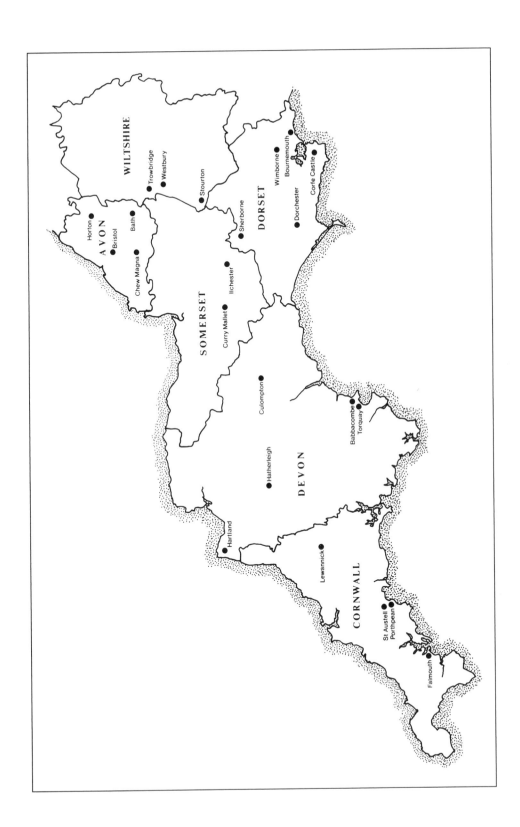

WILTSHIRE

● Trowbridge
● Westbury

● Stourton

AVON

● Horton
● Bristol
● Bath
● Chew Magna

DORSET

● Wimborne
● Bournemouth
● Corfe Castle
● Dorchester

● Sherborne

SOMERSET

● Curry Mallet
● Ilchester

● Culompton

DEVON

● Babbacombe
● Torquay

● Hatherleigh

● Hartland

CORNWALL

● Lewannick

● St Austell
● Porthpean

● Falmouth

THE MURDER CLUB

Background

In the October of 1985, when Steve Wheatley and I first began to mould our mutual interest in Crime and Criminology into some more tangible form, it was as an occasional fireside activity. The first manifestation was the manuscript for a book of Execution Broadsheets. From there, as winter deepened, and the fireside became host to more frequent discussion, the ambitious concept for a new kind of periodical devoted to the Crime of Murder began to creep from our meditations. And the more of the blood-red wine that was sipped, and the more nimbly the shadows from the flickering flames darted about the room, the more of a good idea it seemed. It even stood up to the cold, thin reality of winter daylight.

It was, we decided, to be called *The Murder Club Bulletin* – though heaven knows why, the 'Club' wasn't due to emerge from the moving shadows until the next season's firelight. Indeed, at the time the first rough plans were put on to paper the 'Club' fitted round the editorial desk with more than enough room to spare.

It must have been around the mid-winter of 1986 that somebody said something like: "We've got the *Murder Bulletin*, what about the *Club*?"

I should say, though, that in the intervening months we had gradually begun to put together what will become a complete regional documentation of British Murders since the beginning of the seventeenth century; it's a big job. People in various parts of the country heard about it, and started to send us things – notes about famous local murders, regional press cuttings, pictures. We discovered people like Mr Mackintosh who had traced the last resting place of Bella Wright, the victim of the Green Bicycle Mystery in 1919, and had set up a fund to give Bella a modest memorial. We were becoming a Club!

Discussion began to revolve more and more around what we, as committed enthusiasts, would want out of a Murder Club if we were 'them'. The list on page 191 reveals some of those decisions which have already been adopted; other paths await discovery.

So, in the middle months of 1987 we had a prototype *Bulletin*, we had the partially clad skeleton of *The Murder Club,* and we had something else – we had a series of books demanding to be written; a series of Guides to the darker sides of Britain's landscape. Then came our first meeting with Harrap – long-established publishers of true-crime works – and their Publishing Director, Derek Johns. Derek it was who responded enthusiastically to the proposal for a series of eight *Murder Club Regional Guides;* Derek it was who enthusiastically adopted the suggestion to launch *The Murder Club* on the same date as the first four books – on the 30th of June, this year. And by the next season of flickering fires, Criminology will no longer be the exclusive preserve of the scientists, the lawyers, and the journalists. Our Members will already have become arm-chair detectives.

Brian Lane

London
April 1988

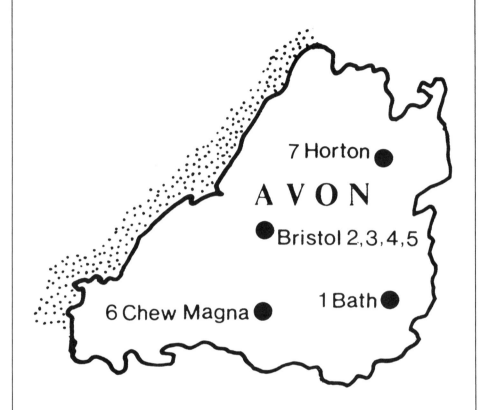

7 Horton ●

AVON

● Bristol 2, 3, 4, 5

6 Chew Magna ●   1 Bath ●

Avon

The Terminal Greed of Reginald Hinks

The Murder of JAMES PULLEN
by REGINALD IVOR HINKS
on Friday December the 1st 1933
at his home 'Wallasey' in Englishcombe Lane, Bath

On May the 4th 1934, after a trial noted for the tenacity of its defence counsel, Reginald Ivor Hinks was hanged at Bristol. Ironically, the only person to mourn the passing of this thoroughly worthless man was his victim's daughter; unfortunately for her, she was also Mrs Hinks.

Hinks had been born in 1900, and after an indifferent education was turned loose on the world to show just what a rotten apple he was. In 1917 he went to lodge with his two brothers in Bath, and managed to secure an apprenticeship as a fitter with a local engineering works. An idle and careless worker, he was also suspected of being responsible for the mysterious disappearances of his workmates' tools. Indeed, had he not left of his own volition in 1921, it is quite likely that the decision would have been made for him. Not so the local branch of the Church Lad's Brigade of which he was a member; they found his behaviour so unacceptable that even that most charitable organization was obliged to dismiss him.

Hinks's time with the Royal Corps of Signals was equally undistinguished. After joining in 1921, they suffered him only until August the 7th 1922, when they opted to do without his further services. His military record reads, in part: "Character indifferent, slack, lazy and untidy." On May the 30th 1923 he joined the Lancashire Fusiliers under the name Hanks; in December 1925 they discharged him as physically unfit. From this point, Reginald Hinks moved about quite a lot, usually for very good reasons – none of them honest. He became a barman in Lambeth, South London; a job which lasted only a few months. His service as a cloakroom attendant with the Royal Automobile Club in Pall Mall lasted for an even shorter period – he was sacked after four weeks. Hinks then had a spell in domestic service in partnership with a girlfriend with whom he was living – he as butler, she as cook. On the 16th of January 1929 Hinks appeared before the magistrates at Westminster on two charges of stealing from his employers and their guests. Later that year his girlfriend received a modest legacy of £225 from a benevolent uncle; money which Reginald Hinks speedily converted to his private use. After a

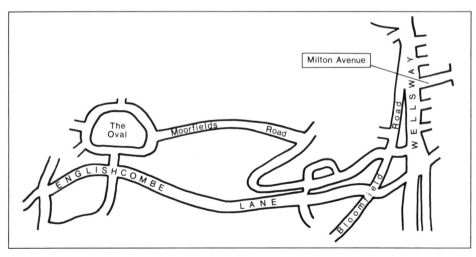

quarrel in which Hinks gave her a severe beating, the couple separated. After a further succession of short-lived jobs – short-lived mainly on account of his dishonesty – and occasional appearances in London police courts, Hinks headed back to Bath.

Arriving in that city on Christmas Eve 1932, Reginald Hinks – presumably unaffected by seasonal goodwill – snatched a lady's handbag containing £100. In early 1933 the Bath branch of Messrs. Hoover Ltd became the latest in a long succession of employers: Hinks was taken on as a vacuum cleaner salesman. In March of the same year he made the acquaintance of Mrs Constance Anne Jeffries (*née* Pullen), a divorced lady who lived with her five-year-old daughter Connie and her ancient father, James Pullen, at 43 Milton Avenue in Bath. Despite his great frailty and the advanced senility that rendered him almost incoherent, Mr Pullen was a great attraction to Reginald Hinks – he had a lot of money. Hinks promptly married Mrs Jeffries and installed himself in her comfortable home. Once settled, Reginald saw no pressing reason to waste his time working while there was so much money around; nonetheless, by way of a small contribution he did economise on poor old Mr Pullen's food – cutting down on both quality and quantity. He also saved the household budget thirty shillings a week through the simple expedient of dismissing Mr Strange, the male nurse on whom the old man was almost totally reliant. But Hinks's heart was set upon higher things, such as larger amounts of money for himself. Within a short time he had embezzled £900 of Mr Pullen's savings and bought a small mock-Tudor house called 'Wallasey' in Englishcombe Lane, a suburb of Bath. The new family home has been appropriately described by Miss Tennyson Jesse in her own perceptive account of the case*: "Wallasey, in short, was a cheap little modern imitation Tudor house and stood in relation to the beautiful houses of Bath much as Hinks must have stood in relation to his honest fellow men."

But Reginald Ivor Hinks was as impatient as he was greedy. When he learned that an order in lunacy had been made out regarding James Pullen, effectively safeguarding his

* *Comments on Cain*, F. Tennyson Jesse.

money from the grasping hands of the likes of himself, and that he was unlikely to have any access to the old man's money until he was dead, Reginald decided to hasten the process. He began, for example, to send the muddled, helpless octogenarian out for walks by himself in the busy city centre in the hope that he might have an accident with the traffic. A local police constable subsequently recalled that on a night in the autumn he had been on patrol and saw James Pullen apparently walking in his sleep; following behind was Reginald Hinks in his car. Hinks breezily explained to the bewildered constable that his father-in-law was on a ten-mile walk, but as they were talking the old man's legs suddenly gave way and he slumped to the ground. Hinks, with some show of concern, bundled him into the back of the car and drove home. On another occasion a different police officer was called to a minor incident aboard a Bath Tramways bus. On his arriving at the scene, the conductor pointed to a customer who had just tendered four match-sticks and a pencil for his fare to Dorking; it was Mr Pullen.

But none of this was proving nearly fatal enough for Reginald Hinks. Clearly, stronger methods were called for.

On the evening of November the 30th 1933, at about 7.30, Hinks called the Bath Fire Brigade Ambulance; his father-in-law, he explained, had been found unconscious in his bath. [It was customary at that time to call the fire brigade in such cases as they had supplies of oxygen in the event of respiratory failure.] One should add that the weekly bath night in the Hinks household was a very bizarre ritual indeed: Once the tub was filled little Connie was bathed, then Mrs Hinks climbed into the same water, succeeded by Reginald Ivor; last of all, old Mr Pullen was immersed in this same poisonous concoction.

Hinks had also summoned the police, and then the doctor, hastening to assure him that he, Hinks, customarily watched over the old man during his ablutions – lest he might do something silly or careless. But on this occasion he had popped downstairs to fetch some clean towels (!), and when he returned he found Mr Pullen with his head under the water: "He was black in the face."

By the time the fire brigade, the Chief

Constable and Dr Gibson arrived, old James Pullen seemed to have made a remarkable recovery – he was sitting up in the now empty bath wrapped in a blanket with a hot-water bottle held to his chest; far from black in the face, he was rather pale. At any rate the doctor could find no cause for alarm, quite the reverse, Mr Pullen was in uncommonly good health for a man of his advanced years. And so the players in Reginald Hinks's elaborately staged scenario gradually left the house. But this had only been the prologue; on the following day the drama proper was to be staged.

Hinks was at home with his father-in-law and step-daughter; Mrs Hinks had gone to the local cinema. On the other side of town the fire brigade was receiving yet another summons to 'Wallasey' via a telephone call from Reginald Hinks. He subsequently called in the police and the doctor. When these players once again found themselves on the stage of Englishcombe Lane they found old Mr Pullen lying in a kitchen smelling strongly of gas; the unfortunate man was still alive, and as a police officer approached him to give assistance, Hinks gratuitously mentioned: "You might find a bruise at the back of his head; I pulled him out of the gas stove and his head fell with a bump on the floor." Hinks later gave an account of his discovery of Mr Pullen: "I found the two gas taps turned on," he began. "I don't think he could turn on taps like that," interrupted the doctor. "He often turned them on and off," replied Hinks. The doctor observed that a raincoat had been draped over the stove – presumably in order to enclose the gas in the oven, and protested that, in Mr Pullen's state of mental degeneration, he would have been unlikely to have coped with the complicated series of actions required to commit suicide in this way. Subsequent pathological examination yielded an even more damaging rebuttal to the suicide theory – the injury to the back of James Pullen's head had been sustained *before* he had inhaled the gas. From this

lead, a case was built up against Reginald Hinks that would lead to his trial at the Old Bailey on a charge of murdering his father-in-law.

For the prosecution, Mr Croom-Johnson KC dismissed the suicide theory totally and absolutely; summing up his case, he told the jury: "This old, tottering man was supposed to have gone upstairs to the bedroom, kissed the little girl asleep, gone downstairs, out of the back door to the lavatory, come back into the kitchen, removed coat and waistcoat, placed a piece of blanket into the stove to make himself happy and comfortable, removed three shelves from the stove, arranged the coats around the oven door, turned on the two taps, removed his slippers, and then laid down with his head in the stove to await his Maker – and all this in the space of twenty-five minutes..."

For Hinks, Mr O'Connor also emphasized the unbalance of the old man's mind, and suggested that not only was he quite capable of suicide, but had on several occasions been heard to threaten to kill himself. He entreated the jury: "I ask you to say that Pullen had the intention of committing suicide if he had the opportunity."

After cautioning them that "You cannot prove a man has murdered another simply by proof that he would be better off if he did so," Mr Justice Branson sent the jury into retirement.

Pronounced guilty, Hinks was sentenced to death. His appeal was heard in April, and once again the decision was against him. In dismissing the appeal, Lord Hewart said that there was clear evidence that James Pullen was neither mentally nor physically capable of committing suicide in the manner suggested; the matter had been finally settled.

There was only one sound to break the hush that fell over the court, it was the anguished sobbing of Constance Hinks, a woman who had stood by her husband to the last.

The Biter Bit

The Murder of an Unnamed Nightwatchman
by JACK SHRIMPTON (alias PARKER)
in Wine Street, Bristol
for which Crime he was Executed in that City
on Friday the 4th of September 1713

John Shrimpton was born of good and reputable parents living at Penns, near High Wycombe, in Buckinghamshire, who, bestowing so much education upon him as might qualify him for a tradesman, put him out an apprentice, when he was between fifteen and sixteen years of age, to a soap-boiler in Little Britain, in London; but not serving out his apprenticeship there, he was turned over to another soap-boiler in Ratcliff Highway.

When he was out of his time he went into the army, where he was some time in the troop of horse commanded by Major-General Wood; but, not finding such preferment as he expected by being a soldier, he came into England and took to the highway. He did always the most damage betwixt London and Oxford, insomuch that scarce a coach or horseman could pass him without being robbed.

Some time after committing one robbery, Mr Shrimpton, being in London, accidentally lit into the company of the common hangman, where he was taking a glass of wine; and coming to the knowledge of his occupation he asked him this question: "What is the reason, when you perform your office, that you put the knot just under the ear? For, in my opinion, was you to fix it in the nape of the neck it would be more easy to the sufferer." The hangman replied: "If one Christian may believe another, I have hanged a great many in my time, but upon my word, sir, I never had any complaint as yet. However, if it should be your good luck to make use of me, I shall, to oblige you, be so civil as to hang you after your own way." But Shrimpton, not approving of the hangman's civility, told him that he desired none of his favours, because they generally proved of a very dangerous consequence.

Another time, Jack Shrimpton, who also called himself Parker, meeting a couple of bailiffs beyond Wycombe carrying a poor farmer to jail, desired to know what the debt might be; and being told six pounds odd money, he requested them to go with him to the next ale-house and he would pay it. They went along with him, where, taking a bond of the farmer, whom he knew very well, he paid the bailiffs their prisoner's debts and fees, and then parted. But Jack Shrimpton, waylaying the bailiffs, had no more mercy on them than they had on the farmer, for he took away what money he paid them, and about forty shillings besides; after which he rode back again to the farmer and, regaling him with a treat of a guinea, cancelled his bond, and then went in pursuit of new adventures.

A little while after, Shrimpton, travelling on the road, met with a poor miller who was going to turn highwayman himself. Thus roving along, and meeting (as above said) with Shrimpton, he held up an oaken plant, for he had no other arms, and bade him stand, thinking that word was sufficient to scare any man out of his money. Shrimpton, perceiving the simplicity of the fellow, fired a pistol at him, which (though he purposely missed him) put our new robber into such an agony that he surrendered himself to Shrimpton's mercy; who presently said: "Surely, friend, thou art but a young highwayman, or else you would have knocked me down first and bade me stand afterwards." The poor miller told him his misfortunes; on which Shrimpton took some compassion, and quoth he: "I am a highwayman myself, and am now waiting on this road for

17

Watchmen arresting a highwayman in London

a certain neighbour of yours, who I expect will come this way by and by with
six-score pounds; therefore if you will be
assisting in the robbery of him, you shall
have half the booty." The miller was very
thankful for this kind offer, and resolved
to stand by him to the very utmost. Then
Shrimpton, having told him again that it
was not long since he had robbed one of
his neighbours of one hundred and fifty
pounds, further said: "Honest friend,
whilst I ride this way, you go that way,

and if you should meet him whom I have told you of, be sure to knock him down and take all he has from him, without telling him why or wherefore; and in case I should meet him, I'll serve him with the same sauce."

They both separated, and went in search of their prey, till at last, upon the joining of two roads, they met together again. Shrimpton, wondering why the person he wanted did not yet come, ordered the miller to follow him still, saying: "Without doubt we shall catch the old cuff anon." But as he was thus encouraging his new companion, who was just at his horse's heels, he took up his stick and gave Shrimpton such a smart blow betwixt neck and shoulders that he felled him to the ground; being then able to deal with him, he robbed him of about fourscore guineas, and bade him go quietly about his business, or otherwise he would have him hanged, according to his own confession, for lately robbing his neighbour. Thus the biter was bitten; but Shrimpton swore he would never more take upon him to teach strangers how to rob on the highway.

This notorious malefactor pursued his wicked courses a long while, till at last, being in Bristol, where he resided for some months, he was drinking one night very late at a bawdy-house in St James's Churchyard, when a watchman, going his rounds, and hearing a great noise of swearing and cursing in the house, compelled Shrimpton to go along with him to the watch-house. As they were going together through Wine Street he shot the watchman through the body and flung his pistol away, that it might not be found; but some men, happening to go by at the same time, apprehended Shrimpton, and the watchman dying on the spot, they secured him till morning, when, carrying him before a magistrate, he was committed to Newgate, in Bristol, where throughout his confinement he behaved himself very audaciously.

At length, being brought to a trial, he was convicted not only for wilful murder but also for five robberies on the highway. When he came to the place of execution at St Michael's Hill he was turned off, without showing any signs of repentance, on Friday, the 4th of September 1713.

He that Loveth not his Brother*
The Murder of Sir JOHN DINELY GOODERE
by his Brother, Captain SAMUEL GOODERE
MATTHEW MAHONY and CHARLES WHITE
on the 10th of January 1741
on board a ship off Bristol

Sir John Dinely Goodere succeeded his father, Sir Edward, in the possession of an estate of three thousand pounds a year, situated near Evesham, in Worcestershire. His brother, Samuel, was bred to the sea, and at length was advanced to the rank of captain of a man-of-war.

Sir John married the daughter of a merchant and received twenty thousand pounds as a marriage portion. But mutual unhappiness was the consequence of this connection, for the husband was brutal in his manners, and the wife perhaps not strictly observant of the sacred vow she had taken: for she was too frequently visited by Sir Robert Jasen; and, after recriminations between the married pair, Sir John brought an action

---

* If a man say, I love God, and hateth his brother, he is a liar; for he that loveth not his brother whom he hath seen, how can he love God whom he hath not seen?

(*The First Epistle General of John*, iv.20)

in the Court of Common Pleas for criminal conversation, and five hundred pounds' damages were awarded by the jury.

Sir John's next step was to indict his lady for a conspiracy, and, a conviction following, she was fined and imprisoned a year in the King's Bench. He likewise petitioned for a divorce; but, the matter being heard in the House of Lords, his petition was thrown out.

Sir John having no children, Captain Samuel Goodere formed very sanguine expectations of possessing the estate; but finding that the brother had docked the entail in favour of his sister's children, the Captain sought the most diabolical means of revenge for the supposed injury.

While the Captain's vessel lay in the port of Bristol, Sir John went to that city on business; and being engaged to dine with an attorney, named Smith, the Captain prevailed on the latter to permit him to make one of their company, under pretence of being reconciled to his brother. Mr Smith consented, and used his good offices to accommodate the difference, and a sincere reconciliation appeared to have taken place.

This visit was made on the 10th of January, 1741, and the Captain, having previously concerted his measures, brought some sailors on shore with him, and left them at a public-house, in waiting to seize the baronet in the evening.

Accordingly, when the company broke up, the Captain attended his brother through the streets, and when they came opposite the public-house the seamen ran out, seized Sir John, and conveyed him to a boat that had been appointed to wait for his reception. As soon as the victim was in the boat he said to his brother: "I know you have an intention to murder me, and if you are ready to do it, let me beg that it be done here without giving yourself the trouble to take me on board." To which the Captain said: "No, brother; I am going to prevent your rotting on land; but, however, I would have you make your peace with God this night."

Being put on board, Sir John appealed to the seamen for help; but the Captain put a stop to any efforts they might have made to assist him, by saying he was a lunatic, and brought on board to prevent his committing an act of suicide.

White and Mahony now conveyed him to the purser's cabin, which the Captain guarded with a drawn sword, while the other villains attempted to strangle him with a handkerchief which they found in his pocket, the wretched victim crying out

"Murder!" and beseeching them not to kill him, and offering all he possessed as a compensation for his life.

As they could not strangle him with the handkerchief the Captain gave them a cord; with which Mahony dispatched him, while White held his hands and trod on his stomach. The Captain now retired to his cabin, and on the murder being committed the perpetrators of it went to him and told him "the job was done"; on which he gave them money, and bade them seek their safety in flight.

The attorney with whom the brothers had dined having heard of the commission of a murder, and knowing of the former animosity of the Captain to his brother, immediately conjectured who it was that had fallen a sacrifice; on which he went to the Mayor of Bristol, who issued his warrant to the water-bailiff, who, going on board, found that the lieutenant and cooper had prudently confined the Captain to his cabin.

The offender, being brought on shore, was committed to Newgate, and Mahony and White, being taken a few hours afterwards, were lodged in the same prison. At the sessions held at Bristol on the 26th of March, 1741, these offenders were brought to trial, and, being convicted on the fullest evidence, received sentence of death. They were hanged near the Hot Wells, Bristol, on the 20th of April, 1741, within view of the place where the ship lay when the murder was committed.

Beyond the Limit of Endurance
The Murder of Miss JEFFERIES
by her Servant SARAH HARRIET THOMAS
in the month of February 1849
at 6 Trenchard Street, Bristol

Though she was reputed to be wealthy – and many reclusive old people are so reputed, with more or less reason – Miss Jefferies was known to have been endowed with an exceptionally mean and grasping nature, which, frustrating though it must have been for her servant, was hardly grounds for murder.

At the time of the occurrence, which was in the early part of the year 1849, Miss Jefferies was residing at 6 Trenchard Street, Bristol. It had been on the 5th of February that Sarah Harriet Jones – by all reports a presentable, even pretty, young woman, if of simple birth – was taken on as an all-purpose servant. In no time at all neighbours began to hear the mistress/servant sounds with which they had become familiar through many changes of domestic staff; that is, the shouting and raving of Miss Jefferies, and the terrified sobbing of Sarah Thomas.

There followed an unexpected day of silence; a succession of days, on which not even the shutters of No. 6 were opened. And they remained closed until the police were

eventually summoned to investigate the unaccustomed lack of activity. The sight that met them on entering Miss Jefferies' house was shocking in the extreme; the lady of the house lay twisted in a puddle of congealed blood on the floor, her head a bloody pulp

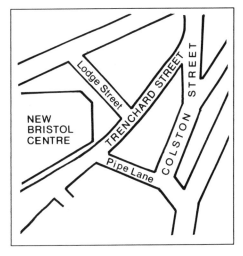

from the severe battering that it had suffered. The body of her small dog was found pushed into the water closet, its throat slashed across.

Missing from the house was Sarah Thomas, upon whose head suspicion immediately fell. The unfortunate girl was eventually found hiding in the coal cellar of her parents' house in Pensford, surrounded by the money and jewellery which she had ransacked from her late employer's home.

Brought to trial, Sarah Thomas related the most heart-rending account of the cruelty of her mistress, of the constant fear of further ill-usage, and finally the hatred, the blind

rage that had caused her to destroy the single source of all her misery.

Found guilty, and despite a petition signed by 3,500 Bristol women, Sarah Thomas was condemned to the gallows; but it was to be one of the most difficult and harrowing executions of hangman Calcraft's long career.* On the fatal day, the prisoner refused absolutely to co-operate in her own death, and it took half-a-dozen burly warders to drag their struggling, screaming victim to her fate.

* For an account of the life and career of William Calcraft see *Murder Club Guide No.3.*

Did he fall, or was he pushed?
The Death of THOMAS FARRANT
on Thursday the 26th of December 1867
at the *Colston's Arms*, Hotwell Road, Bristol
and the Acquittal of GILES CLIFT of his Murder

ALLEGED HOMICIDE IN HOTWELL-ROAD*

On Thursday evening a tragedy, which has caused a great deal of excitement, not merely in the locality where the occurrence took place – the Hotwell-road – but also throughout the city generally, was enacted at a beer-house called the *Colston's Arms*, situated in the thoroughfare just referred to. A young man named Thomas Farrant, aged 25 years, was killed under circumstances of the most suspicious character; and a blind man, named Giles Clift, 53 years of age, is in custody on the charge of having killed him through throwing him from a top storey window of the *Colston's Arms* into the street.

Giles Clift has for some time past kept a lodging-house at No.1 Little-street, St James's-back, in this city [Bristol]. He has been married about twelve years [the "four years" stated below is probably more correct], and the marriage proved a most unhappy one, frequent quarrels having taken place between him and his wife leading to magisterial proceedings and an agreement to live separated. Clift accuses his wife of having taken away goods belonging to him, and of having gone to live at the *Colston's Arms* beer-house with the deceased Thomas Farrant, a vendor of fruit, and a grand-nephew of Clift. On Thursday evening [26 December 1827], about six o'clock, Clift hearing that his wife and Farrant were at the *Colston's Arms* went there, led by a youth named Lyons who lived with him at his house in Little St James's-back. He ascended the stairs and alone entered the room where Farrant, Mrs Clift and the daughter of the latter, about three years of age, were. Lyons remained downstairs until he heard a great noise overhead; and judging from the screaming which followed immediately afterwards, a quarrel and a struggle at once commenced. The young man rushed into the room, rescued Mrs Clift from the grasp of her husband, who was beating her with the leg of a bedstead, and took her downstairs. She, however, went

* Adapted from various issues of the *Bristol Mercury*, December 1867-January 1868

again upstairs to fetch her child, and there was a renewal of screams and other noises. At this moment some persons who were passing by the house were horrified to see a man fall head foremost from the top window on to a ledge which projects over the window of the basement, and then roll on to the pavement. This man, on examination, proved to be Farrant, and it was at once apparent to those who were on the spot that the injuries he had received were of a very serious character, for blood poured from him in a copious stream, and in a few moments formed a pool around him. A lad was sent in haste to the Clifton Police-station, and he reported that a man had been thrown from the top window of a house in Hotwell-road. Mr Inspector Attwood, who was on duty, immediately directed Pc Dawes and another constable to go to the spot and take a stretcher with them. On accompanying the lad to the Hotwell-road, they found the body of a man lying on the pavement in front of the *Colston's Arms* beer-house, which by the by is situated nearly opposite the 'Daedalus' training ship. The man was insensible, and had bled freely from the ears, nose, and mouth, etc. He was conveyed to the station, and life must have been quite extinct though blood was still streaming from him. Mr Attwood did everything for him which kindness could suggest. He had him placed in front of a fire, and bathed his face with warm water. In the meantime he also sent for Mr Bernard, of Victoria-square, the police surgeon, and Mr Steele, one of the medical officers of Clifton Union, was also fetched. These gentlemen examined him, and found that death was occasioned by the dislocation of the neck. Soon after the fatal occurrence, and before the deceased's body was moved, one of the city constables, who happened to be at hand, went up to the room of the beer-house from the window of which the man fell; it is of considerable height from the street. The distance he fell – 27ft. 10in. – fully accounts for the fatal nature of the injuries he received; it would have been little less than a miracle if he had escaped with his life. The room, when examined by the city policeman, bore clear indication of a struggle having taken place there, the chimney-glass and other articles being smashed. Clift was apprehended at once by PC 179 (Fletcher) who was passing the house at the time in plain clothes, and was conveyed to the Clifton Police-station, where he was locked up. He says that he never touched the deceased, and did not know that he was in the room. He spoke to no-one but his wife, and did not hear Farrant say a single word. It is suggested that Farrant, in endeavouring to get away from Clift, fell through the window, which is only 2 feet square, and Clift, who is a thin and apparently weak man, bears not the slightest mark of having been engaged in any encounter.

It is generally asserted that the prisoner, exasperated at finding his wife – who, it should be stated, was the aunt of the deceased – in the company of another man, seized hold of him and threw him out of the window. The evidence of the wife, the only other person in the room, cannot, we believe, be legally taken against her husband, but she asserts that he said to the deceased: "---- thee, I'll break thee ---- neck out of the window."

At the Council-house yesterday morning Mr M. Alman, solicitor, appeared before the sitting magistrates, Mr S.V. Hare and Mr W.H. Wills, and inquired if Giles Clift, who was in custody charged with causing the death of Thomas Farrant in the Hotwell-road, would be brought up that day. Mr Williams said that the practice of the magistrates was to leave such a case to be dealt with first by the coroner, and if they were dissatisfied with the verdict of the jury then they would have the accused brought before them. Mr Alman rejoined that the deputy-coroner, Mr Wasbrough, was out of town, and it was a hardship to his client to be detained in custody; but Mr Brice said as Clift was charged with occasioning the death of a man there could not be much hardship in detaining him in custody for a day. The deputy-coroner subsequently sent word that he would hold the inquest on Saturday afternoon, at the *Hope and Anchor* public house, Jacob's-wells. There are four witnesses summoned to attend, Mrs Clift, Lyons, a person who lived in the basement of the beer-house, and a man who it is said saw the deceased fall from the window. The beer-house where the tragic affair took place is the same premises which a few years ago the notorious Willey set fire to, for which he was sentenced to twenty years' penal servitude.

On Saturday afternoon, Mr H.S. Wasbrough, the deputy-coroner, held an inquest at the Clifton Police-station, Brandonhill, on the body of Thomas Farrant, an itinerant fruit vendor, whose death occurred under mysterious circumstances in the Hotwell-road. The jury having viewed the body, which was on the premises, they afterwards went to the room in which the scuffle had taken place. The room was in confusion, and fragments of broken pan were scattered on the floor, but as the contents of the apartment had been interfered with, nothing could be judged from these appearances. The window is a very small one, and the sash can only be raised to the height of 17½ inches, and there seemed a general opinion that Farrant could not have fallen through it by accident. On the outside ledge of it were marks resembling finger-marks, and it was suggested that the deceased might have tried to drop out, with a view to avoid Clift's knowledge of his presence in the house. On a ledge over the lowest front window of the house was a mark, apparently of a heel, on the lead with which it was covered. The testimony of several witnesses was taken, and the proceedings lasted three hours. The prisoner Clift, for whom Mr Alman appeared, was present in custody of a constable during the inquiry. He was apparently very nervous, but paid close attention to the statements made.

The following evidence was taken:

Henry Lyons, a carpenter, stated that he lived with Clift at Little St James's-back. In consequence of information received to the effect that Mrs Clift and the deceased were living together at the *Colston's Arms,* he accompanied the prisoner to that tavern. They went upstairs together, and when nearly at the top Mrs Clift came out of a room with a candle in her hand, and on seeing her husband ran back into the apartment, and was followed by Clift. Witness remained outside, but in a few moments he heard screams and cries for help, and on rushing into the room he saw the prisoner and his wife struggling together on the floor. He pulled Mrs Clift out of the room, and she ran downstairs. The deceased was not in the room. The window was open. He and the prisoner then commenced to pack up the bedding, etc. and whilst engaged in this operation they were informed that Farrant was lying on the pavement in the front of the house dead. On hearing this the prisoner said: Well, I didn't do it, for I didn't see him or hear him; I didn't know he was here." The pan was standing behind the door, and it was broken by the prisoner when he ran into the room. Witness subsequently shifted some of the fragments nearer the window. The witness went on to state that the deceased and Mrs Clift had been co-habiting together for six weeks. Mrs Clift is about 28 years old and her husband 53, and they had been married about four years [see above]. The prisoner was the deceased's great-uncle. Prisoner and his wife frequently quarrelled, and on Christmas Eve she came to his house and broke seven panes of glass. He never heard Clift use any threatening language towards the deceased.

Eliza Evans, a widow living in a room situated immediately underneath the apartment occupied by Farrant and Mrs Clift, deposed she heard a scuffle in the room which she thought sounded near the window. She heard a woman come downstairs, and then the sound ceased, and she did not hear the window thrown up.

Mr Butler, who was passing along Hotwell-road, stated that he saw the deceased falling from a window, his heel caught the lead of a ledge over the front window and he fell into the street.

A young man named *Griffin* deposed to seeing the deceased descend into the street.

Mr Charles Steele M.R.C.S., who had made a post-mortem examination of the body, stated that the cause of death was a fracture to the skull. He described the appearance of the deceased. There was a bruise under the chin, and on the underside of the lower lip outside, and a corresponding cut inside, from the teeth. The front teeth of the upper jaw had been clearly forced up into their sockets. His opinion was that these appearances were produced by the deceased's chin being struck violently against the window sill as he was getting out. He believed that he was in the act of getting out of the window hurriedly, when his fingers slipped, and his chin struck violently against the window sill, thereby precipitating him on to the edge of the ledge below; his heel then slipped, throwing him forward, and his head came in contact with the ground.

Pc Fletcher having deposed to apprehending the prisoner, Mr Wasbrough summed up, remarking that the great probability was that the deceased was anxious to escape from his uncle's just wrath, and attempted to escape by the window, and in doing so lost his life. After a short consultation the foreman informed the deputy-coroner that the jury had come to the conclusion that the deceased's death was caused by his attempting to get out of the window to avoid meeting his uncle, the husband of the woman he was co-habiting with. A verdict to that effect was recorded.

According to the verdict of the coroner's jury in the above case, there was no murder charge to answer; and perhaps we have no justification in calling that verdict into question. However, it seems in retrospect that enough doubt can be cast on the extent of the evidence [and we must not forget that newspaper accounts of court hearings at that time were virtually verbatim reports] to have warranted further investigation. Readers can be left to pick their own holes in the statements and conclusions reached; but it is worth considering why James Farrant should have chosen to squeeze through a window 17½×24 inches, almost 30 feet above the street, when there was a perfectly adequate door to the room. It is hard to accept that 25-year-old Farrant had such fear of a *blind* man described as being "thin and apparently weak", as to sacrifice his neck out of the window.

The Bristol Taxi Murder
The Murder of WILLIAM TRIPP
by JOHN ROGERS
on Friday the 29th of July 1960
at the Powderhall Farm Cross Roads, outside Chew Magna

Although the likelihood of a person being murdered in Britain is statistically very low, there have always been occupations which, by their nature, carry with them a proportionately higher risk of lethal assault. As most killings that are committed by people not known to the victim are the accompaniment of robbery, those who carry cash about with them as part of their job are among the most vulnerable. Tradespeople like milkmen are regularly the victims of violent attack, and in the days before wide acceptance of cheques and credit cards, rent-collectors and tallymen were at the top of the high-risk occupations – not least because the regular pattern of their calls made them easily identifiable.

But perhaps the most vulnerable of all have been taxi-drivers. From the days when highwaymen terrorized the roads, cab-drivers have frequently been victims of robbery, physical assault and even murder. The cabbie, locked in a confined space for most of his working life with total strangers, needs all his wits and instincts functioning, as well as a lot of luck, to help him avoid attack; and with the proliferation of such assaults it is no surprise that cab-men and women the world over are arming themselves against such an eventuality.

William Tripp was a taxi-driver; and at the age of forty-one had tens of thousands of miles of service behind him. By all reports he was a gentle, homely man, well liked and respected; indeed, as his wife Sybil said after his tragic death: "It could only have been done by a madman." Because William Tripp had been brutally murdered in his cab – his only 'fault' was the possession of £20.

Late on the night of Friday the 29th of July 1960, Cyril Farrow was cycling towards the Powderhall Farm Cross Roads between Chew Magna and Winford (in those days part of Somerset). As he neared the junction he could hear the sound of a car horn blaring out pointlessly at the night; then, in front of him, he saw the overturned car, its lights staring into the darkness: "As I approached the overturned cab on my bicycle, a man ran past me. I was wondering what to do when suddenly I heard the footsteps stop. They did not sound again for ten minutes." Ten minutes during which Farrow crouched in the shadow of the car, expecting any minute to end up as dead as the cab's occupant.

When the police arrived, they found William Tripp slumped over the steering wheel, dead from a gunshot wound; on the back seat lay a tartan duffel-bag, in it the .22 rifle that had so recently blasted its deadly charge into the back of its victim's head. The taxi's meter had stopped, showing a fare of 39s. 2d.

Inside a few hours, investigating officers led by Detective Superintendent A.C. Brown, head of Somerset CID, had begun to piece together a picture of their suspect and the sequence of events that led up to the murder. Tripp had been observed picking up a fare in Bristol city centre at 10.40 pm; the distance to Powderhall Farm Cross Roads

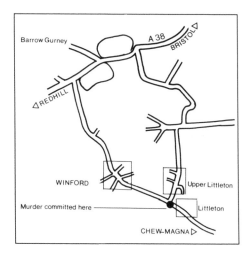

27

BRISTOL EVENING POST

RENAULT DAUPHINE SALOON

COVENTRY & JEFFS, LTD.
52, WHITELADIES RD., BRISTOL 8. Tel. 3-7076

A STEELS GROUP GARAGE

PARKES CLASSIC CONFECTIONERY
DAIRY BUTTER MINTS

No. 8,801—2½d.   The paper all Bristol asked for and helped to create   Wed., Oct. 19 1960

Tripp case opens—clerk's accident defence

TAXIMAN MURDERED FOR GREED IN COLD BLOOD
—prosecution

The defence of John Rogers, 20-year-old brewer's clerk, accused at Taunton Assizes today of the capital murder of Bristol taxi-driver William Tripp (44), would be that the shooting was an accident, Mr. N. R. Fox-Andrews, Q.C., prosecuting, disclosed today.

In his 25-minute opening speech to the all male jury, Mr. Fox-Andrews said: " If you accept the evidence which is to be put before you on behalf of the prosecution you will see that this murder is one of the most calculated and cold-blooded types of murder imaginable.

" You will also see that it was a murder dictated simply and solely by greed."

Furtherance of theft

Rogers, of Church Road, Bishopsworth, stood firmly to attention and crossed his hands as the charge was read out to him.

It accused him of the capital murder of Mr. Tripp by shooting him in the furtherance of theft on July 29.

Mr. Fox-Andrews said Rogers had taken a rifle from the rifle club of which he was a member, sawn off part of the barrel and stock, and disposed of these parts in a stream.

He deliberately shot Mr. Tripp as he was driving along, said counsel.

On the defence that it was an accident, Mr. Fox-Andrews asked, if so, what would a man do ? He alleged that Roger's next day went to the Beaulieu Jazz Festival " to enjoy himself."

The case is expected to end tomorrow

(Full report on Page 2.)

Woman (84) missing for three days

Bath police are looking for an 84-year-old woman who has been missing from an old people's home in Bathwick Hill since Sunday.

She is Mrs. Ada Foot, a resident at Casa Bianca, one of Bath Welfare Committee's homes for elderly people.

Police and officials of the home are most concerned about Mrs. Foot, because she was due to receive an insulin injection on Monday morning.

The old lady is a diabetic and has not been seen since she walked out of the home at 10 a.m. on Sunday.

Today the Chief Constable of Bath (Mr. G. E. T. Nichols) issued an appeal for information as to Mrs. Foot's whereabouts.

She is 5ft. 10in., well built and although she walks slowly is very erect. All her clothes are marked with the name of the home and when she was last seen Mrs. Foot was wearing a brown overcoat.

Police have contacted all known relatives of Mrs. Foot without results.

20 Marines hurt —four seriously— in lorry crash

Twenty Royal Marines were injured—four believed critically—when the lorry in which they were travelling on an exercise crashed at Marytavy, near Tavistock, Devon, today.

The lorry hit the bank of the road, part stone and part grass, and overturned.

The injured, all from the infantry training centre, Lympstone, Exeter, were taken to Tavistock Hospital.

Later seven of the injured were moved to the Royal Naval hospital at Plymouth. Two were on the seriously injured list and next of kin had been informed.

The party had been on a 17-week training course and were finishing up with an exercise on Dartmoor.

The leading truck had just rounded a corner when it hit the left bank, possibly after skidding.

truck saw nothing until it came across the smashed and splintered lorry lying at the foot of a four-foot bank.

THROWN OUT

Almost the entire party were thrown out, some into the field on the other side of the road.

Apparently nobody saw the accident, the road being clear at the time.

The occupants of the second

Gas in house children die

Three young children were taken to hospital from a house in Foleshill Road, Coventry, today.

Two of them were found to be dead and the third was suffering from the effects of coal gas poisoning.

The children were found in the house in the early hours. Gas was escaping from the oven.

The dead children were an month-old girl, and her four-year-old brother. The third child, a three-year-old sister, was treated at hospital.

The house was occupied by Indians.

ONE-WAY CONVERSATION PIECE 'as a new friend introduces herself to Julie Lewis (2), of Shirehampton, the youngest patient in Ward 11 of Frenchay Hospital, Bristol, who with other children in the ward were presented with this huge Dutch doll by Mr. F. T. Tjolle, a Bristol travel agent.

VIOLENCE WAVE SWEEPS CONGO —MINISTER HELD

Colonel Mobutu's troops in the Congo today arrested a group of leading supporters of Mr. Patrice Lumumba, including his Information Minister, Mr. Anicet Kashamura.

Also arrested were Mr. Jason Sendwe, leader of the Balubakat party and a member of Mr. Lumumba's Cabinet, and 13 others.

The arrests, ordered by Colonel Mobutu's student council running the Congo, follow a wave of violence and hooliganism which Mr. Lumumba's enemies claim was organised by his M.N.C. party's youth movement.

10 DEAD REPORT

Yesterday, a curfew was clamped down on the city after loads of youth had been seen roving the city, breaking into empty houses.

Unofficial reports say that about 10 Africans have been found killed in the past few days.

Mr. Sendwe and Mr. Kashamura were later released, but a number of youths, believed to be M.N.C. members, who were found with revolvers and machetes (two-edged knives) were kept in gaol.

A crowd of onlookers and U.N. Ghana soldiers gathered as Mr. Sendwe was being arrested.

Two Congolese soldiers ripped the film out of the camera of a U.N. official taking snapshots.

SIDDELEY ENGINES' UNOFFICIAL STRIKE CONTINUES—150 MEN OUT

Bristol Siddeley Engines Ltd.'s electricians unofficial strike — it involves about 120 day men and 30 night shift staff at the Patchway and Whitchurch factories goes on, writes BRIN CLIFFORD.

The men met today—and voted unanimously to stay out, pending further consideration by the management of their wage claim.

A strike spokesman said after today's meeting: "We accept the fact that the ability system exists in the engineering industry set up. But the management offer would mean a further increase in

shared uniformly between all grades—and say the management are seeking to enlarge the daily differential which already exists.

It is this wage claim—the men say it has been in since June—which caused yesterday's walk-out.

The men want extra pay

the differential and this we are not prepared to accept.

"The pay claim's total cost to the company is acceptable to us. We are not asking for any more; but we do want the

PAGE TWO ★

was seven miles – a fare of 39s. 2d. Combining information from this witness and from Mr Farrow, the police were able to issue a description of the young man they wanted to interview: 5ft. 8in. tall, slim build, wearing a dark suit, drain-pipe trousers and thick rubber-soled shoes.* Officers had meanwhile identified the gun as one stolen from a local brewery's rifle club. That it had been stolen with the express purpose of crime was evidenced by the sawing down of the barrel and stock so that it could be concealed beneath a coat.

Five days later, a suspect was taken into custody; he was twenty-year-old John Rogers, clerk in a Bristol brewery and living with his parents in the town. After being cautioned, Rogers remarked: "It was not the intention of murder, definitely not."

The trial opened at the Somerset Assizes in Taunton in October 1960. Mr Justice Cassels presided and Mr N.R. Fox-Andrews QC led for the Crown. What defence Rogers could make was entrusted to Mr Hugh Park QC.

Rogers did not – could not – deny stealing and 'adapting' the rifle for the sole purpose of armed robbery; nor that on the night of July the 29th, a taxi-driver was to be the object of that intention. With this in mind he hired William Tripp to drive him from Bristol to Winford. Rogers's version of the 'accident' was as follows: "I took the .22 gun from the duffel-bag, with intentions of robbing the driver. I told him to pull into the side. He turned round, and I jumped up. As I did so I flipped the trigger of the gun and he flopped over the wheel. I do not know where I shot him, or if I hit him. When he flopped the taxi lurched forward and we went into a hedge and overturned. It took me about three minutes to get out of the thing."

Having escaped from the car and from the attentions of Cyril Farrow, Rogers spent the rest of the August Bank Holiday with friends at the annual Beaulieu Jazz Festival – no

* These were characteristics of the clothing worn by the youth cult of the '50s called 'Teddy Boys'.

doubt spending freely of the £20 known to have been in William Tripp's possession up to the night of his death – it was his weekly takings due to be paid to the taxi company.

When Crown witness Dr Edward Parkes, Director of the South-Western Forensic Science Laboratory, took the stand, he described the tests which had been undertaken by the ballistics experts and the pathologist, the result of which led to the clear conclusion that: "The fatal shot was fired with the gun when the driver was looking forward. The gun was held virtually horizontally and pointed at the back of his head."

Summing up at the end of the trial, Mr Justice Cassels instructed the jury: "If a wicked, intentional mind, bent on killing or seriously injuring, has accompanied an act which does in fact kill, then in law there is malice aforethought, and that is murder... If you come to the conclusion that this may have been an accident you have to ask yourselves, was it an accident with criminal negligence and was there reckless disregard for the safety of the taxi driver. If you conclude that there was, he would be guilty of manslaughter."

The jury, quite rightly, opted for the former verdict – guilty of capital murder.

Though John Rogers was sentenced to death, he did not finally suffer 'the ultimate sanction'. On December the 6th, the day before he was due to hang, Rogers was removed from Horfield Gaol's condemned cell by order of the then Home Secretary, Mr R.A. Butler, who had granted an eleventh-hour reprieve.

Quite why this callous, brutal young man should have received the benefit of clemency we will never know because a Home Secretary is not obliged to give his reasons for granting or refusing a reprieve. It may be that the obligatory inquiry into the state of mental health of a condemned man revealed some factor that indicated a diminished responsibility. He may have been, as in Mrs Tripp's earlier estimate "a madman." But it was of little comfort to Sybil Tripp; even less to her husband William.

A Killer Sent by God*
The Murder of COLYN BEDALE-TAYLOR
by GRAHAM BACKHOUSE
on Monday the 30th of April 1984
at Widden Hill Farm, Horton, near Chipping Sodbury

Forty-three-year-old farmer Graham Backhouse, appearing at Bristol Crown Court, stood charged with the attempted murder of his wife Margaret in order to collect the sum of £100,000 on her life insurance, and the murder of neighbour Mr Colyn Bedale-Taylor in order to divert police suspicion from himself.

Mr James Black, QC for the prosecution, described Backhouse as a "devious, dangerous and determined man, who had carefully planned both crimes and carried them out in cold blood". Mr Black went on to tell the jury how Backhouse had invented a scenario whereby he and his family were the victims of a supposed village vendetta; he had gone as far as to impale a sheep's head on a stake close to the house bearing a note reading "You Next". The police had had constant complaints from Mr Backhouse of threatening letters and telephone calls – which latter obligingly ceased when a listening device was installed.

On April the 9th 1984, Margaret Backhouse climbed into the driver's seat of the family's Volvo estate car and turned on the ignition; the resulting explosion left her with severe injuries to her legs and buttocks. Although the injuries were said by consultant surgeon Colin Davidson to be "extensive and extremely serious", they were mercifully not fatal, due in large part to the solid design of the vehicle. Believed at the time to be the intended victim, Graham Backhouse was given 24-hour police protection.

On the 18th of April, at Backhouse's request, the police watch was taken off, and a 'panic button' linked to the local police station fitted. On April the 30th the alarm went off.

When police constable Richard Yeadon arrived at the farm he found sixty-three-year-old Colyn Bedale-Taylor lying dead from shotgun wounds to the chest; in his hand was a Stanley handyman's knife. Pc Yeadon then noticed Mr Backhouse lying in the entrance to the lounge, sobbing; he was covered in blood coming from wounds to the face and chest.

In a statement read to the court by Mr Lionel Read QC, acting for Backhouse, his client claimed that Bedale-Taylor had called at the farmhouse on the evening of the 30th and told him that he had come to repair furniture: "I told him there was no furniture to repair, and he said that God had sent him." Bedale-Taylor then went on to accuse Mr Backhouse of being responsible for the death of his son Digby – who had in fact died as the result of a car crash some eighteen months previously. The visitor later confessed to having planted the car bomb, and then lunged at Backhouse with the Stanley knife: "I ran into the hallway and grabbed a gun; Bedale-Taylor was still after me. I shouted I had got a gun but he still kept coming and I shot him. He fell back and I shot him again and that was it."

This version of the events leading to Bedale-Taylor's death was at variance with the findings of the forensic investigation, alleged the Crown prosecutor, and from the witness stand Mr Geoffrey Robinson from the Home Office forensic laboratory at Chepstow, Gwent, advanced the proposition that Mr Backhouse's wounds were self-inflicted, and that he placed the knife in his victim's hand after death. Backhouse, he suggested, must have splashed blood in the kitchen after the shooting to simulate an attack on himself. Although there were bloodstains in the kitchen and around the area where the body lay, there was none in the hallway or on the murder weapon (the prisoner and the deceased had different blood groups, he

* This account derives from contemporary court and newspaper reports of the trial.

Mrs Margaret Backhouse

Mr Graham Backhouse

emphasized). When Backhouse placed the knife in the dead man's hand, he could not have noticed that the palms were completely covered with blood through clutching at his wounds after being shot. If his story was true, and Bedale-Taylor had been holding the knife, then at least part of the palm should have been clear of blood.

Evidence was then offered to the court indicating that even after arrest the prisoner continued in his efforts to incriminate Bedale-Taylor. From his cell at Horfield Prison, Bristol, Backhouse wrote to his wife asking her to smuggle in writing materials: "The police are fabricating evidence against me and my case is looking black. However, with your help I can improve the case considerably. I want to fabricate a letter to the Press. So please help me. I must get out of this hell hole."

The jury was told that Backhouse persuaded a fellow-prisoner to smuggle out an unsigned letter which implicated Mr Bedale-Taylor in the bombing addressed to the editor of the Bristol *Evening Post*. Forensic examination proved that the handwriting matched the threatening letters supposed to have been received by Graham Backhouse, and that they both matched the handwriting of Backhouse himself.

Presenting evidence of motive, Mr Black for the Crown examined Richard Martin, manager of the Chipping Sodbury branch of the National Westminster Bank. Mr Martin stated that the prisoner had been left to run the farm after his father's death in 1979. As the result of bad harvests and poor management the farm had turned into a liability; within four years, Backhouse had accumulated debts of more than £70,000. The jury was also told that up to 1984 Margaret Backhouse's life had been insured for £50,000; in March of that year a further policy had been taken out for the same amount "in event of her death or serious injury".

———————

On Monday the 19th of February, 1985, the jury of eight men and five women retired to consider their verdict; after five-and-a-half hours, by a majority of ten to two, they returned a verdict of guilty on both charges. Mr Justice Stuart-Smith, in giving Backhouse two terms of life imprisonment, made no recommendation on the sentences.

On his way from the dock, escorted by prison officers, Graham Backhouse passed within feet of his wife sitting in the public gallery; he did not glance in her direction.

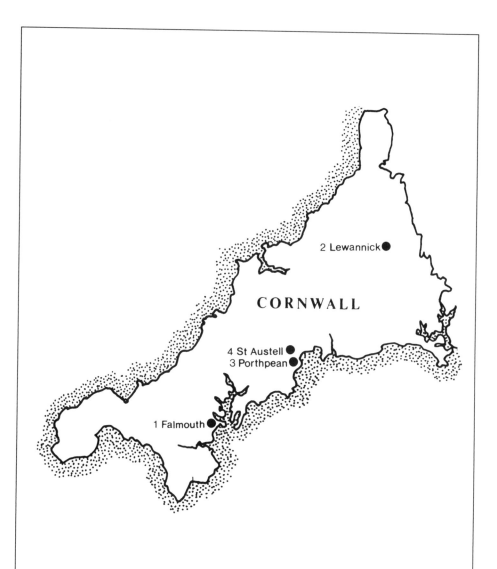

2 Lewannick●

CORNWALL

4 St Austell●
3 Porthpean●

1 Falmouth●

Cornwall

Ship's Rations

The Murder of RICHARD PARKER
by THOMAS DUDLEY and EDWIN STEPHENS
in the month of July 1884
on board the *Mignonette*

Cannibalism is not a thing that we tend to associate with the year 1884. It was the year Parsons invented his turbine. It was the great age of the railway, of Britain's huge industrial expansion; the hey-day of our world-wide reputation as builders of ships, large and small.

And that, really, is where the strange story of the *Mignonette* began; in a boat-yard in Southampton in 1884. She was a thirty-one-ton sailing yacht which had been purchased by an Australian named J.H. Want, and for the purpose of taking her to Sydney, a crew was hired consisting of thirty-one-year-old Thomas Dudley, who acted as captain, Edwin Stephens, aged thirty-six, and Edmund Brooks, thirty-nine; and like all good crews it had a cabin boy in the person of seventeen-year-old Richard Parker.

The *Mignonette* sailed out of Southampton on the 19th of May and on the 17th of June crossed the Equator. At the beginning of July the yacht ran into heavy storms and by the 3rd had shipped so much water that crew were forced to abandon her, taking to a lifeboat with no water and no provisions save a couple of cans of vegetables. Nature provided some nourishment in the form of a turtle, but after eight days adrift the food had run out. With reckless desperation, young Richard Parker made the fatal mistake of drinking sea water, which combined with lack of sustenance caused his mind to break. It was before this desperate background that captain Dudley proposed that they should kill the boy and eat him; Stephens agreed, but Edmund Brooks voiced strong disapproval. Having outnumbered Brooks, the captain informed the cabin boy that he was about to become supper and dispatched him with a stab to the throat.

By the time Parker had been all but consumed, the castaways were picked up by the *Montezuma*, a German vessel which set them ashore at Falmouth. Here they were arrested on a charge of murdering Richard Parker, which they did not deny. Edmund Brooks was subsequently released and Thomas Dudley and Edwin Stephens appeared before Baron Huddleston at the Cornwall Assizes on November the 6th 1884. From here the case was adjourned to the Royal Courts of Justice where Sir Henry James presented the evidence for the prosecution and the defence of Dudley and Stephens was entrusted to Mr Collins QC. Both men were found guilty of the charge against them and were sentenced to death.

There was widespread public sympathy for the extreme circumstances in which the men had found themselves and on December the 13th their sentence was commuted to a token 'six months without hard labour'.

Thomas Dudley and Edwin Stephens

An early woodcut depicting the results of a shipwreck. The woman in the centre of the picture is cutting a dead man's throat, probably in order to drink his blood.

CANNIBALISM FROM TIME TO TIME

The following stories derive from recent newspaper reports:

Stone Age Cannibalism?

Human bones bearing cut marks discovered last week inside Gough's Cave in Cheddar Gorge, Somerset, are being examined by scientists at the British Museum.

Recent excavations have yielded an almost complete lower jaw and part of an upper jaw (thought to be from a 12-year-old boy), the base of another skull and further bone fragments, all provisionally dated from 11,000 to 10,000 BC.

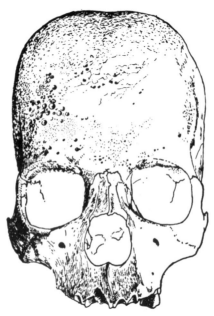

Archaeologists believe that the cut marks, inflicted with stone tools to the base of the skull, indicate that the head had been removed after death. The possibility has also been advanced that the flesh was systematically and ritually removed from the bones.

Whether these activities were for ritual cannibalistic purposes is now a matter of speculation among archaeologists.

The Body in the Freezer

The court in Bangui where Jean-Bedel Bokassa, ousted emperor of Central Africa, is on trial on charges of cannibalism heard yesterday [March 2nd 1987] from witnesses testifying to seeing human corpses – some with missing limbs – in the emperor's palace. One witness said she had seen two human bodies lying on the floor and another in a large freezer. Court sources say the testimony of Bokassa's former chef will be crucial.

Man, like other animals, does not eat blue food*

The Poisoning of ALICE ('ANNIE') THOMAS
on Saturday October the 18th 1930
in a café in Bude
and the Trial and Acquittal of SARAH ANN HEARN
for her Murder

At the time Mrs Sarah Ann Hearn began to attract the attention of the nation she was in her middle forties. Although she claimed to be a widow, there were circumstances surrounding her 'marriage' which make the opening to this story as curious as its development and its conclusion. To start with, there was no record of Sarah Ann's marriage certificate in the official registry at Somerset House. Her story was that she had married Leonard Wilmot Hearn in 1919 in a London register office; Leonard had been a medical student at the time and for reasons she never disclosed he and Sarah separated after only a few days. Shortly after that, so she said, Mrs Hearn read in a Harrogate newspaper that her husband had died. After such a tragic incident it was obvious that she would be asked by sympathetic friends and relatives to see a picture of the late Leonard Hearn. The photograph she chose to show them was subsequently discovered to be of Lieutenant Charles Stewart Vane-Tempest, who had been killed in action in the Great War. Mrs Hearn had bought his photograph. This incident, unimportant as it seems in isolation, does perhaps help us to understand what sort of attitude underlay Mrs Hearn's reactions to her later 'troubles'.

Immediately after the 'separation' from Leonard Hearn, Sarah had gone to stay in the house of an aunt who ran a cookery school in Harrogate. In 1921 the aunt retired and in company with Sarah and Sarah's invalid sister Lydia (called 'Minnie') removed to Cornwall where they shared Trenhorne House, in the small village of Lewannick.

Towards the end of the decade Mrs Hearn's aunt died, and shortly afterwards sister Minnie was nearing the end of a long illness, an illness characterized by severe gastric pains – though the unfortunate woman had for many years suffered problems with her heart and eyes. Minnie succumbed in early 1930, not long after complaining that her medicine tasted "too strong". She was buried in Lewannick churchyard.

Throughout this troubled time, Sarah Hearn had found great comfort in the friendship of her neighbours William and Alice ('Annie') Thomas. The Thomases occupied the next property to Mrs Hearn, called Trenhorne Farm – though one must add that neighbour is a word that is relative in country terms; in fact, the farm was some distance from Trenhorne House. The Thomases had always been on friendly terms with the two sisters and their aunt, but since Sarah Hearn had been left alone the kindly couple had shown her extra little attentions; they would take Sarah on short outings with them in the family car, and Annie would always think of her if she was doing some baking, making a few extra treats for her neighbour. Mr Thomas had also made Mrs Hearn a small loan of thirty-eight pounds to tide her over a difficult financial period.

On October the 18th, William and Annie Thomas invited Mrs Hearn to go with them on a trip to Bude, a seaside resort not far from Lewannick. Accepting gladly, Sarah made them all some tinned salmon sandwiches to take with them – apparently not an unusual gesture of reciprocation. As was customary on these outings they stopped for afternoon tea in a café, on this occasion supplementing their repast with some of Mrs

* Editorial from *Blue Food No.1*, ed. John Lyle, 1970.

... available to the public

The following compounds of arsenic are used for various purposes, and most of them are available to the public: sodium and potassium arsenite, sold as such and in arsenical sheep-dips, weed-killers, cattle-dips, hide preservers, worm powders and tablets for animals, fly powders for external application to sheep, preparations for foot-rot of sheep, and preservative solutions for wood; arsenious oxide in arsenical sheep-dips, powder for destruction of ants, and fly powders for external application to sheep; sodium arsenate in arsenical sheep-dips and fly powders for external application to sheep; arsenic sulphides and thioarsenates in arsenical sheep-dips and fly powders for external application to sheep; arsenic acid in arsenical weed-killers; copper arsenite and arsenate in arsenical worm powders for animals; lead arsenate—either $PbHAsO_4$ or $Pb_3(AsO_4)_2$—in horticultural spray or dust; calcium arsenate, magnesium arsenate, manganese arsenate, and zinc arsenite in horticultural spray or dust; London purple—calcium arsenite and calcium arsenate—in horticultural spray or dust; and Paris green—copper aceto-arsenite—in horticultural spray. Arsenical soaps also are probably in fairly general use, and certain arsenical compounds are used as ingredients in anti-fouling paints for ships' bottoms. With the possible exception of soaps and anti-fouling composition all the above-mentioned compounds can produce fatal poisoning if taken by man.

(*Toxicology*, Dr Gerald Roche Lynch)

Hearn's sandwiches. On the return journey to Lewannick Mrs Thomas became violently ill with stomach cramps and vomiting; once home, she became worse, and the abdominal pains grew so severe that Annie Thomas was rushed to Plymouth Hospital, where she died on the 4th of November.

A post mortem examination of Mrs Hearn's body revealed 0.85 grain of white arsenic – in those days freely available in the form of weed-killer.

In such small, insular communities as Lewannick, it is inevitable that a sudden mysterious death should result in speculation and gossip. William Thomas was well aware of the fact and told Mrs Hearn as much – that one of them was likely to be blamed and that she would be more open to suspicion than he. At Annie Thomas's funeral the gossips were out in force, pointing fingers, and one of the deceased's brothers, Mr Percy Parsons, did more than just point a finger when he heard that it was Mrs Hearn who had prepared the sandwiches; he fixed her with his eye and promised: "The matter must be cleared up."

A few days later Mr Thomas received a letter from Sarah Hearn, postmarked 'Launceston', and suggesting that she might be about to take her own life:

Dear Mr Thomas
Good-bye. I am going out if I can. I cannot forget that awful man [Percy Parsons] and the things he said. I am innocent, innocent, but she is dead and it was my lunch she ate. I cannot stay, when I am dead they will be sure I am guilty and you at least will be clear. May your dear wife's presence guard and comfort you still.
        Yours, A.H.
PS. My life is not a great thing now that dear Minnie's gone. I should be glad if you send my love to Bessie and tell her not to worry about me. My conscience is clear, I am not afraid of the afterwards. I am giving instructions to Webb [a solicitor] about selling the things and hope you will be paid in full. That is all I can do now.

A police description of Mrs Hearn was immediately circulated nationwide.

Before long a woman's coat and hat were found on the cliff-top at Looe, and it seemed possible that Sarah Hearn had, after all, committed suicide. But the police were still not convinced. In December they obtained a Home Office order for the exhumation of Mrs Hearn's sister and aunt. Both bodies were found to contain traces of arsenic.

Meanwhile, Sarah Hearn had adopted an

assumed name and taken up employment in Torquay, where she served as housekeeper to Mr Cecil Powell, an architect. Some weeks after Mrs Hearn's appointment, Mr Powell recognized her photograph printed in the *Daily Mail* alongside an offer of £500 reward for information on her whereabouts. As a model citizen, the architect immediately informed the Devonshire police of his suspicions; as a compassionate man, he immediately used the reward money to secure for his housekeeper the very best legal advice.

And so it was through this act of generosity that when Sarah Hearn stood before Mr Justice Roche at the Bodmin Assizes on July 15th 1931, her case was in the able hands of Mr Norman Birkett, one of the most successful defence attorneys of his day. The Crown was led by Mr H. du Parcq KC (later Lord du Parcq) assisted by Mr Patrick Devlin (later Lord Devlin).

It was with evidence relating to the fatal sandwiches eaten by Mrs Thomas at Bude that the prosecution case opened, though under cross-examination by Norman Birkett, William Thomas agreed that there had been nothing suspicious about the circumstances, no apparent 'forcing' of particular sandwiches onto his wife.

The chief chemist of the firm who manufactured the tinned salmon from which the sandwiches were made agreed that, though every care was obviously taken to sterilize the food before canning, it was possible that toxins could remain that would cause food poisoning. And furthermore, that there were cases on medical record in which one person may succumb to such poisoning while others may not.

Mr Birkett, in contesting the medical testimony on the deaths of Mrs Hearn's sister and aunt, established first that the soil in the graveyard in which they had been interred yielded a high natural arsenic content on analysis – higher, in fact, than that found in either of the corpses – and then began to attack the evidence of Dr Eric Wordley, the pathologist who had conducted the exhumation. Birkett suggested that it was possible for contaminated soil to have entered the jars in which the organs to be used for analysis were being stored, concluding with

the question: "Am I right in saying that a piece of soil, so small you could hold it between your fingers, dropped on to the body would make every single calculation wrong?" "Yes."

Mr du Parcq quoted the findings of the redoubtable Dr Roche Lynch, senior Home Office analyst, that pathological evidence indicated that Mrs Hearn's sister Minnie had been ingesting small doses of arsenic for some seven months before her death; and the court was further reminded of the patient's complaint that the medicine tasted "too strong".

A seminal piece of evidence in the Crown case was that Mrs Hearn had once purchased some weed-killer which contained arsenic – the manufacturers, however, as was the custom, had mixed a blue dye with the poison to prevent its being mistaken for some less toxic substance. In his cross-examination of Dr Roche Lynch, Norman Birkett asked:

Birkett: You say that in your opinion the weed-killer was used in solid form? – *Dr Roche Lynch*: I suggest so.

Have you taken a sandwich and put 14.3 grains in it? – No.

You have shown that arsenic put in Benger's Food discolours the white food? – Yes.

That is with two grains? – Yes.

Seven times as much as would greatly discolour it? – Yes.

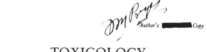

TOXICOLOGY
I.–HOMICIDAL, SUICIDAL, AND ACCIDENTAL POISONING

By G. ROCHE LYNCH, O.B.E., M.B., B.S., D.P.H., F.I.C.
Director of the Department of, and Lecturer in, Chemical Pathology, St. Mary's Hospital; Lecturer in Forensic Medicine and Toxicology, St. Mary's and Westminster Hospitals, London; Senior Official Analyst to the Home Office; Member of the Poisons Board

AND

D. M. PRYCE, M.D.
First Assistant, Department of Morbid Anatomy and Histology, St. Mary's Hospital, London

From
THE BRITISH ENCYCLOPAEDIA OF MEDICAL PRACTICE
Vol. XII, pp. 59-126

Roche Lynch on 'Homicidal Poisoning'

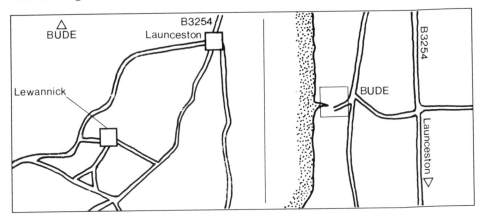

If you put fourteen grains of blue weed-killer on a sandwich and carried it for hours, I suggest it would be blue? – I have not tried it; but my opinion, for what it is worth, is that it would not be.

But you have not tried it! On the theory of the prosecution, surely it was a most terrible risk to run? – Personally I don't think so.

If you have sandwiches in two piles of three each, assume for the moment that the topmost sandwich in one of these piles contains arsenic, am I right in assuming that the sandwich with the blue weed-killer would stain downwards? – Yes.

The white bread, like the white Benger's Food, would make the stains instantly discernible? – I agree, and the white bread being more localized, the blue would come through in spots and stains.

When the prosecution case was complete and it was time for Norman Birkett to begin presenting his case, he opened with a common, if regularly unsuccessful, gambit. He suggested to Mr Justice Roche that, on the basis of the Crown case, there was insufficient evidence to go to the jury. Predictably, the judge responded that he thought there was ample evidence on which to continue, and Mr Birkett immediately put his main, and only, witness into the box.

As witnesses go, counsel could have asked no better than Mrs Sarah Ann Hearn; modest and unflappable, straightforward and eloquent in her own defence, she defied the best efforts of the prosecution to shake her testimony. She had left Lewannick, she

stated, because malicious gossip was making her life unbearable; indeed, she *had* contemplated suicide on that cliff-top in Looe, but had not had the courage to jump. The suggestion that she had been emotionally involved with Mr Thomas – the first and only hint of a motive to come out in the case against her – was vehemently denied. To emphasize her rebuttal of this implication, Norman Birkett concluded his cross-examination:

Birkett: I want you to understand that it is now suggested that you killed Mrs Thomas in order to do that [marry William Thomas]. Is there a word of truth in that? – *Mrs Hearn*: Not an atom.

Did you ever conceive a passion, guilty or otherwise, for Mr Thomas? – No.

On the following day, after a summing-up considered by many to be sympathetic in favour of the accused, Mr Justice Roche sent the jury into retirement with a final observation: "I do not suppose you have any doubt in your mind that the issue is now down to two people – Mrs Hearn and Mr Thomas. It is no use beating about the bush or failing to face facts. If, at the end of this case, you cannot say which it is, you ought to acquit Mrs Hearn, just as, if you were trying Mr Thomas, you would have to acquit him."

The jury did acquit Mrs Hearn, and the untimely death of Mrs Thomas remains a mystery. With no tangible evidence even to investigate William Thomas, the case was closed – and is likely to remain so.

Born to Lose

The Murder of CHARLES HENRY GIFFARD and his Wife by their Son MILES GIFFARD

on Friday November the 7th 1952 at 'Carrickowl', Porthpean

Miles Giffard was born in 1927 at 'Carrickowl', the extensive family residence overlooking Carlyon Bay, Porthpean, near St Austell, where Charles Henry Giffard was Clerk to the Magistrates.

Young Miles was to prove a grave disappointment to his parents, a disappointment that was first focused in 1940 when his masters at the exclusive Rugby public school found him uncooperative and virtually impossible to teach and were constrained to remove him. In fairness to Miles, his subsequent examination by Devon psychiatrist Dr Roy Craig revealed him to be suffering from a form of schizophrenia – a condition for which he was never given treatment.

Giffard then failed to make any progress in the study of law and enjoyed even less success in a course in estate management. At the age of twenty-five he inherited the sum of £750, gave up hope of mastering the estate agent's profession and settled comfortably into the day-to-day routine of a wastrel. Within four months he had squandered his inheritance and, pausing briefly to spend a couple of weeks selling ice-cream in Bournemouth, returned in June 1952 to his parents in Porthpean. Here, he set about frittering away his father's money as he had his own.

From Porthpean, Giffard began to make frequent sorties to London, where he became enamoured of nineteen-year-old Gabrielle Vallance, who lived with her mother at 40 Tite Street, Chelsea. By this time an exasperated Charles Giffard was prepared to go to extreme lengths to try to preserve both his son and what was left of his money. He recalled Miles to Porthpean, and after an ugly domestic scene forbade him – on pain of losing his allowance – to return to London. Miles, at the age of twenty-six, totally dependent on his father for financial support, had been forced into a corner. On November ber the 3rd 1952 he wrote in a letter to Gabrielle Vallance: "I am dreadfully fed up as I was looking forward to seeing you... Short of doing him in, I see no future in the world at all. I love you terribly..."

At 5.30pm on the 7th of November he telephoned Gabrielle that he would be travelling up to London later that night, adding that he would phone again in a few hours to confirm it. At 7.30pm Miles Giffard

Mrs Giffard

41

walked into the garage where his father was at work on his car. Leaving the old man unconscious from a crushing blow to the head with an iron pipe, Miles made his way to the kitchen, where he felled Mrs Giffard with a series of blows from the same blunt instrument.

He now made the promised call to Miss Vallance announcing his imminent departure for London, and returned to complete the job of killing his parents. Having tipped the victims of his murderous attack over the cliff some small distance from the house, Miles took the family car and drove to Chelsea, where he was knocking on Gabrielle Vallance's door at 8 o'clock the following morning. Taking a short time out to pawn some of his mother's jewellery, Giffard and his girlfriend went on the town. That evening, in a public house in Chelsea Mews, Miles confessed the murders to her, observing later: "it upset her..."

While Miles Giffard had been busy raising cash on his unfortunate mother's jewellery that morning, the Cornish police had been busy investigating the discovery of two bodies on the beach below the cliffs at Carlyon Bay; though Giffard, in his ineptitude, had left very little to tax the resources of the investigating officers. A trail of blood led along the cliff path into the kitchen and garage of 'Carrickowl', where only the most rudimentary attempt had been made to clean up the evidence of the previous evening's brutal killings. Giffard had disappeared along with the family car. Within hours, the London police had located Charles Giffard's Triumph outside the house in Tite Street. As Miles and Gabrielle returned that night from drinking they were met by a squad of policemen.

Held overnight on a charge of car stealing, Giffard was interviewed on the Sunday morning by Superintendent Julian, head of the Cornish CID, to whom he admitted killing his parents: "I wish to tell you everything about it with as little trouble as possible... I want to be frank. I did it."

Driven back to St Austell, Miles Giffard was formally charged with murder in the small courtroom in which his father had been Clerk for twenty-five years. In a statement he had said: "I can only say that I have had a brainstorm. I cannot account for my actions.

Miles Giffard

I had drunk about half a bottle of whisky on the Friday afternoon, before all this happened."

Giffard's trial opened at Bodmin Assizes in February 1953; he pleaded not guilty by reason of insanity. Contesting this defence, Mr John Scott Henderson QC pointed out to the jury that this had been a most calculated and cold-blooded murder; that Giffard had killed his father in order to take his car to London, and his mother in order to steal jewellery with which to finance his further extravagance. The fact that he had made little attempt to evade capture was due not to insanity, but to thorough incompetence.

In Giffard's defence, Mr John Maude QC said that there had been no attempt to deny the killings, but that the defence would rely on a proven history of mental instability. In the witness box Dr Roy Craig, who had subsequently retired from practice, recalled his examination of Giffard after his removal from Rugby: "I do not consider that he has ever been normal mentally. It was found that the origins of his terrors came from some sadistic nurse, who had not only beaten him as a tiny child, but had locked him in a dark cupboard." Questioned on the probable state of Giffard's mind at the time of the murders, Dr Craig replied: "I think at the time he did this thing he was in a schizophrenic episode. He would know what he was doing, but in schizophrenia there is a split in the mind – a split between the unconscious or primitive part of the mind and the more superficial, conventional part. When the split takes place the primitive mind takes charge, uncontrolled any longer by the conventional part. People in this condition know what they are doing and know the consequences of what they are doing."

Nevertheless, after a trial lasting four days, Mr Maude had clearly failed to convince the ten men and two women who comprised the jury that Miles Giffard was insane at the time he killed his parents. After a deliberation of only thirty-two minutes they found the prisoner guilty of murder. Miles Giffard was hanged at Bristol on February 24 1953.

The Drama Of Tregonissey
The Murder of Mrs ANNIE BLACK
by her Husband EDWARD ERNEST BLACK
in October 1921
at their home in Tregonissey, near St Austell

The tiny village of Tregonissey, near St Austell, might have remained forever in happy obscurity; but the murder of Annie Black in the autumn of 1921, under dramatic circumstances, thrust it into the glare of national publicity.

In 1914, when Annie was 54, she married Edward Ernest Black, a man eighteen years her junior. As the owner of the village confectionery shop she was a popular local figure, and her marriage to a clay-pit worker so much younger than herself must have caused its share of gossip. Nevertheless, the couple settled down happily enough in the home above the shop, which they shared with Edward's 17-year-old step-daughter Marion, and Black gave up the pits for a job as an insurance agent.

The business prospered and all went well until October 31, 1921, when Mrs Black became ill. She had just finished a breakfast of bread-and-butter, cake and a cup of tea, poured by her husband, when she was stricken with violent sickness and diarrhoea. Dr Edwin Andrew was called and concluded that she was yet another victim of a bout of gastro-enteritis that was doing the rounds at the time. He prescribed the customary bismuth mixture and carried on to his next call. Mrs Black, however, got steadily worse, and friends and neighbours felt anxious enough to sit with her day and night – always with Mr Black in close attendance. They found it touching that his concern for his wife's health made him so insistent upon giving her the medicine himself; and even though each time he did so she complained of a terrible burning in the throat, he refused to let her stop the treatment. Strangely, the medicine seemed not to have this adverse effect on the patient on the few occasions when it was administered by someone other than her husband – but at the time this was not remarked.

After three days the illness had not abated, and Black spread the story among their neighbours that his wife was gravely ill and had a diseased heart – solely Black's diagnosis, as the doctor had expressed no anxiety at this stage. Eight days later, when Mrs Black was still in the grip of the sickness, her husband mysteriously disappeared; and with his departure the symptoms abated – but the invalid was now so weak that little hope was held out for her life. The doctor now realized that something more malignant than gastro-enteritis was killing his patient and he was finally obliged to diagnose suspected poisoning. Three days later, on 11th November, Mrs Annie Black was dead. The doctor, refusing to sign the death certificate, called for the intervention of the coroner.

And where was Edward Black?

We now know that the unhappy man was in grave financial difficulties. Having taken people's money for insurance policies that they never received, he was running from imminent arrest on charges of fraud. But at the time of his disappearance, the national press splashed story and photographs of a possible runaway murderer, and when the post-mortem confirmed Dr Andrew's suspicions the hunt intensified; the inquest which had started on November 14th was adjourned three times while attempts were made to locate Edward Black.

Meanwhile, Mrs Black's internal organs had been removed and sent for chemical analysis. Arsenic was found, but only in a minute quantity – one-seventeenth of a grain (3.73 mg) – far less than the two grains normally considered a fatal dose. It was suggested that the prolonged period of vomiting and diarrhoea could account for this; but why had Mrs Black died three days *after* her husband's desertion? The answer was then given that she had in fact died from failure of the kidneys – but failure of the kidneys due to the effects of arsenic on those already weakened organs; the improvement of the last three days of illness was due to the removal of the source of the irritant arsenic – by then the damage had already been done, the woman already fated to die.

The newspapers continued to make much of the story, and then, at midnight on November 21st, Black was found in the most extraordinarily dramatic circumstances. His trail had been followed to Cashin's Temperance Hotel, Bell Street, in Liverpool, and when a local detective burst into the room rented by the runaway, he found him sitting in the darkness, fully-clothed by the side of the bed with his hands to his throat. Blood was streaming through his fingers and, as the detective approached, a pocket knife clattered from the blood-drenched hands onto the floor.

Black was rushed to hospital and by January 5th was well enough to attend the adjourned inquest at St Austell. There he was charged with the murder of his wife.

The trial at Bodmin Assizes which started on February 2nd 1922 was a short one, due to the weight of evidence against the accused (albeit mostly circumstantial). The case was heard before Mr Justice Rowlatt, Black was defended by John Lhind Pratt, a junior barrister provided under the Poor Prisoners Defence Regulations. The evidence for the Crown was presented by Mr Holman Gregory KC. Seldom could evidence have seemed so damning; first, a local chemist and his assistant identified Edward Black as the customer who had bought two ounces of indigo-coloured arsenic (enough to provide about 500 fatal doses) from their St Austell shop on October 29th. They claimed to be positive of their identification because they had served him before, and he was a well-known member of the local church choir. Black insisted that he bought arsenic in order to dispose of rats, though his daughter testified that to her knowledge there had never been a sign of a single rat, either in the shop or in their home above it. Black's signature was identified in the chemist's poison book by several witnesses, including the superintendent of the insurance company for which the accused had worked and who would be expected to be familiar with the signature. "Forgery," said Black, "it is not my signature." The flatness of Black's denials were losing progressively more of the jury's sympathy...

Next, the neighbours gave evidence of his strange behaviour in the administering of his wife's medicine; traces of arsenic had also been found in the bottles – and though these could not be treated as conclusive evidence (the amounts were small and were consistent with impurities in the bismuth) other scientific evidence was more substantial. The experts explained that even indigo-stained arsenic could easily be disguised in medicine or in a cup of tea; the jury, requesting proof of this hypothesis, were shown cups of tea with and without the offending ingredient for comparison. Finally, in a search of the Blacks' home, the police discovered a Red Cross book with the page dealing with arsenic and other poisons neatly turned down at the corner. Black, characteristically, denied having seen the book since the end of the war.

The accused man could not provide one piece of evidence in his defence. But a letter written by Edward Black just before his suicide attempt, addressed to his friend Joseph Kelly – the local butcher – was read out in court and the pathetic document visibly moved those present.

Dear Joe,

No doubt this letter will give you a shock, but I have always looked to you as a pal, and being the last letter I shall ever write in this world kindly forgive me for sending it to you. Joe, I am heart broken and can't stand it any longer, so now I am going to Annie. God bless her; she will forgive me if nobody else will. So farewell to all my friends I never thought you would have kicked me when I was down, but never mind old friend you can't hurt a dead man, and the people who are telling such horrible lies about me will have their day. For remember 'Vengeance is mine said the Lord. I will repay.' and don't forget the devil is not so black as he is painted. Well, Joe, for one thing, I can't understand. For God's sake why doesn't Dr. Andrew tell the others the state of Annie's heart, the same what he told it to me. Ask him to be a man and not a cad. What does he mean by suggesting arsenic. My God, Joe, you know me better than

that. I made the greatest mistake of my life when I came away. What made me do it I can't say, but we all make mistakes, old friend, and now I am about to pay a big price for mine; so good-bye all. Kiss Marion for me, look after her, and ask her if she will forgive me, Tell her to be a good girl, and Heaven will bless her, and Annie, and Grannie, and I will be watching for her, for the time comes when there will be no more deaths, neither sighing nor weeping, for God shall wipe away all tears from their eyes. Remember me to all my friends, if I have any left, and oh, my God, how I should like to clasp you all by the hand, but that is forbidden now. Well Joe, you can do what you like with this letter, but it is my wish that you read it to all, and those in particular who are trying to brand me. I don't know where this letter will be posted from. A friend is going to post it for me, but one thing is sure, my body won't be found in England as I am already several hundred of miles away. Now, kind friend, break the news gently to Marion, and tell her I won't trouble her any more. So now farewell to you from a heart broken miserable man whom I hope God will forgive (signed) Ted Black.

[Then followed at the end of the letter about 60 crosses marked "For Marion."]

In view of his attempted suicide, and the signs of a possibly psychotic personality revealed in this letter, it is surprising that no plea of insanity was advanced in his defence. The case, though, proceeded; and the jury, with sample cups of tea and other evidence, retired for forty-five minutes. They returned with a verdict of 'Guilty'.

Black was sentenced to death and, after the rejection of his appeal, he was hanged at Exeter on March 24 1922.

It would seem to have been an open and shut case; but what possible motive did Edward Black have to murder his wife? He had no emotional attachment to another woman; financially Annie Black was more of an asset to him alive than dead, with her successful running of the shop and her generous attitude towards money. True, they had been overheard on occasion arguing over shortage of finance, but this would hardly have been solved by the £60-odd that Mrs Black left on her death. Perhaps there was some still-secret reason for his wishing her dead; or maybe Black was the victim of some deep neurotic disturbance and no suitable case for execution.

Postscript

In doing the original research for his book *Scales of Justice** in the 1970s, Fenton Bresler made a startling discovery in the official Register of Deaths for St Austell. Duly recorded was the death of Annie Black on November 11th 1921, and against 'Cause of Death' was written "Murder. Arsenical poisoning by Edward Ernest Black". No

surprise in that; after all, it was the verdict of the Court. But Bresler looked again, looked at the date of the recording – January 10th 1922. Twenty-two days *before* Black was put into the dock at Bodmin!

For twenty-two days, then, this judgement-by-Deputy-Registrar was common property around the town of St Austell. One is tempted to ask what sort of chance Edward Black stood with the evidence of neighbours; with a local jury, for whom his guilt had already been officially recorded.

*Weidenfeld and Nicholson, London, 1973.

[Based on 'The Drama of Tregonissey' by Susan Dunkley]

Hartland 3

2 Culompton

Hatherleigh 4

DEVON

1 Babbacombe
5 Torquay

Devon

The Man They Couldn't Hang
The Murder of Miss EMMA KEYSE
by JOHN LEE
on Saturday the 15th of November 1884
in her house at Babbacombe

Along with stories of people being hanged in error* – of which, due mainly to the unsound foundations of the law enforcement system and the huge number of capital offences on the statute in former centuries, there were many – are a host of legends of people who were hanged several times, hanged and then revived, or reprieved just as they had been "launched into eternity". In fact, there are a number of reliably recorded cases where, for reasons generally connected with the crudeness of the method of execution, the prisoner simply would not hang.

The most celebrated such case was that of John Lee, the Babbacombe Murderer, who, in 1884, at the age of nineteen years, was convicted of the brutal murder of the elderly spinster for whom he served as footman.

John Lee was the son of a yeoman farmer living at 3 Town Cottages, Abbotskerswell, near Newton Abbot, in which village he

---

* See *Murder Club Guide No.5* for a note on Hanging in Error.

lived with his mother. Shortly after his fifteenth birthday, John was taken into service by Miss Emma Keyse of Babbacombe; she had once been a maid to Queen Victoria and around the village was known and loved for her kindness and generosity. Among her servants she was known for her strictness and parsimony.

Though John did well in his employment, it was barely eighteen months before the spirit of adventure rose in him, and the dreams inspired by the passing ships and the tales of the fishermen and seafarers that clustered around the quayside along that stretch of the Devon coast decided him on a life in the Royal Navy. Sadly, the youthful enthusiasm was not equalled by physical strength, and his weak chest failed John Lee in all but the lightest duties. Finally disaster struck – after developing pneumonia on board, he was invalided out of the service.

Now whether it was disappointment, depression after his illness, or simply a natural tendency that had not yet manifested itself,

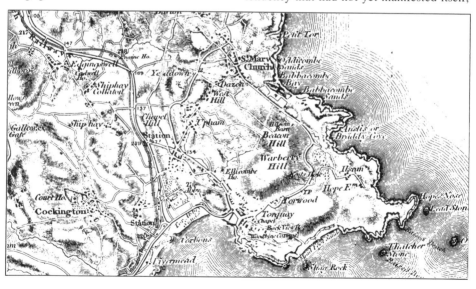

John 'Babbacombe' Lee

James Berry

back on shore John Lee was a changed young man. A youth who had changed to such a degree that he may already have been marked for the gallows.

From his next employer on dry land, Lee took to stealing; and was rewarded with six months' hard labour. And this might have proved the salutary lesson that he needed; but Miss Keyse, hearing of his predicament and with more generosity than foresight, wrote to the prison Governor offering to take John back into service if he should be released. And so he was. And so John Lee came to return to the house by the sea.

In the early hours of Saturday morning, the 15th of November 1884, one of the maids woke to the strong smell of smoke. When the household had been roused with cries of "Fire!", it was discovered that there were no less than five separate fires – all of them started with paraffin, but only one burning human fuel. With utter horror and disbelief, the party which had been despatched to deal with the fire in the dining-room came upon the body of Miss Keyse, her head terribly injured, her throat cut through to the vertebra. Around the body, like a ghastly funeral pyre were smouldering newspapers soaked in a mixture of blood and paraffin.

When John Lee's blood-soaked knife and towel were found next to the body of Miss Keyse he was immediately arrested and charged with murder. At his trial, the prisoner owned that it was revenge that had turned him into a killer, resentment that his weekly wage had been reduced by sixpence to two shillings on account of some minor lapse.

On December the 4th 1884, Lee was condemned to death. He was to have been executed at Exeter by James Berry, then the official hangman, whose competence had never been held in doubt. The prisoner was in position beneath the gallows, a hood over his head and a rope round his neck. Berry pulled the lever. The trap remained stuck fast, with John Lee standing on it. The hangman pulled again; and again; still the prisoner could not drop. Berry stamped several times on the doors of the trap, so did the Warders; still they remained firmly together.

With Lee removed from the 'machine', it was tested and checked and worked perfectly. Until they tried to hang John Lee for the second time.

A much embarrassed James Berry once

49

again tested his apparatus; once again completed a successful test drop. And was once again unsuccessful in launching Lee, as they say, "into Eternity". To the dismay, and by now more than a little disgust, of the observers, the trap refused to open for a third time. The chaplain recorded: "The lever was pulled again and again. A great noise was heard, which sounded like the falling of the drop. But to my horror, when I turned my eyes to the scaffold, I saw the poor convict standing upon the drop as I had seen him twice before. I refused to stay any longer."

The only person not surprised by the strange occurrence was Lee himself, for he had dreamed that he would not hang; "The Lord will never permit me to be executed", he said. And, indeed, He did not. John Lee's sentence was commuted to imprisonment and he was released in 1907.

Of the subsequent explanations (including many concerning Divine intervention), the most likely seems to be that the flaps of the trap had become swollen as a result of soaking up the recent heavy rain and when a weight was put directly on them the edges bound.

[*See also Appendix One – The Ones They Couldn't Hang*]

JAMES BERRY'S ACCOUNT

Executioner's Office,
1, Bilton Place, City Road,
Bradford, Yorks.,
4th March, 1885.

Re John Lee

Sir,
    In accordance with the request contained in your letter of the 30th inst., I beg to say that on the morning of Friday, the 20th ult., I travelled from Bradford to Bristol, and on the morning of Saturday, the 21st, from Bristol to Exeter, arriving at Exeter at 11-50 a.m., when I walked direct to the County Gaol, signed my name in your Gaol Register Book at 12 o'clock exactly. I was shown to the Governor's office, and arranged with him that I would go and dine and return to the Gaol at 2-00 p.m. I accordingly left the Gaol, partook of dinner, and returned at 1-50 p.m., when I was shown to the bedroom allotted to me which was an officer's room in the new Hospital Ward. Shortly afterwards I made an inspection of the place of Execution. The execution was to take place in a Coach-house in which the Prison Van was usually kept. Two Warders accompanied me on the inspection. In the Coach-house I found a Beam about four inches thick, and about a foot in depth, was placed across the top of the Coach-house. Through this beam an iron bolt was fastened with an iron-nut on the upper side, and to this bolt a wrought-iron rod was fixed, about three-quarters of a yard long with a hole at the lower end to which the rope was to be attached. Two Trap-doors were placed in the floor of the Coach-house, which is flagged with stone, and these doors cover a pit about 2 yards by 1½ yards across, and about 11 feet deep. On inspecting these doors I found they were only about an inch thick, but to have been constructed properly should have been three or four inches thick. The ironwork of the doors was of a frail kind, and much too weak for the purpose. There was a lever to these doors, and it was placed near the top of them. I pulled the lever and the doors dropped, the catches acting all right. I had the doors raised, and tried the lever a second time, when the catch again acted all right. The Governor was watching me through the window of his office and saw me try the doors. After the examination I went to him, explained how I found the doors, and suggested to him that for future executions new trap-doors should be made about three times as thick as those then fixed. I also suggested that a spring should be fixed in the Wall to hold the doors back when they fell, so that no rebounding occurred, and that the ironwork of the doors

should be stronger. The Governor said he would see to these matters in future. I spent all the Sunday in the room allotted to me, and did not go outside the Gaol. I retired to bed about 9-45 that night. The execution was fixed to take place at eight o'clock on the morning of Monday the 23rd ultimo.

On the Monday morning I arose at 6-30, and was conducted from the Bedroom by a Warder, at 7-30, to the place of execution. Everything appeared to be as I had left it on the Saturday afternoon. I fixed the rope in my ordinary manner, and placed everything in readiness. I did not try the Trap-doors as they appeared to be just as I had left them. It had rained heavily during the nights of Saturday and Sunday. About four minutes to eight o'clock I was conducted by the Governor to the condemned Cell and introduced to John Lee. I proceeded at once to pinion him, which was done in the usual manner, and then gave a signal to the Governor that I was ready. The procession was formed, headed by the Governor, the Chief Warder, and the Chaplain followed by Lee. I walked behind Lee and 6 or 8 warders came after me. On reaching the place of execution I found you were there with the Prison Surgeon. Lee was at once placed upon the trap-doors. I pinioned his legs, pulled down the white cap, adjusted the Rope, stepped on one side, and drew the lever – but the trap-door did not fall. I had previously stood upon the doors and thought they would fall quite easily. I unloosed the strap from his legs, took the rope from his neck, removed the White Cap, and took Lee away into an adjoining room until I made an examination of the doors. I worked the lever after Lee had been taken off, drew it, and the doors fell easily. With the assistance of the warders the doors were pulled up, and the lever drawn a second time, when the doors again fell easily. Lee was then brought from the adjoining room, placed in position, the cap and rope adjusted, but when I again pulled the lever it did not act, and in trying to force it the lever was slightly strained. Lee was then taken off a second time and conducted to the adjoining room.

It was suggested to me that the woodwork fitted too tightly in the centre of the doors, and one of the warders fetched an axe and another a plane. I again tried the lever but it did not act. A piece of wood was then sawn off one of the doors close to where the iron catches were, and by the aid of an iron crowbar the catches were knocked off, and the doors fell down. You then gave orders that the execution should not be proceeded with until you have communicated with the Home Secretary, and Lee was taken back to the Condemned Cell. I am of opinion that the ironwork catches of the trap-doors were not strong enough for the purpose, that the woodwork of the doors should have been about three or four times as heavy, and with iron-work to correspond, so that when a man of Lee's weight was placed upon the doors the iron catches would not have become locked, as I feel sure they did on this occasion, but would respond readily. So far as I am concerned, everything was performed in a careful manner, and had the iron and woodwork been sufficiently strong, the execution would have been satisfactorily accomplished.

I am, Sir,
Your obedient Servant,

James Berry.

Henry M. James, Esq.,
   Under-Sheriff of Devon,
      The Close, Exeter.

A Black Unnatural Monster
The Murder of his Aunt and her Five Children
his Wife and his own Two Children
by the Highwayman THOMAS AUSTIN
near Culompton
and his Execution at Exeter in August 1694

Thomas Austin was born at Culompton, in Devonshire, of very honest parents, who at their death left him a farm of their own, worth about eighty pounds per annum, which is a pretty estate in that country; and as his land was without encumbrances, and he had a good character at that time, he soon got a wife with a suitable fortune, she having no less than eight hundred pounds to her portion. But this increase of his riches, and the thought of having so much ready money by him, made him neglect the improvement of his living and take to an idle, extravagant course, by means of which, in less than four years' time, he had consumed all that his wife had brought him and mortgaged his own estate.

Being now reduced to pinching circumstances and not knowing which way to turn himself for a livelihood, the devil so far got the upper hand of him as to excite him to the commission of all manner of unlawful actions for the support of himself and his family. Several frauds he was detected in, which his neighbours were so good as to forgive, out of respect to his family and to what he had once been. At last he was so desperate as to venture on the highway, where, assaulting Sir Zachary Wilmot on the road between Wellington and Taunton Dean, that unfortunate gentleman was murdered by him for making some attempts to save his money.

The booty he got from Sir Zachary was forty-six guineas and a silver-hilted sword, with which he got home undiscovered and unsuspected. This did not, however, last him long, for he followed his old riotous course. When it was all spent he pretended a visit to an uncle of his, who lived at about a mile from his own habitation, and it was one of the bloodiest visits that ever was made.

When he came to the house he found nobody at home but his aunt and five small children, who informed him that his uncle was gone out on business and would not be at home till evening, and desired him to stay a little and keep them company. He seemingly consented to stay; but had not sat many minutes before he snatched up a hatchet that was at hand and cleaved the skull of his aunt in two; after which he cut the throats of all the children and laid the dead bodies in a heap, all weltering in their gore. Then he went upstairs and robbed the house.

He made all the haste he could home to his wife, who, perceiving some drops of blood on his clothes, asked him how they came there. "You bitch," says he, "I'll soon show you the manner of it!" pulling at the same time the bloody razor which he had before used out of his pocket and cutting her throat from ear to ear. When he had gone thus far, to complete the tragedy he ripped out the bowels of his own two chidren, the elder of whom was not three years of age.

Scarcely had he finished all his butcheries before his uncle, whom he had been to visit, came accidentally to pay him the same compliment on his way home; when, entering the house and beholding the horrid spectacle, he was almost thunderstruck with the sight, though as yet he little thought the same tragedy had been acted on all his family too, as he soon after fatally found. What he saw, however, was enough to point out the offender, whom he immediately laid hold of, and carried him before a magistrate, who sent him to Exeter Jail.

In the month of August, 1694, this inhuman wretch suffered the punishment provided by the law, which appears much too mild for such a black unnatural monster.

A Wolf in Sheep's Clothing

The Murder of ROGER ASHTON
by the Reverend PETER VINE

in or around the month of April 1811
at Heartland [Hartland]

EXECUTION
of the
REV. PETER VINE

Being an impartial Account of the Life, Character, Behaviour, and last Dying Words of the Rev. Peter Vine, Vicar of Heartland, who was Executed at Heavy-Tree-Gallows, in the County of Devon, on Monday August the 8th [1811], for a Rape and Murder, the first committed on the Body of a Child Eleven Years of Age, belonging to Mrs Dark, in the aforesaid County, & the second on the Body of Roger Ashton, who went to apprehend him after he had committed the Fact. With the remarkable Speech he made to the Populace at the Place of Execution.

Together with a Prayer he made use of while under Sentence of Death

With a Copy of Verses

EXECUTION OF THE REV. PETER VINE

It must certainly have been a dismal shock to all Christians, especially those of the Clergy, when they heard of the inhuman actions of the Rev. Peter Vine, a gentleman who was once respected by every body for his seeming good behaviour to both God and Man. He was greatly respected by the Gentry, who were very desirous of his instructions in their Family, and more especially by the mother of the unhappy child, Mrs Dark, who was very desirous of his company, that he might instruct her Daughter (who was about eleven years of Age) in the principles of Religion.

He who was sent to be a messenger over a flock, to guard and preserve them from the devouring Beast, should cast off that Heavenly garment, and clothe himself with the habit of a wolf. One who was designed to instruct and convert sinners to repentance, should desert his Heavenly Master, who shed his own precious Blood, for lost souls, and 'list himself in the Devil's Regiment.

I say then how dreadful is the case of this man, who at the day of Judgement can find no one to plead for him; even his new Master, in whom he once put such confidence, will then leave him; I hope the following Relation, which is certainly true, may be a means to reclaim the most hardened Sinner on Earth.

This Unhappy Gentleman, the Rev. Mr Peter Vine, was Vicar of Heartland, in the County of Devon, and went frequently to Mrs. Dark's, who always desired his company, that he might instruct her Daughter, which seemingly he did to all outward appearance.

There was a pleasant Garden belonging to the house, in which they walked together; and one day the gentlewoman, leaving the child and the wolf in sheep's clothing by themselves, he being prompted by the instigation of the devil, he ravished the Infant, at which time the child screaming out, he made his escape over the garden wall. The mother of the child coming up, saw her daughter in a horrid state and in a terrible fit; the sight of which struck her with such surprise that she swooned away, and lay till one of her servants came to know what occasioned her stay. As soon as she came to herself, she went in search of him, but he could not be found. The mother fell sick with grief, and the infant lay indisposed for some time; as soon as the gentlewoman was recovered she promised a reward of twenty Guineas for any one who should find him out, so that he might be apprehended and brought to Justice.

He absconded from his habitation near three months, and notwithstanding he was acquainted with the reward that was offered for his being secured, he ventured home on Sunday the 17th of April, and had the undaunted assurance to swear by God that he would shoot the first man who should attempt to take him. The neighbourhood being informed of his coming home, sent word to Mrs Dark who immediately went to Justice Saltern, who granted her a Warrant to apprehend him, and the Constable to whom she gave it took one Roger Ashton, and William Blake to assist him.

When they came to the house they found they could have no admittance without violence, and with much difficulty they at last entered the house and then were obliged at last to break open several locks before they came to the room where he was. The first that entered it was Roger Ashton, who seeing the Prisoner with a pistol in his hand made up to him, but before he could come at him, Vine discharged it, and shot him dead on the spot. Then the other two secured him, and being carried before Justice Saltern, he was under examination two hours.

The Justice first informed him of the abominable Crime laid to his charge, and said with a seeming tenderness that there had been too sufficient Proof of his being guilty, he could not believe it, for says he, the sad condition of the Infant and your flying from Justice thoroughly confirms your Guilt. He appeared very undaunted, and strongly denied the Fact laid to his charge of the Rape. Before his committments were finished his aged Father came, who accosted him in the following manner: With what a load of grief have I at last arrived, to see this dreadful sight of Infamy, and you, which cuts my very soul to see, should be the sole occasion of it. O! that I had died in my mother's Womb that I could not have seen the sea of sorrow; you in whom lay all my delight and pleasure of this life, now proves the destroyer of it. Having repeated these words, while floods of tears bedewed his cheeks, he was sent home and put to bed where he lay ten days before he expired.

On Monday the 25th Instant, he was tried at the Guild-Hall for the city of Exeter, for the aforesaid Rape and Murder, and found Guilty; but did not seem daunted in the least when Sentence of Death was pronounced against him, and said he did not fear dying for that he was entirely innocent of the Rape, and as to the Murder he stood in his own defence.

On Thursday the 4th [of May], the Warrant for his Execution came down to him, for his Execution on the Monday following, which he did not seem to mind, but hoped as he was Innocent to have the forgiveness from Almighty God, who was able to reward him for all his sufferings on Earth.

He was near 35 years of age, born of honest reputable parents; he was the son of Mr John Vine, of Heartland, in the county of Devon, who spared no cost to accomplish him in the practice of Divinity, and as soon as he was put in Orders, he was made Vicar of Heartland. His father doted on him, and thought himself to be one of the happiest Parents in the whole Universe. Vine's behaviour was seemingly good while under sentence, and he was heard often to say the following Prayer:

THE PRAYER

O God who hath not given Laws to be Traps and Snares, nor on purpose that they may be broken, and poor mortals be brought under the Lash of the Law and be sentenced to damnation, hear me, O Lord, and have mercy upon me, for I have sinned against thee; I heartily pray and beseech thee, in the bowels of thy mercy, to look down from Heaven upon me thy poor servant, whom thou chose as a shepherd, to watch thy Flock, and whose sins be infinite and immeasurable, most heinous and insupportable, but as they be grievous without number, so is thy Mercy more abundant and without end. Turn not thy Face away from me that lies prostrate, lamenting for his sinful Life before thy Mercy gate; which thou dost open wide to those that do lament their sins; O shut it not against me Lord, when I depart this sinful World; but let me enter in, and call me not to a strict account how I have lived here. Thy Mercy is above all thy Works; more able to save than my sins to condemn. Therefore, O Sweet Saviour, for thy bitter Death and Passion, and for the Glory of thy Name, be merciful unto me, and forgive me all my Sins, as I heartily repent, and the Lord Jesus Christ remain with me now and for evermore. Amen.

He was so well respected among his Parishioners that he was invited to dinner at one house or another almost every Day. All good Christians that knew him thought it was an honour to be in his company as his conversation was so good, and certainy he bore a fine character before the commission of the Rape and Murder. Whilst he was under sentence he would not suffer any Clergyman to come nigh him, saying if the learning and education which I received from my tender indulgent Father is not sufficient, I ought to receive no Mercy.

AT THE PLACE OF EXECUTION

The Morning of his Execution, he behaved with becoming decency, and after receiving the Blessed Sacrament, he walked to the fatal Tree in a suit of mourning, attended by the Sheriff's officers, and as soon as he mounted the Ladder, he spoke in the following manner:

"Loving people,
I see there are numbers of you assembled to see me depart this Sinful Life, in shame, and as I am a dying Parson no doubt but you expect to hear something of the fact for which I suffer, especially from me who was sent as a Messenger from God to instruct his people, and not to learn them more Wickedness, by breaking into evil paths, following not the righteous ways.

I say as there is a just God, who sitteth on the Judgement seat in Heaven, before whom I must presently appear to answer for all my sins, that I am not guilty of the Rape which I am charged with, committed on the body of Mrs Dark's child. I own that I committed the Murder on the body of Roger

Ashton, but that I stood on my own defence, therefore I think I have the less sin to answer for, because he never told me his business when he came to take me, and I being in fear of being robbed discharged the pistol which shot him dead on the Spot.

As for my absconding, it was on account of my Father's ill state of health, on whose death was an hundred pounds depending, and who is dead since with grief for this unhappy affair. I pray God be with you all, and beg you all to pray for my departing Soul, and desire you to shun all treacherous persons' company, in doing which you will do good both to God and to yourselves."

After reading Prayers and singing a Psalm, he was turned off the Ladder, crying: "Lord Jesus receive my Spirit."

A Copy of Verses

You tender Christians all, of high and low
    degree,
Stop a few moments, and listen unto me,
A shocking tale you now shall hear,
Will surely draw forth many a tear.

In Heartland town, it's known full well,
The Rev. Peter Vine, he there did dwell,
Minister of that Parish Church was he,
Respected by all, of high and low degree.

A widow lady in this same town did
    dwell,
Had a daughter eleven years old, that she
    lov'd full well,
To this Minister she sent without delay,
To have her brought up in virtuous ways.

Surely the devil must him possess,

For to commit such wickedness,
On her he did commit a rape,
And left her in a shocking state.

A reward was offered then with speed,
They went to apprehend him for this
    deed,
Soon as the room they entered,
He quickly shot one of them dead.

When at the Bar he did appear,
The court with horror was fill'd we hear,
To see a man in holy degrees,
Found quilty of such crimes as these.

Now he's executed for the same,
Great numbers went to see him die in
    shame,
By this Minister's fate, be warn'd I pray,
Never let your passions lead you astray.

The Cost of Living
The Murder of JOHN TRENAMAN
by JANE COX
on Tuesday the 25th of June 1811
at Hatherleigh, near Exeter

Jane Cox was indicted at Exeter Assizes, on the 9th of August 1811, for the wilful murder of one John Trenaman, an infant, sixteen months old, and Arthur Tucker was charged as an accessory. The latter was a respectable farmer, living in Hatherleigh, in this county, and the infant was his natural child. It appeared that Jane Cox had, on the 25th of June 1811, administered to the child a quantity of arsenic, by putting it into the child's hands. The child put the arsenic in its mouth, in consequence of which it died in about two hours. The prisoner, in her written confession, had implicated Tucker, as having persuaded her to do the deed, and stated his having taken the arsenic from under the roof of a cottage, and given it to her, and promised her a one-pound note if she would administer it to the child. This was not believed.

The prisoner, Jane Cox, after a trial of seven hours, was convicted, and hanged on the following Monday. Tucker was acquitted. He called a number of respectable witnesses who gave him a very high character.

On Monday, the 12th of August 1811, pursuant to her sentence, this unfortunate woman was brought to the 'new drop', the place of execution, and underwent the dread sentence of the law.

She addressed the spectators at some length, and lamented that the person who had instigated her to the commission of the horrid deed was not also to suffer with her.

The Haunting of 'Castel-a-Mare'
Ghostly Manifestations following a Brutal Murder
that took place around 1870
at 'Castel-a-Mare', Middle Warberry Road, near Torquay

That ghosts and murders are frequently linked in the popular imagination comes as no surprise to serious psychical researchers. It is a long-held theory that the manifestations we label 'ghosts' can be simply explained if we use the 'tape-recorder' theory. One of the pioneers of this hypothesis was the celebrated English physicist Sir Oliver Lodge; in his *Man and the Universe*, Lodge explained that it was "as if strong emotions could be unconsciously recorded in matter, so that the deposit shall thereafter affect a sufficiently sensitive organism and cause similar emotions to reproduce themselves in his subconsciousness, in a manner analogous to the customary conscious interpretation of photographic or phonographic records... Take for example a haunted house... wherein some one room is the scene of a ghostly representation of some long past tragedy. On a psychometric hypothesis the original tragedy has been literally *photographed* on its material surroundings, nay, even on the ether itself, by reason of the intensity of emotion felt by those who enacted it... It is this theory that is made to account for the feeling one has on entering certain rooms,

that there is an alien presence therein, though it is invisible and inaudible to mortal sense..."

This 'psychometric hypothesis' will also explain why, in the majority of cases, a ghost seems quite unaware of the presence of human beings – who clearly would not have been part of its 'recording'. Similarly, the fact that manifestations seem sometimes to "just disappear", or to "walk through a wall", indicates that when the image was transferred – when the ghost was 'created' – there was some obstruction, a partition, a wall, that would have kept it from view or, in the second case, that there was once a door, or opening, where that section of wall now is – the spirit is simply walking through it.

Most researchers will agree that the release of violent, often malevolent, energy that accompanies a brutal killing will more effectively imprint itself onto its surroundings; awaiting those conditions sympathetic to rendering it visible, audible and possibly destructive.

Because criminologists seldom concern

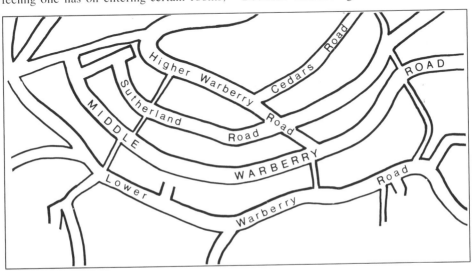

themselves with such ethereal matters as the 'spirit world', hauntings that are associated with murders are rarely documented in any detail. Similarly, as it is frequently only the *fact* of a killing that interests the ghost-hunter, details of the crime itself are often scantily recorded.

The following case is of the latter kind, and is included here because what little we do know of the murder – which was never discovered in its own time – comes direct from the 'mouths' of those involved via a spirit-medium.

'Castel-a-Mare' was an unimpressive, three-storey edifice "standing on the left-hand side of Middle Warberry Road opposite 'Edwinstowe', the back of the premises opening on to the road."* The house was demolished in 1920 and the site now provides the garden for its former neighbour.

As far as can be determined, the crime took place around 1870; the participants in the drama seem to have been the master of the

house, his maid, and a mysterious doctor – possibly of 'foreign' extraction. The trouble with spirits is that they cannot always be relied upon to give the correct information in the correct narrative sequence. Consequently, we are by no means certain of the course of events of that dreadful evening that were to etch themselves so indelibly into the fabric of 'Castel-a-Mare'. Our best analysis of the facts is that the guest – the foreign doctor – went berserk and first killed the master of the house and then strangled his maid. The fact that the murder remained undiscovered until the ghosts started talking may be due to the fact that the doctor could himself have issued a certificate stating that his victim's death had been due to natural causes; as for maids, they were being hired and fired all the time, prone to "going off" with young grooms, or simply getting home-sick and packing their bags.

We are fortunate in having a first-hand account of an investigation of this celebrated haunting recorded by Violet Tweedale* which, in an edited form, follows:

* *Devon Mysteries*, Judy Chard. Bossiney Books, Bodmin, 1979.

* *Ghosts I Have Seen*, Violet Tweedale. Herbert Jenkins Ltd, London.

THE HAUNTING OF 'CASTEL-A-MARE'

In 1917 a friend rang me up and asked me if I would form one of a party of investigation at 'Castel-a-Mare'. The services of a medium had been secured and a soldier on leave, who was deeply immersed in psychic research, was in high hopes of getting some genuine results.

On reaching the house I found a small crowd assembled.

The medium, myself, and four other women. The soldier, and an elderly and burly builder belonging to the neighbourhood, who was interested in psychic research. Eight persons in all.

As there was no chair or furniture of any description in the house, we carried in a small empty box from a rubbish heap outside and followed the medium through the rooms. She selected to remain in the large bedroom on the first floor, out of which opened the bathroom, and she sat down on the box and leaned her back against the wall, whilst we lounged about the room and awaited events. It was a sunny summer afternoon and the many broken panes of glass throughout the house admitted plenty of air.

After some minutes it was plain to see that the medium had fallen into a trance. Her eyes were closed and she lay back as if in sound sleep. Time passed, nothing happened, we were all rather silent, as I had warned the party that though we were in a room at the side of the house farthest from the road, our voices could plainly be heard by passers-by, and we wanted no interference.

Just as we were all beginning to feel rather bored and tired of standing, the medium sprang to her feet with surprising agility, pouring out a volley of violent language. Her voice had taken on the deep growling tones of an infuriated man, who advanced menacingly towards those of us who were nearest to him. In harsh, threatening voice he demanded to know what right we had to intrude on his privacy.

There was a general scattering of the scared party before this unlooked-for attack and the soldier gave it as his opinion that the medium was now controlled by the spirit of a very violent male entity. I had no doubt upon the point.

The entity that controlled her possessed super-human strength. His voice was like the bellow of a bull, as he told us to be gone, or he would throw us out himself and his language was shocking.

The majority of our party were keeping at a safe distance, but suddenly the control rushed full tilt at the soldier, who had stood his ground, and attacking him with a tigerish fury drew blood at once. The big builder and I rushed forward to his aid. The rest of the party forsook us and fled, pell-mell out of the house and into the garden. Glancing through a window, near which we fought, I saw below a row of scared faces staring up in awed wonder.

The scene being enacted was really amazing. This frail little creature threw us off like feathers, and drove us foot by foot before her, always heading us off the bathroom. We tried to stand our ground and dodge her furious lunges, but she was too much for us. After a desperate scuffle, which lasted quite seven or eight minutes and resulted in much torn clothing, she drove us out of the room and on to the landing. Then suddenly, without warning, the entity seemed to evacuate the body he had controlled and the medium went down with a crash and lay at our feet, just a little crumpled, dishevelled heap.

For some considerable time I thought that she was dead.

After about ten minutes, she gradually regained her consciousness and seemingy none the worse for her experiences she sat up and asked what had happened.

We did not give her the truth in its entirety, and contrived to account for the blood-stained soldier and the torn clothing without unduly shocking and distressing her. We then dispersed; the medium walking off as if nothing whatever had occurred to deplete her strength.

Some days after this the soldier begged for another experiment with the medium. He had no doubts as to her genuineness and he was sure that if we tried again we would get further developments. She was willing to try again, and so was the builder, but with one exception the rest of the party refused to have anything more to do with the unpleasant affair, and the one exception stipulated to remain in the garden.

After the medium had remained entranced for some minutes, the same male entity again controlled her. The same violence, the same attacks began once more, but this time we were better prepared to defend ourselves. The soldier and the stalwart builder warded off the attacks, and tried conciliatory expostulations, but all to no purpose. Then the soldier, who seemed to have considerable experience in such matters, tried a system of exorcising, sternly bidding the malignant entity depart. There ensued a very curious spiritual conflict between the exorcist and the entity, in which sometimes it seemed as if one, then the other, was about to triumph.

Those wavering moments were useful in giving us breathing space from the assaults, and at length, having failed, as we desired, to get into the bathroom, we drove him back against the wall at the far end of the room. Finally the exorcist triumphed, and the medium collapsed on the floor as the strength of the control left her.

For a few moments we allowed the crumpled-up little heap to remain where she lay, but quite suddenly a new development began.

She raised her head, and still crouching on the floor with closed eyes she began to cry bitterly. Wailing and moaning, and uttering inarticulate words, she had become the picture of absolute woe.

"Another entity has got hold of her," announced the soldier. It certainly appeared to be so.

All signs of violence had gone. The medium had become a heart-broken woman.

'Will no one set us free?', Francisco de Goya, 1799

We raised her to her feet, her condition was pitiable, but her words became more coherent.

"Poor master! On the bed. Help him! Help him!" she moaned, and pointed to one side of the room. Again and again she indicated, by clenching her hands on her throat, that death by strangulation was the culmination of some terrible tragedy that had been enacted in that room.

She wandered, in a desolate manner, about the floor, wringing her hands, the tears pouring down her cheeks, whilst she pointed to the bed, then towards the bathroom with shuddering horror.

Suddenly we were startled out of our compassionate sympathy by a piercing scream.

The medium had turned at bay, and began a frantic encounter with some entity unseen by us. Wildly she wrestled and fought, as if for her life, whilst she emitted piercing shrieks for "help". We rushed to the rescue, dragging her away from her invisible assailant, but a disembodied fighter has a considerable pull over a fighter in the flesh, who possesses something tangible that can be seized. I placed the medium behind me, with her back to the wall, but though I pressed her close she continued to fight and I had to defend myself as well as defend her. Her assailant was undoubtedly the first terrible entity which had controlled her. At intervals she gasped out, "Terrible doctor – will kill me – he's killed master – help! help!"

Gradually she ceased to fight. The soldier was exorcising with all his force and was gaining power; finally he triumphed, inasmuch as he banished the "terrible doctor".

The medium was, however, still under the control of the broken-hearted entity and began again to wander about the room. We extracted from her further details. An approximate date of the tragedy. Her master's name, that he was mentally deficient when the murder took place. She was a maidservant in the house and after witnessing the crime she appeared to have shared her master's fate, though by what means we could not determine. The doctor was a resident physician of foreign origin.

At last we induced her to enter the bathroom, which she seemed to dread, and there she fell to lamenting over the dead body of her master, which had lain hidden there when the room was used as a large cupboard. It was a very painful scene, which was ended abruptly by her falling down insensible.

This was the last time I set foot in the haunted house, which is now being demolished.

The date and names the medium had given us were later on verified by means of a record of villa residenters, which for many years had been kept in the town of Torquay.

If there is any truth in the story it falls under the category of undiscovered crimes. The murderer was able somehow to hide his iniquities and escape suspicion and punishment.

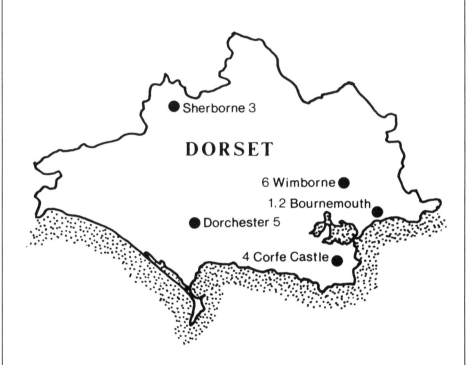

Dorset

With a 'V' or a 'W'? *

The Murder of IRENE WILKINS
by THOMAS HENRY ALLAWAY
on Thursday the 22nd of December 1921
at Fifteen-Acre-Meadow, outside Bournemouth

Lady Cook, 31, requires post in a school. Experienced in a school with forty boarders. Disengaged. Salary £65. Miss Irene Wilkins, 21 Thirlmere Road, Streatham, S.W.16.

So read the advertisement in December the 20th 1921's edition of *The Morning Post.* By mid-day on Thursday the 22nd, Miss Wilkins had already received a reply; the telegram instructed her:

Morning Post. Come immediately 4.30 train Waterloo Bournmouth Central. Car will meet train. Expence no object. Urgent. Wood, Beech House.

After sending a hasty telegram of confirmation, Irene left her home at 3.00pm carrying a few necessaries in a small attache case; she arrived in Bournemouth at 7.03. What she did not know was that her telegram had just been returned – address unknown.

At 7.30 on the following morning, Friday December 23rd, labourer Charles Nicklen was well into his regular morning constitutional and had reached a plot of rough ground known locally as the Fifteen-Acre-Meadow, at the point where the Seafield Road meets the Iford to Tuckton lane. With nothing much else to look at, Nicklen's attention wandered to the comparatively interesting sight of two cows worrying at a bundle on the ground; a bundle which on closer inspection turned out to be the body of a young woman.

By 8.00am the police had arrived. At 9.00 Dr Harold Summons, the police surgeon, began his examination of the victim's injuries, concluding that the most severe head injuries had been caused by blows from a

heavy instrument such as a hammer, and the more superficial bruising probably by a clenched fist.

Meanwhile the police had determined from signs of a struggle on the path and a trail of blood, that the woman had been attacked before being deposited in the field. In the mud they found footprints belonging to a man and a woman and the tracks of a car fitted with characteristic Dunlop Magnum tyres. Time of death was estimated as being between 7.45 and 8.20 on the previous evening.

Already alarmed by the return of their daughter's telegram, Mr and Mrs Wilkins were no less distressed when they read in their evening paper of the discovery of a young woman's body, wearing a gold watch engraved with the initials 'IMW', and clothes embroidered with the name 'I. Wilkins'. They lost no time in expressing their worst fears to the Streatham police.

In this way the threads were joined together; the unhappy Wilkins family learned the fate of their daughter, the police learned of the advertisement and the telegrams.

Indeed, in the succeeding days they learned of two further similar telegrams, sent from the same area and in response to similar advertisements. It was a matter of great good fortune that neither of the other recipients felt inclined to keep the assignation. The post office clerks in all three cases were vague about their description of the man who sent the messages, though Alice Waters said he might have been a chauffeur, and that he had a "rough voice".

It also transpired that Irene Wilkins had been observed on her fateful journey to Bournemouth by a fellow-passenger. Frank Humphris also recalled seeing the girl get into a chauffeur-driven grey Mercedes at the station. Mr Humphris had no reason to make

---

* "Do you spell it with a 'V' or a 'W'?" inquired the judge. "That depends upon the taste and fancy of the speller, My Lord," replied Sam.
(Charles Dickens, *Pickwick Papers,* ch.34)

66

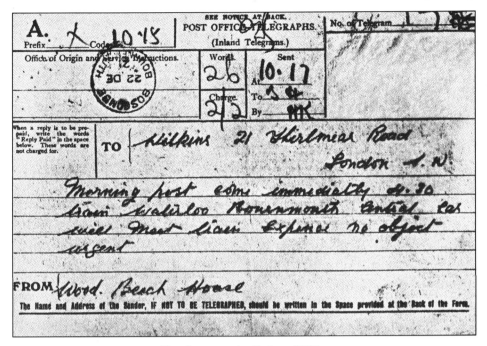

The telegram received by Irene Wilkins

a note of the vehicle's registration number, but he was to get a second glimpse of the same car driven by the same man on January the 4th 1922 – this time with full awareness of its significance – and took the number down and passed it on to the police (it was LK 7405). Had the police not, for some unaccountable reason, ignored this information, Irene Wilkins's killer might have been caught a lot earlier.

As it was, all this talk of a dark Mercedes car and chauffeurs was making one of that latter calling decidedly nervous – especially after a routine visit from the police. Thomas Henry Allaway, driver to Mr Sutton, a resident of nearby Boscombe, fled his lodgings taking with him a book of his employer's cheques. Eight days later, Allaway was traced to Reading, whence he had gone to rendezvous with his wife; when he was arrested, police found a number of betting slips in his pockets, the handwriting on which matched the telegram messages. Further examples of Allaway's handwriting were found at his Boscombe address, and while in custody, Allaway agreed to write out, to the dictation of a police officer, the texts of the three telegrams. Although he made every attempt to disguise

his writing, Allaway convicted himself with his bad spelling – reproducing faithfully the 'Bournmouth' and 'expence' of the Wilkins telegram as well as other obvious inaccuracies and illiteracies.

Thomas Allaway was then identified by the postal clerks who had taken his telegram messages, by Mr Humphris, and by a railway signalman who saw him standing at Bournemouth station on the day of the murder.

On July the 3rd, 1922, Allaway was put on trial at the Summer Assizes at Winchester, before Mr Justice Avory. In his defence, Allaway attempted to prove an alibi – that he had been at his lodgings on the night of the murder, and had spoken to his landlord. It was an alibi that held only until that landlord was called as a witness; his recollection was that not only had he not spoken to the prisoner, but that it would have been very difficult to have done so, as he had been out of the house since early evening.

Thomas Allaway was found guilty of the murder of Irene Wilkins, and on the morning of August the 19th, 1922, he was hanged at Winchester. Shortly before his death, Allaway confessed his guilt to the prison governor.

Thomas Allaway on his way to trial

The Great Bournemouth Mystery

AS GIVEN THROUGH
Mrs. C. STARKEY, Sensitive.

Just before Christmas, 1921, the nation was stirred by a brutal murder in the neighbourhood of Bournemouth, a murder that seemed lacking motive. The murderer appeared to have covered up all his tracks and it looked as if what was known as the "Great Bournemouth Mystery" would be relegated to those regions of undiscovered crimes so rampant the last few years.

It will be remembered that use was made of a decoy telegram sent from Boscombe Post Office, and by its means a lady cook, Miss Irene Wilkins, was inveigled from London to Bournemouth where she was done to death. I will not recapitulate the evidence of the witnesses that brought the murderer to his doom, as these can always be referred to in files of newspapers by persons interested, but suffice it to say that all ordinary means had been tried and exhausted, and for some weeks the case was a dormant one.

I have a friend who is a born Clairvoyant and Psychometrist, and I repeatedly tried to persuade her to see if she could get anything that would throw light on the state of darkness existing. I might not have been so persistent had Mrs S. not declared *from the time the murder took place that she felt the murderer was in Boscombe or its immediate neighbourhood.* She demurred to my repeated suggestion, saying that as she had not done any psychic work for several years (having had to give it up through a prolonged illness) she was not sure such sittings would prove of value; also pointing out that there was no article left behind by the murderer, and she did not see how she could get in touch with the case unless she could handle *something he had handled.* I suggested getting the originals of the telegrams, and she countered this suggestion by pointing out that these had been handled by so many persons and she would get so many influences that it would be next to impossible to pick out with any degree of certainty the writer of the missives. Readers may wonder what handling the article would have to do with the matter. Well, there is a psychic gift known as Psychometry or Soul reading, and persons who possess this gift can by handling an article describe the person to whom such article has belonged, go into his movements, and sometimes (but rarely) get names connected with it. In this particular case it looked as if matters were a bit hopeless owing to this lack of articles and I fully realized the difficulties. However, I got the lady to walk down with me to view the spot where the body was found, and while she stood passively gazing at the place with every sympathy aroused in her for the murdered woman, I began to look around hoping against hope to find some little trifle – if only a bit of cloth that had been left behind. As Sir A. Conan Doyle says, in his 'Wanderings of a Spiritualist': "A piece of clothing is, as a rule, to a psychometrist what it would be to a bloodhound – the starting point of a chase which runs down its victim."

All I could find was a quantity of match sticks; that struck me as strange, for they were all at a rounded corner of the curbing of the path opposite the spot where the body was found. And this would be about the position where the motor car stood that conveyed the body of the murdered woman to the spot. These I carefully collected up, there were about 50 in all, and I noticed that there seemed no signs of matches either up or down the roadway, hence the possibility was that they *might* have been handled by the murderer.

Mrs S. had also been busy as she said she had got a vision of a man standing inside the wire fencing near where the cut furze bushes lay. We took the matches home and she placed the little parcel on her pillow – she got influences of three men but could not get one to stand out plainer than another. But she said "The man who did the deed has not left Boscombe, he is close by us – and I cannot go further than Fisherman's Walk on the one side and Boscombe Gardens on the other." When I tell you that Allaway stored the car he drove about 100 yards from our house and that his employer's son where he constantly attended was about 500 yards away, and that Allaway lived within about 500 yards of us, readers will realize how true Mrs S.'s statement proved to be.

I again tried my persuasion to get Mrs S. to take the matter up, but got no promise. The next thing that happened was one afternoon we suddenly missed her – no one knew where she was – but about two hours after we noted her absence she came home looking quite ill and told us she had been walking through the Manor and up the roads at the back of Christchurch Road, and she was upset by violent tremblings and had to sit down on a seat before she could get home. I realized at once what this meant, that she was being impelled by our unseen friends to go into the matter we had been discussing.

A few days after this incident she sent the maid out for an *Express*, and the peculiar thing is that I never knew her to buy a copy of this paper before, but more peculiar still – in that issue of the *Express* was a reproduction of an anonymous letter that bore a striking resemblance to the writing in the original draft of the telegrams published. I got a magnifying glass and compared the reproductions and told her I did not think it was the same handwriting, as there were some little differences in the formation of certain letters. I presume Mr Guerin came to the same conclusion, as although these documents were in the hands of the police they did not appear in the evidence given by this noted expert in handwriting.

No more was said till I came in at night, when Mrs S. told me she had written to the *Express* people to try and get the original document they had reproduced to psychometrize. I told her I doubted if she would get it, that if any notice was taken of her letter they would send a messenger along with the document as they would not part with it to a stranger. I also told her if they knew nothing of Psychic work they would throw the letter aside as the work of a crank, attaching no importance to it. The application remained unanswered. She felt greatly hurt that they had not even replied to her and I could see she meant to be up and doing. I therefore, without telling Mrs S., wrote to Inspector Garrett of the Bournemouth police and told him there was one thing they had not yet tried, viz. Psychometry, which I went on to expain as briefly as possible, and wound my letter up by saying that it was possible, given suitable conditions, to get in touch with the spirit of Irene herself. I am afraid that winding up settled him and that he regarded me as a crank, no reply coming to my letter.

And now I must digress and tell you by what means I got in touch with the police. The poet said: "God moves in a mysterious way His wonders to perform," and He certainly did in this case. Just before Xmas. we advertised a large American doll in the "Bazaar, Exchange and Mart", and in reply had an application for the doll from a town in the Midlands. The reply looked quite a genuine one, and as it only wanted three days to Christmas and Mrs S. thought the lady might want the doll urgently she decided to send it along without having the purchase price deposited with the Editor of the paper, which is the usual custom, I therefore packed the doll up for her and took it myself to the G.P.O., Boscombe (the same office from which the decoy telegram had been dispatched) and it was posted from there on the evening of the day in which a few hours later the terrible tragedy was enacted. We

little thought when the doll was posted what a remarkable chain of incidents would be the outcome. It was through that doll posted in the very district in which the murderer lived that touch with the police was established and they were made by the aid of a lost toy to listen to me. Several days passed and as no acknowledgment of the doll came, I wrote to the applicant and getting no answer I wrote again; still getting no reply I thought the transaction looked fraudulent and then I wrote to the police at the town the doll was posted to. The Assistant Superintendent of Police there said the woman in question was the wife of a police constable, and as there had been other complaints of a similar nature he advised me to write to the Chief Superintendent. I did so and he communicated with the police at Boscombe. The upshot was that one day a ring came at the door, I answered the call and a gentleman standing there said "I am from the police." I said "Oh, walk in, I have for some time been expecting one of you gentlemen to call." I thought he looked a bit surprised; anyhow he came in and asked about the lost doll. I answered all his queries, and when he had placed the documents relating to this in his pocket, he said "You said you were expecting one of us to call, was it on this matter?" I said "No, it was on a totally different matter – 'The Murder Case'." I then told him what I had written to Inspector Garrett and described a few details of things I had seen done by a sensitive handling articles, and cited a case at Bourne, in Lincolnshire, where a man had been traced and caught by the police in two days after a sitting with Mrs S., and gave other instances in which she had been of service.

In this case a man had been professing to sell railway surplus stock and had a few articles with him that he sold at a ridiculously cheap rate. He then booked orders for articles of higher value demanding prepayment for which a receipt was given – but the articles were not forthcoming. The only clues left were three written receipts. My friend, who had seen Mrs Starkey's gifts exercised on one occasion asked me whether I thought she could throw any light on the matter, if so the police would, he was sure, welcome it, and it might help the people who had been too trustful of the stranger's statements. I asked him if all the receipts had been handled. He thought he could get one that had been kept in an evelope since it was given, and it was that receipt that proved the undoing of the wrongdoer. I told my friend to get one of the police to come in and we would see what could be done. He came in plain clothes and was introduced to the Medium as a friend of my friend. No word or clue of any kind was given to the sensitive. I handed her the envelope containing the receipt and asked her to put her fingers inside the envelope and see what she sensed from it. As soon as her fingers touched the receipt she said she was taken to a long building and could see bales of materials – that it was right away from where we were – that she got a man with it and he had a horse and cart. She said he had another man with him, and gave a name afterwards which proved to be right. She stated he had collected a little over £9 out of this small town (which was quite correct), and that if the police went to the north east they would find the man. On the strength of this a warrant was taken out by my friend the next morning, and in two days the man was taken at Boston due north east of where the sensitive had given the psychometric reading.

I cited another case of a personal friend who lost a diamond ring, about which she was greatly concerned. She was told it had been taken by a person who had taken her a cup of tea up to her in her bedroom on a certain day. Now on that day two people had taken her tea up, one early and one later, and the lady had noticed that different tea pots were used. She asked the sensitive whether she could pick out the tea pot that was carried by the person who stole the ring. She said she could. She was taken to the pantry where there was a row of no less than 10 tea pots. She picked out a certain tea pot. The lady said that was one of those that had been used and the result was the person who carried that particular tea pot up was charged with the theft and she owned to it and returned the ring.

The representative of the police force seemed impressed, and reported to his superior at Boscombe. It was not long before Sergt. Fisher gave me a call, he said he wanted to know more about what his man had told him, and I put the matter quite clearly before him. I also told him that Sir Basil Thompson, of Scotland Yard, in a letter to the newspapers was urging increased effort be made and said that "no stone should be left unturned" to try and solve the mystery. I pointed out that we made the offer in the cause of humanity at large. *That time might be wasted and no result obtained, but that on the other hand we might get things that would help them considerably. I also said we had no axe to grind; we were open to give our time freely if he and any of his colleagues were willing to give theirs.* I told them we should only take the matter in hand on the understanding that some of their people should attend every sitting to take down their own notes as to what the sensitive gave. He queried whether the lady was a local lady. I said "Yes, you can see her in two minutes as she resides in this house." I called Mrs S. and

after a short chat with her he said he would go and report to his chief. He was a man of open mind and I could tell he was impressed by what I had said. I told him we should need articles to handle, and told him as far as possible we wanted articles that had not been handled by many people. He reported to Inspector Brewer, another man of open mind, and they decided to try what mediumship could do.

I told Sergt. Fisher that they were like men groping in the dark and the only chance of light I could see was what I suggested. He acknowledged they were going round and round in a circle and would welcome any suggestion that would give them a fresh jumping-off point. Sergt. Fisher said they would help us in any way possible, what did I suggest? I told him we should by handling the clothing of the murdered woman, try and put the sensitive in touch with the assailant. My theory was that to get the body in the field in which it was found the man must have placed his arms round the woman to throw her over the barbed wire fence, or else would be likely to place his hands under the arm pits and drag her through the fence, hence if the fingers of the sensitive touched such portions of the clothing that might result in getting useful matter for their guidance.

A message came that the clothes worn by the girl at death could be obtained and a sitting was arranged, and this led up to a series of sittings that will for ever be memorable to those who participated therein; and the thanks of the world are due to Inspector Garrett for supplying the various articles for the sittings, and to Inspector Brewer and Sergeant Fisher and others, official and non-official, for their careful, patient and painstaking work in the unravelling of the mystery of 1921.

The night of the sitting arrived – a suitcase was brought containing Irene's clothes. The sitters were a few personal friends (absolute strangers to the seance room and the subject of Psychic research in the form of trance mediumship under control), together with members of the police force, none of whom had ever been at a seance before. I had provided pencils and paper, so that each could take their own notes; and told them before Mrs S. came into the room that things strange to them might happen, but that they were to simply use eyes, ears, and pencils, and that should Mrs S. need looking after I would undertake that, and that I should probably not be able to take my own notes as I must look after the sensitive.

Mrs S. came into the room and after a few minutes began to show signs of a controlling influence, and she made for the case of clothes and took therefrom the stockings and from these she gave us the description of a man. Long sallow face, high cheek bones, dark brown hair, eyes hazel, medium height and build, big ears, weight 10 to 11 stone; he did not seem to be over 11 stone, and the sensitive gave details even to the size of the boots he wore. More details of appearance were given at later sittings, and one policeman was told he had already spoken with the assailant. Not only did Irene give us this description of the man, but other intelligences who controlled the medium gave corroborative evidence. *The description never varied and fitted the man Allaway perfectly.* She said the hair was thrown up at the sides, that he sometimes wore a lightish-coloured coat and a cap (this was a tweed mixture coat that he wore throughout the trial), and that he also had a dark one with buttons and a driving coat – that he was a "cute man but would not be cute enough." The medium wanted to know who "May" was, and as this name cropped up several times in the sittings, it seems somewhat significant as Allaway's wife was named "May".

On handling the coat, however, a change came over the scene, the medium being controlled, thrown upon the floor, and an impersonation of the death of the victim given. The body was absolutely rigid as though *rigor mortis* had set in. In going under control she gradually sank down upon the floor, shot her legs forward, and in some way this crumpling up and shortening of the medium's body resulted in the medium's clothes being drawn upwards till they were level with the knees. This was marked and significant, as the clothes of Irene were drawn right up to the waist when the body was discovered, the result of dragging the woman through the fence by pulling the ankles. The medium's body lay in the exact attitude in which the police found Irene. The legs were stretched apart, the feet turned toes outwards, the hand was clenched, and the clothes were somewhat pulled towards the trunk. In a little time signs of returning consciousness were apparent; and the spirit professing to be Irene, who had taken control of the medium, spoke to us through her organism. The messages given were short messages in themselves, but collated and pieced together formed themselves into a clear and homogeneous whole.

The sittings were numerous and covered the period from the 31st January, 1922, to the 30th June, 1922, five months in all. At the first sitting this spirit told us that she arrived at the station, that she picked up her case and umbrella, and alighted from the train, and that she stood waiting for someone to accost her. She looked round but could not see who she wanted. Someone beckoned her, she answered "Yes," and went with a man whom she described. This description was identical with that given by the sensitive when she handled the stockings, and fitted the man who was arrested in March, some three months after he was described. Continuing her narrative, the control stated that she got into a waiting motor car, the door of which was already open. She stated she had nothing in her hands, as her belongings had been taken from her. She described the car as a dark coloured car, a comfortable nice car, that it was a car of medium size, not one of the very big ones, that when she got in the car there was a screen in the front of her, and described the man sitting to the right behind this screen, giving the time as 10 minutes past 7. The car Allaway drove was peculiar as to colour, for evidence was given that it appeared a different colour at night (darker than it did by day) due to some peculiarity in the paint used on same. The sensitive, when recovering, said she felt the owner of this car had travelled a great deal, in fact had been all over the world. This we afterwards found to be correct. She noticed a grey horse in a cart; also that there were tram lines not far off the station; that their car cut up a road, passed a few shops, went down an incline, then up into a long road. That she then saw more shops, and got to more tram lines and a church, and that they then got to a place where there were a few houses dotted about. The car then made a turning movement and they arrived at a house. During this drive she seems to have had her eyes about her for she gives the name of "Chessel" and the name "St. Mary's;" these are names of places that would be visible by the light of a motor lamp when travelling, viz., Chessel Avenue clearly shown by a sign at the corner, and "St. Mary's," being the name of a house in that avenue. She said the house was not far from where we were sitting.

"St. Mary's" is very peculiar in its significance, for not only does a house of this name exist near to the house of the son of the employer of Allaway, but there is a "St. Mary's" right opposite his employer's house, so Allaway was daily near one or the other. We were sitting within 500 yards of "St. Mary's," and not above 50 yards from the commencement of Chessel Avenue.

She said it was a detached house with a garage attached – not far from St. Mary's, she described the approach, that there were steps to it, that the hall was square "not a long passage hall." She also noticed certain articles of furniture in the hall, and that she sensed the presence of a dog. That there was a hose pipe there for washing a car. She gave a description of a man connected with this place, sometimes talkative, sometimes reticent, also described a lady that frequented the house. She said the house had large window panes, and she gave an indication of the position of this house, that there was a drive up to it, and that it looked out upon trees. In the hall we were told of an antique table and that there was a writing table under a window in the room she was taken into. When they arrived at this house the lights on the car were put out and Allaway took a key from his pocket and opened the door, and there were not others in the house. In another sitting she told us there was some statuary in the house and she described the same.

Irene seems to have had some sort of a premonition, as she described that something seemed to pull her eyeball and that she was all of a tremble when she entered the house. We were told indecent overtures were made to her and the medium's face changed and expressed disgust while the hands of the medium pushed as though pushing someone away from her. No words can convey the realism of the actions, such things must be seen to be understood.

She told us that she sat down on a chair given to her, not modern and not very old and not tall, and when immoral overtures were made to her she got up making objection, and went dazed through disgust and nervousness. (The medium went by action through the whole scene in a most realistic fashion.) "*Oh, no, certainly not.*" "*Oh, not that, oh, Mother, Mother.*" On another occasion "Father, Father", is given, so she may have appealed to both. The Mother being in the body would be most in her mind. She said "I was not having any of that rudeness."

She then states the man hit her and shook her violently, that she "did fight" and "took the peaked hat off the man"; she states his coat was buttoned over. The medium then stooped towards the fireplace and indicated picking up something (later on we were told this was a poker – a short poker) and indicated the head being struck twice. Something was indicated as being pulled off a table and tightly wrapped round her head (probably a table cloth which would keep blood in bounds), she was taken by the arms but not till, we are told, she was nearly dead, that the blows in the house did not actually kill and that before dragging her into the car the man struck her again. She states she was dragged out of the house by the arms and taken into a place, and that she was struck in the face – that her hand was hurt by gripping something (the police tell me this was correct). The throat rattled before she left the house and she seems to indicate that this led up to the blow in the face as he wanted to make sure. She tells us of her clothes being all

wet (blood) and said "I seem to be hurt." The medium on coming to herself complained of a feeling as though she had been swallowing blood, in fact she kept putting her hand to her lips and then looking at it as though she expected to see blood there. This is of interest, as the doctor gave evidence of much blood being found in Irene's stomach. She also complained of her left eye on more than one occasion. Since Allaway paid the penalty I have seen photographs of Irene's wounds and one terrible wound occurred under that eye.

She then goes on to describe her journey across the tram lines, down a lonely hill and that she was pulled out of the car and dragged along by the feet and that the time was about 8 o'clock. By actual experiment, it was proved in court that there was ample time for the girl to have been murdered and car safely housed between 7 and 8. She always in speaking of the place where the body was found uses the phrase "my grave."

Through the medium, who lay on the floor as if dead, with limbs and neck absolutely rigid and unbendable and with hand clenched, an exact reproduction of the body as found by the police, we got the following, given as she was recovering from this rigid state, "Oh, my poor brains." She also, when opening the eyes, turned her head from side to side and moaned "It's all fields," and she showed great concern about her condition as she said "put my clothes down, don't show my bloomers," and kept repeating "put my clothes down, put my clothes down, I want to go home to Mother," and made use of this peculiar phrase "There's me and here's me," evidently the spirit looking at the body and unable to realize what it signified. The writer has personally on two occasions had this peculiar experience of being as it were outside the body and looking at it, on each occasion this occurred when in ill health and much run down. I queried whether Irene had bloomers on and the police verified the correctness. In dragging Irene through the barbed wire fence by the legs into the field where the body was found the clothes were all pulled upwards uncovering the legs, so you see the significance of this ejaculation. On another occasion we were told she is "Part here and part there," that means she is in a state partly on the earth plane and partly on the spirit plane. This may account for her power of so quickly getting into touch with and controlling the medium.

Among other information given by Irene herself and information given by other spirits who helped us in this case, we get the following statements: that when she resisted the overtures made to her "she was laughed and jeered at," one can easily imagine that this would be the attitude of a man who could not get his way; that she seemed to be sitting in a big room.

On another occasion she began crying "Why did I come, why didn't I go to the other place?" This seems to indicate she had the choice of more than one situation. She also said "my poor brains have come outside" (at one of the early sittings when the medium was returning to consciousness her hand went to her head and she couldn't make out what was the matter with her head – she fingered it and indicated picking up something between finger and thumb and said "I don't like this, what is wrong with my head?" Next day she stated her head had been funny all the night and her hand again travelled up to the head and she looked at her fingers as though she expected to see something adhering to them).

The police explained this by saying Irene's brains protruded and were full of prickles from the furze bushes she had been drawn through.

Irene made a statement that her case had been left in the house by an oversight. (This case you will remember was thrown into bushes at Branksome near the house of the sister of Allaway's employer, where he used to take his mistress visiting.)

Irene stated that the blood ran down all over her collar and neck. "Didn't the blood run down, all over my collar and neck, my head was covered with a cloth, I felt smothered, not killed outright at first." In another place she says "Don't think he intended murder, had to do it he thought to protect himself."

The medium, we were told by a control, had a great deal of opposition to fight as there were spirits present trying to prevent others giving information; that these were spirits who knew the man. On one occasion there was a deliberate attempt made to dash the medium's head against the wall. The lady at whose house we were sitting had been impressed to move during the day a sewing machine out of the room used for the seance. Had this not been done I believe the medium would have been seriously injured if not killed. She was under control when another spirit suddenly took control and shot her towards the wall head first just as if she had been propelled from a gun. None of us could stop her from falling – I, though on the alert, was powerless, and although I got my hand to her head the impact overbalanced me and I was thrown violently across the room. If that sewing machine had not been removed there must have been a very serious accident.

On March 26th we were told "you are on the right man, he did not mean to do it, he was afraid." On March 30th this was again emphasised. "You have got the right man, *have no fear when the time comes.*"

On the 2nd of May two letters were handed to the medium. When she handled these she selected one written by Allaway and said "I don't like the conditions of this letter, the man is a bit of a bully, and a man who would fight, he could do terrible things." "You have him in your power" (was given us by automatic writing). A query was made as to how the charge could be brought home to him, and the reply was "You have him in your power, why don't you act?" This was given at a sitting on May 5th, and on May 6th Allaway was charged with murder. At another meeting the two letters were handed to another control, when the pencilled letter was at once selected with "There's your man." One control on handling the pencilled letter of Allaway's, said at once "There's blood with this man. Yes, there's blood with this man – nasty too – creepy – and there's a child with it." (Allaway had a child, a little girl.) Another control, a foreign spirit whom we know as Zurah, to whom the letter was handed, by dumb show, enacted the scene, went to fireplace, tried to pick up a poker. I took the poker from the fender and gave Zurah a lead pencil. In her acting she is often too realistic in her efforts to make us understand her meaning, and I did not feel like risking a broken head. She indicated the length of the poker, indicated how Irene's hair was done up, showed the damage to her head by taking her hand from the side of head and trying to shake something off her fingers, seeming to have difficulty in doing so (brains and prickles). She got out the words "It's him," indicated brushing hair back – threw letter away angrily and *spat upon it.* Now how could a spirit, or a person not knowing how to speak a language, express more contempt than by *spitting* upon what she did not like?

Irene stated "That someone else wanted her," not the man himself; this looks very much as if Allaway was acting the part of a procurer and was being used to test the feelings of the subjects on such a proposition. The motive given was Money and Lust. Irene said "I suffer and he must suffer." We obtained the description of another man, "a man who has travelled much and receives something from under the Crown," the owner of a dog was described, and had some very distinctive detail given which so far has not been verified, together with the description of certain other people in this man's surroundings. On this matter I can say no more. In May Irene said, "I want Mother, I want my Mother, oh what is it, I wanted Mother, I want to give her a message, I want to go home, *I have done all I can do."*

Allaway had disposed of the body, but the attaché case inadvertently left in the house still remained, and it was policy to get that out of the way, and we were told through the medium "We go from Boscombe to where the man left the case, the man goes back alone, a lovely drive down trees (County gates, evidently). To the left and up a hill, the car stops on the top of the hill, there are trees on both sides and lots of bushes, he was not there a tick. Car gone, dark car, nice car, went back same way. It was night when car left."

Pat, an Irish control, told us: "You are going at a snail's pace, but it will be all right." This was given as encouragement to the sitters, and to the police in particular. There are opposing influences at work trying to shield the man and trying to block us. We were told these were spirits trying to help Allaway and hinder us. "It will be around June before it is brought home." This was correct; the trial began July 3rd, 1922. The opposing influences however were weak, as the result proved. In an early sitting we were given the figure of a large Owl. The control stated this was given symbolically. I cogitated, an owl is a bird of prey, an owl sits up aloft, an owl comes out at night, an owl is a thing devoid of pity for a victim; but the correct signification was "Owl's Road." In Owl's Road is the Burlington Hotel, and from the balcony of the hotel there was visible the house where Allaway lived, and houses where he went upon his daily business. The medium made reference to this at one sitting. "I've been running about a lot, I'm always along that road looking as if from the balcony of the Burlington." The medium said "From the top of the road I can see the Arcade, I cannot see further *than that first corner shop* (Baker's shop). I am on the other side of the road and I cannot get away from this locality." This position is remarkable, as Allaway lived a few doors from that corner shop. Suspicion was centred upon a certain house in this immediate locality, with the result that the police concentrated their efforts and were given an increased zest in their search.

The name, "May," was given several times, and on June 30th, 1922, we had a description of the woman: long face, high cheek bones, nose turned up at tip, age about 33, hair brushed up and taken back, and the statement made "She did not know where he was the night of the crime;" later on "there is a little child connected" (Allaway had a little girl, *vide* trial).

On February 7th we made a very interesting experiment, and it proved a very convincing experience. I had made arrangements for the medium to motor with two friends down to the spot where Irene was found, to see whether we could get into still closer touch with the conditions of the actors in the great drama. We alighted from the car, and in a few minutes Mrs S. (the sensitive) went into a partial trance, and gave as follows: "When the man got there he took her out of the car by the shoulders backwards." In evidence given at the trial you will see there "were many impressions of a man's foot, but only one impression of a lady's boot heel." Now if she were taken out of the car as stated, it is fair to assume that the whole weight of Irene's body might be temporarily thrown on to the foot that touched the ground, hence that definite impression of the one heel. We are told he laid her on the ground and took something off her head and threw it into the car, it was a biggish thing and it was very tight over the head. We were afterwards told that he destroyed this by burning in a furnace; this might have been in a fire at one of the glass houses at his employer's house. The medium, under partial control in the roadway, then undid her own coat and began fingering her clothing, telling us what Irene wore, and how they were placed upon her body. She said, "Blue thing, two woollies (my blouse – a woollie, and another woollie, and my coat)." She also said her shoulders were hurt (not scratched as I suggested, said she had too may clothes on for that). She also said her umbrella was broken and was stood up by the fence *outside* the barbed wire. This was quite correct the police told me. She said there were not many stains on the man, he was protected, but there were stains in the car. Fingering round the neck she said "My blouse is all red." As a matter of fact Irene's blouse was absolutely saturated with blood. She was concerned about something on her breast, fingering her breast she said "My name is on it – a kind of monogram, I want my Mother to have it." This referred to a watch she wore that pinned on her clothing, later on she said her Mother had got it. Irene would have the car we were using turned round, and remarked "It's better there, door deeper down than this." She was evidently comparing the car she was conveyed in to this spot with our car, and pointing out how it differed. Pressing the semi-conscious medium to get in the car she said "I don't like to get in that again." I asked her why, was she not well, she threw her head up and said "Oh, I'm all right." We all got in the car; I had previously instructed the driver the route to take, and at a certain point to gradually slow down. As we went along Chessel Avenue, I noticed the medium's shoulders begin to tremble, and a movement was made as though a shudder went right through her body, her breathing got deeper, and she made an effort to stand up in the car. She began to get in an excited condition, looking from side to side and behind her. When we got near the Burlington Hotel she got very excited, stood up in the car and said "Take me away – take me out of this. Take me out or I shall jump out." A lady friend in the car clung round the medium's legs, and had to exert all her weight to keep her in the car. I told the driver to put on speed, and Mrs S. was very uneasy and kept saying "I wouldn't live down here rent free, I don't like there roads at all." This is rendered doubly interesting as Allaway was constantly travelling up and down there roads. *The mills of God are said to grind slow but sure, and this case seems a striking example to illustrate its truth.* Another control said "The end justifies the means," and that this case had been lifted out of darkness from a humane point of view, that they would work round the man *to make him give himself away.*

The man Allaway had been charged with the crime of murder and absolutely denied it, but thoughts are things, and under some conditions can be collected, and we had some striking examples of this peculiar phase of Psychic science. At one seance we got "So you've locked me up like a caged bird or a tiger. What a terrible struggle, it's a terrible struggle" (evidently meaning mental struggle). On one occasion he said "I've had a thick night." "You've walled me in for something, but it will come home. I'll fight to the end." "What am I walled up for? I've saved myself for something sour." "Oh yes, I did go to Kingston-on-Thames. I've been to Hampton Court, I went after *I did that.*" We were told that there was a band of spirits who would go to and fro to give the medium information, and this was clearly proved during the trial, by notes taken at her home by the medium as the trial proceeded. We had many interesting things given in regard to the trial itself. We were told that "They have a cute man" (Lawman), "that there was a deficiency in money," that he (Allaway) would give himself away and it would be a little thing that would do it. And a little thing it truly was, for it was simply the mis-spelling of the word Arthur in one of the cheques stolen from his employer's son and which caused him to fall into the hands of the police. He, in forging the cheque, spelt it *Arther.* Mistakes in spelling were apparent on the forged telegrams, this led to comparisons of hand writing on the telegrams and cheques. The description of the man tallied also with that given the police by us, and in handling letters written by the prisoner there was a denouncement emphatically given and without hesitation. Another little thing also told heavily against him which was a duplicate

garage key that Allaway left in his lodgings. This was found there by the chauffeur who took Allaway's place, and handed by him to the police. Mrs Allaway said this belonged to a lavatory at a place she was employed at two years previously.

We were again told that we had the right man, and that everything would work round as Irene wished. We were told that he had been recognised by four people; and also that during the trial "we should shake one day, but the next would put it all right," and that "what will make it a bit weak, will turn out strong." The exact words read, "The elements against you are not so many, but will swear to have seen the man, what will make it a bit weak – but will turn out strong." This was regarding the evidence given for the defence, and was quite true. During the trial a date was asked for, this had been forgotten, and much depended on that date. *That date was given by Psychic means and all went smoothly afterwards.* A witness (one of our sitters) was called into the witness box and suddenly asked for a certain date. He said "My mind was a perfect blank," and he mentally said "Pat, you promised to help us; now if you are here, help me." The response was immediate. He said it seemed as if a sheet of office paper was placed before his eyes and a big January 6th upon it. *That was the needed date.* I may here explain that this "Pat" is a spirit who seems to be always in attendance at our sittings, and through his aid we obtain knowledge that is often unknown to the sitters, and which has to be afterwards verified, entirely doing away with the idea of thought reading or thought transmission.

We were told that as the case was nearing a finish we should have a surprise, "something that makes them look at each other – draw their breath – even the public look at one another." This clearly refers to the incident of the calling of Mr Lawman, the solicitor for the defence, into the witness box, to swear to a certain statement which caused a great excitement in Court. Another point was that on the 30th of June, the medium scribbled something on a piece of paper and demanded we should get an envelope and seal it up in her presence, extracting a promise that it would not be opened until after the trial, *as it was a forecast of the Verdict.* This scrap of paper was placed in an envelope by Sergt. Fisher, sealed and dated by him, and immediately after sentence had been passed it was opened by him in my presence, and on it we found in automatic writing "Guilty, Hanged." This has here been photographically reproduced for the reader's satisfaction.

We were told witnesses for the defence would want to back out, which was correct.

We were told to watch Allaway in the dock, as when things were going wrong for him he would be made to put his hand up to his face. You see by this extract from the *Daily Mail*, Saturday, July 8, 1922, that this was noticeable to the reporters: "Allaway received his sentence without emotion, but there had been fear in his staring eyes from the moment he was cross-examined in the witness-box and his futile attempt to deny writing letters and post-cards to his wife was exposed. He has a loose tremulous mouth, whose trembling betrayed his anxiety, and frequently during his evidence he clutched his right cheek with nervous fingers."

There is also a foreshadowing of the confession in these words "Will come out at last when he sees that it is no use and no hope."

Another strange incident occurred. As soon as the Judge had pronounced sentence a bugle was heard from the neighbouring barracks sounding "The Defaulters' Call," – Allaway as an old soldier would no doubt note its significance.

During the progress of the trial at Winchester the medium took notes of various things that were happening in the Court House at Winchester while she was seated at home at Boscombe, such as the incident of the wanted date, the time Allaway was in the box giving evidence, the Lawman incident, the dropping of the head of the Judge.

"At 4 o'clock the Judge has rather dropped his head, different to anything before, in a manner not noticed before, downed his head. The Judge himself within himself thinks the man has done it. It's deeply impressed him this afternoon, I know the verdict, deeply moved."

"8 past 6 – Telling a different tale now. What do they mean by clear the gangway? What is an usher?"

And for a time there was a terrible hush that could be felt by the medium and those with her, at her house; as she described it, "there was a terrible hush in the spirit world."

The deliberation of the Jury ended and the Verdict was given, when the Judge donned the black cap and pronounced those fatal words in a quiet but forceful way, –
"And you, too, shall die."

Allaway had protested his innocence throughout, even in his last messages to his wife, and hundreds believed his protestations of innocence. Hence it was a great relief to all concerned when it was given out from the Home Office that Allaway owned up to the acutal murdering of the girl.

I have tried to condense the foregoing matter into a clear and readable form, and the readers must weigh it up for themselves. Every item recorded is as it was given us *and could be sworn to in any court of law.*

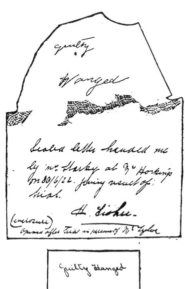

The automatic writing foretelling the verdict is shown at the top. At the bottom the same words in the medium's normal handwriting

A Damned Unworthy Son

The Murder of MARGERY GARDNER; and DOREEN MARSHALL by NEVILLE GEORGE CLEVELY HEATH

on Thursday the 20th of June 1946; and Wednesday the 3rd of July 1946 at the Pembridge Court Hotel, London; and Branksome Dene Chine, Dorset

Margery Aimée Bramwell Gardner, a twenty-two-year-old occasional film extra, first met the young man who had introduced himself as Lieutenant Colonel Heath in May 1946. Somewhat the worse for drink, they booked into the Pembridge Court Hotel, 34 Pembridge Gardens, in London's Notting Hill Gate area. There Mrs Gardner was stripped, tied up and flogged by Heath. In short, they were doing what they enjoyed most – which was bondage and flagellation. It must have been a very bewildered hotel detective who, attracted by Margery Gardner's screams, rushed through the door to find they were cries of pleasure.

On June the 15th, nineteen-year-old Yvonne Symonds was the focus of attention for the amorous officer. Miss Symonds was staying at the Overseas Club in London, and on the night of the encounter had gone to a WRNS dance in Chelsea. Though he was ten years her senior, Yvonne, like so many girls be-fore her, had succumbed to the gentle manners and easy charm of the man calling himself Lieutenant Colonel Heath. They visited the Panama Club in South Kensington before the gallant officer escorted his companion back to the Overseas Club. After spending the following Sunday in each other's company, and after – perhaps *only* after – Heath had proposed marriage, Yvonne Symonds consented to being booked into the Pembridge Court Hotel under the rather premature title 'Mrs N.G.C. Heath'. Sex, if it took place at all, was by Heath's standards disarmingly normal; Miss Symonds was not attracted to flagellation. On the following morning she departed for her parents' home in Worthing leaving Heath to his own devices.

The second time that Margery Gardner shared Heath's room at the Pembridge Court Hotel, on Thursday June the 20th, it was the last. On the following afternoon a

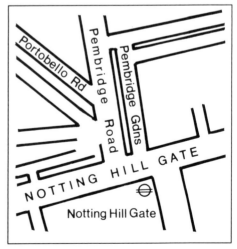

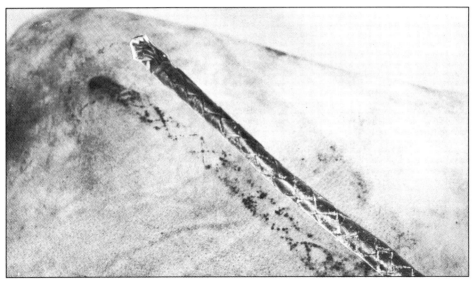

*Characteristic pattern of the skin marks on Margery
Gardner, with the whip used by Heath*

chambermaid, irritated by not being able to get in to clean the room, used her pass key. What she found was enough to send her scurrying for the manageress – on the bed nearest the door, covered by bedclothes was the shape of a person, a very still, stiff person. The sight *beneath* the covers was too much even for Sergeant Fred Averill, sent over from the nearby Notting Hill police station. Margery Gardner's naked body lay on its back, her feet tied together with a handkerchief; her wrists, judging by the marks, had also been bound, though the ligature had been removed. Her face had been severely bruised consistent with having been punched repeatedly. There were no less than seventeen vicious lash marks on various parts of her body – marks with a distinctive diamond criss-cross pattern. In addition the breasts had been bitten, the nipples almost bitten off. Finally, some rough object had been forced into her vagina causing excessive bleeding. The unspeakable savagery of the injuries were compounded by the fact that Margery Gardner had been alive when they were inflicted; death had come later, from suffocation.

On that same morning, Heath's 'fiancée' received a telephone call, the result of which was Heath taking a train to Worthing. After booking himself into the Ocean Hotel, they lunched. On the Saturday morning – for no

explicable reason – Heath told Miss Symonds that a terrible murder had occurred in London and that he would tell her about it later. And tell her he did, over dinner at the Blue Peter Club in Angmering. It took place at the Pembridge Court Hotel, he said, in the room that *he* had booked; what was more, he had actually seen the body: "a very gruesome sight". Quite how this was affecting Yvonne Symonds's digestion we can only guess, but in her subsequent statement she recalled that her companion had said he met the victim earlier on the evening of her death and that he had lent her his room to entertain a gentleman friend, and that on the following day Inspector Barrett had personally invited him to view the body. Heath suggested that a poker had been "stuck up her".

It was with understandable dismay that the Symonds family – over breakfast this time – learned not only the details of the murder from the Sunday newspapers, but also that the police were anxious to interview one Neville George Clevely Heath. When Yvonne Symonds relayed their disquiet to her fiancé over the telephone, he sympathized with her parents' upset and assured her that he was at that moment on his way to London to "clear things up".

Of course he did no such thing. Instead he moved along the coast to Bournemouth from where he posted a preposterous letter to Scotland Yard's Inspector Barrett, in which he claimed to have met the late Margery Gardner and lent her his hotel room key in order to accommodate a man friend with whom "for mainly financial reasons" she was obliged to sleep. He continued: "Mrs Gardner asked if she could use my hotel room until two o'clock and intimated that if I returned after that, I might spend the remainder of the night with her. I gave her my keys and told her to leave the hotel door open. It must have been nearly 3am when I returned to the hotel and found her in the condition of which you are aware. I realized that I was in an invidious position, and rather than notify the police, I packed my belongings and left. Since then I have been in several minds whether to come forward or not but in view of the circumstances I have been afraid to. I can give you a description of the man. He was aged approximately thirty, dark hair (black), with small moustache. Height about 5ft. 9in., slim build. His name was Jack and I gathered he was a friend of Mrs Gardner of some long standing... I have the instrument with which Mrs Gardner was beaten and am forwarding this to you today. You will find my fingerprints on it, but you should also find others there as well." The letter was signed "N.G.C. Heath". The alleged 'instrument' never arrived.

Heath arrived at the Tollard Royal Hotel on the West Cliff in Bournemouth on Sunday June the 23rd and checked in under the name of Group Captain Rupert Brooke. He occupied room 81. On the morning of the 3rd of July 'Brooke' met twenty-one-year-old Doreen Marshall and entertained her to afternoon tea. In a later statement to the police – when they finally caught up with him – Heath described the events of that Wednesday: "I met her along the promenade about 2.45 in the afternoon, and after a short stroll we went to the Tollard Royal for tea about 3.45. The conversation was fairly general and covered the fact that she had served with the WRNS. She mentioned the fact that she had been ill and was down in Bournemouth to recuperate. She left the hotel at about 5.45 after accepting my invitation to dinner in the evening. At approximately 7.15 I was standing outside the hotel when I saw Miss Marshall approaching the hotel on foot down West Hill Road. I entered the hotel, went to my room to get some tobacco, and came down again just as she was entering the lounge. We dined at about 8.15pm and sat talking in the lounge after dinner, moving into the writing room at about 10pm. The conversation was again general but she told me she was considering cutting short her holiday and returning home [she lived in Pinner] on Friday instead of Monday. She mentioned an American

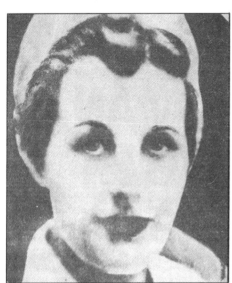

Margery Gardner

Doreen Marshall

Heath's re-entry route to the Tollard Royal Hotel after the murder of Doreen Marshall

staying at her hotel and told me that he had taken her for car rides into the country and to Poole. She also mentioned an invitation to go with him to Exeter, but I gathered, although she did not actually say so, that she did not intend to go. Another American was mentioned – I believe his name was Pat – to whom I believe she was unofficially engaged some while ago. Conversation continued general until approximately 11.30pm. At 11pm (approx) Miss Marshall suggested going away, but I persuaded her to stay a little longer. At about 11.30 the weather was clear and we left the hotel and sat on a seat overlooking the sea."

When 'Group Captain Brooke' returned to his hotel he "decided to practice a small deception" on the night porter: "I guessed he would be waiting for me to come in, and as a ladder had that day been placed up against my window... [I] entered my hotel bedroom via the ladder."

On the 5th of July the Norfolk Hotel's manager notified the local police that one of his guests – Miss Doreen Marshall – had been missing since the 3rd. At the same time he telephoned his opposite number at the Tollard Royal, a Mr Relf, who on the following morning asked 'Brooke' whether his guest of the previous Wednesday had been the missing Miss Marshall from Pinner. "Oh, no," Brooke laughed. "I've known that lady for a long while and she certainly doesn't come from Pinner." Nevertheless, Relf suggested, it might be a good idea to get in touch with the police.

And with amazing bravado, he did just that; presenting himself at Bournemouth police station at 5.30pm. Here, through Detective Constable George Suter, he met Doreen Marshall's father and sister who had travelled down from Pinner to be close to the search for Doreen. Brooke was shown a photograph of the missing girl and with a great show of surprise and sorrow admitted that it was, after all, the same young woman with whom he had dined on the night of her disappearance. Throughout this exchange, DC Suter had been scrutinising his guest carefully; he bore an uncanny resemblance to the photograph of the man Heath that Scotland Yard were anxious to interview. Finally, he gave voice to his thoughts: "Brooke, is your real name Heath?" "Good Lord no!" he replied, "But I agree it is like me."

Nonetheless, with a good detective's instinctive caution, Suter detained his visitor until the Inspector arrived, at which point Brooke's meagre belongings were brought from the Tollard Royal Hotel to the police station. Searched in front of him, Brooke's jacket pockets yielded a left-luggage ticket issued at Bournemouth West station, the return half of a first-class railway ticket issued to Doreen Marshall, and a single artificial pearl from a necklace. When Detective Inspector George Gates redeemed the deposited suitcase from Bournemouth West, a further damning array of evidence was revealed: clothing and a hat marked with the name 'Heath', and a blue woollen scarf and a neckerchief, both stained with blood and bearing hairs later proved to have come from Doreen Marshall's head. At the bottom of the case was a leather riding switch; a riding switch with a distinctive diamond pattern weave.

Early the following day Detective Inspector Reg Spooner arrived from London, and on Monday the 8th of July Heath was removed to Scotland Yard, where he was charged with the murder of Margery Gardner.

Meanwhile, that same day Kathleen Evans, a young waitress, had been exercising her dog at Branksome Dene Chine on the Dorset/Hampshire border when she noticed a swarm of flies around some rhododendron bushes. When she later read of Doreen Marshall's continued disappearance she was reminded of the flies and voiced her suspicions to her father. When Kathleen and Mr Evans returned to the chine later that evening they solved the riddle of Doreen Marshall.

When the police arrived they found the body naked but for a left shoe and covered by the victim's clothing and some branches of fir-tree. Close to the body, police searchers found Doreen's torn stockings, a powder compact and a broken string of artificial pearls; on the following morning her handbag was located behind a beach-hut at Durley Chine.

The direct cause of Doreen Marshall's death had been two deep cuts across her throat, though these were but two of a dreadful series of injuries and mutilations committed on the body both before and after death. She had been bludgeoned a number of times on the back of the head and there were bruises and abrasions to most of the upper body. One rib had been fractured and had pierced the left lung; Doreen's hands, which had been tied at the wrists, bore deep cuts, indicating that she had tried to grab the knife from her attacker. But even in death, the tragic girl had suffered further appalling treatment; one nipple had been bitten off, and a ragged knife cut reached from her

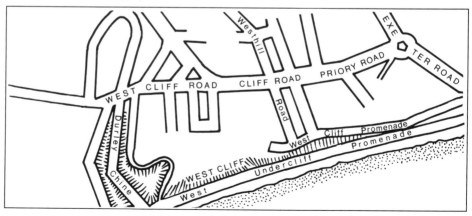

Neville Heath (left) under arrest

vagina to her chest where it met a further diagonal slash from each nipple to the middle of her body. In addition, an instrument, probably the branch of a tree, had been forced into her vagina and anus.

The trial of Neville George Clevely Heath opened in the Old Bailey's No. 1 Court on Tuesday the 24th of September 1946. Mr Justice Morris presided and Mr E.A. Hawke and Mr J.D. Casswell led, respectively, the prosecution and defence cases. Heath was charged only with the murder of Margery Gardner; he pleaded not guilty.

There was never any question of Heath's guilt – he was quite patently a vicious and sadistic killer. The question was, was he insane? Mr Casswell's defence rested heavily on the fact that a man simply *had* to be mad to have committed such grotesque crimes; that though Heath may well have known what he was doing, he was so morally bankrupt that he had no conception at the time that what he was doing was wrong. For the

Crown, two prison doctors, while allowing that Heath was both a sexual pervert and a psychopath, refused to agree that he was, within the scope of the McNaghten Rules* – which determined such matters in law – definitely not insane.

As for the prisoner himself, he seemed throughout the three days of the trial to be quite indifferent to the proceedings – even bored. He said not one word in his own

---

* See *Murder Club Guide No.3* for a note on the McNaghten Rules.

defence, nor exhibited the slightest remorse. After a retirement of one hour, the jury were unanimous in their verdict – guilty of murder.

Heath made no appeal and no last-minute confession; his sole gesture to decency was to admit, in a letter to his parents, that he had been "damned unworthy of you both". On October the 16th he stood on the scaffold at Pentonville Prison. Before hangman Albert Pierrepoint carried out his public duty, Neville Heath is said to have asked the prison governor for a whisky, adding: "You might as well make that a double."

Eureka
The Murder of FREDERICK BRYANT
by his Wife CHARLOTTE
between the 11th and 21st of December 1935
at their home in Coombe, near Sherborne

At the age of twenty-five Frederick Bryant was a corporal in the military police serving in Ireland; this had been during 'The Troubles' of 1920-21, and despite the savage guerrilla warfare that had been waged against the British troops, the awful bloodshed that was to result in a divided Ireland, Bryant had come through unscathed. It was to be another fifteen years before one of Erin's children would be the cause of his untimely death.

During his service in Londonderry, Frederick had met Charlotte McHugh, at the time just nineteen, illiterate and careless both in appearance and morals. Quite why the sober, upright corporal found her attractive is a mystery, but he brought her back home to Somerset where, in March 1922, they married.

But life for Frederick Bryant, a soldier without a battle to fight, was proving a sad disappointment. After the glamour and camaraderie of the Service, to find himself unemployed was more than his dignity could stand. Desperately clutching at the respectability of honest toil, Bryant accepted a job as a labourer on a farm at Over Compton, on the Somerset/Dorset border. In 1925, he and his new wife moved into the tied cottage that

had come with the job.

Before long, Charlotte had settled down and resumed some of the small daily routines

Charlotte Bryant

The Bryants' cottage at Coombe Farm

that she had enjoyed in Ulster – mainly drinking and sex; both in varying degrees of excess. Squalid as she was in both mind and appearance, toothless and verminous, her reputation grew; as did her list of amours and her brood of children. Not that Frederick Bryant was in much of a position to complain – feeding seven mouths on a labourer's wage was not easy; as he once confided to a neighbour: "Four pound a week is better than thirty bob – I don't care a damn what she does."

Around Christmas 1933, an eighth mouth was sitting at table in the Bryants' shabby abode; a lodger in the person of Leonard Parsons, itinerant gypsy horse-dealer and pedlar. Needless to say, Charlotte's favours were included in the rent.

When even the tolerant people of Compton tired of the 'goings-on' of the Bryant household, and Frederick was thrown out of job and home, he simply removed his rag-bag of family and possessions on to Coombe, to another farm, another cottage. Life here resumed its familiar pattern, though by now Leonard Parsons was spending less time at the Bryants' hovel and more time with his

'wife' Priscilla Loveridge – also a gypsy, and the mother of his four children. Thus did jealousy become an aggravating complication in Charlotte Bryant's life.

It must have been about this time that she made up her mind that Frederick alone was the obstacle in the path of her true happiness with Leonard Parsons. On May the 14th 1935 Bryant fell ill with vomiting and acute stomach pains, diagnosed – wrongly as it turned out – as gastro-enteritis. On August 6th of the same year he had a further similar attack. Now whether it was because he suspected foul-play and feared for his own safety, or that he simply tired of Charlotte's sluttish ways, Parsons packed his bags and made it clear that he was going for good. Between the 11th and 21st of December Frederick Bryant was once again in pain, his suffering becoming so acute that he could barely move or speak. On Sunday the 22nd, he died in the Yeatman Hospital at Sherborne.

Suspicious now, Dr McCarthy refused to sign the death certificate and quicky made known his misgivings to the local police. As a result, Frederick's earthly remains were

The bedroom in which Frederick John Bryant received his fatal dose of arsenic

given into the charge of Home Office analyst Dr Roche Lynch, who would have been blind not to have noticed the lethal 4.09 grains of arsenic in the body. Scotland Yard had meanwhile been alerted to this possibility, and were already making an exhaustive search of the Bryants' cottage. Of the 146 samples of dust and dirt collected from various surfaces in the building, an astonishing thirty-two were later to show traces of arsenic. In a pile of rubbish found outside, the police also recovered a battered tin that had onced contained 'Eureka', a weed-killer with a high arsenic content.

Charlotte Bryant appeared at the Dorset Assizes in May 1936, charged with the murder of her husband. While she sat in the dock munching caramels, the chief witness for the prosecution, Leonard Parsons, recalled for the benefit of the court an occasion in the previous October when Mrs Bryant had assured him that she was soon to become a widow. Mrs Lucy Ostler, a recent lodger with the Bryants, told how on December the 21st Charlotte had almost forced her husband to drink a cup of Oxo meat extract and subsequently disposed of a tin of weed-killer with the words: "I must get rid of this."

On Saturday the 30th of May 1936 Charlotte Bryant was found guilty and sentenced to death. On the 15th of July that sentence was carried out at Exeter Prison. The priest who attended Mrs Bryant in her final hours said later: "Her last moments were truly edifying."

Edward, Martyr King of England
The Assassination of KING EDWARD
by a Servant of his Step-Mother ELFRIDA
in March 979
at the gate of Corfe Castle

Edward was born in about the year 963, son of Edgar the Peaceful, sovereign of all England, and his first wife Ethelfleda. The queen did not long survive Edward's birth and Edgar remarried, to Elfrida by whom he had another son, Ethelred.

On the king's death in 975, Edward, as the eldest son, succeeded to the throne at the start of a reign that was to be as unpopular as it was short. Though we know little of the political life of Edward, his adherence to the strict guidance of St Dunstan (then

Archbishop of Canterbury), and his own irrepressible ill-temper, made him many powerful enemies. Opposition was particularly strong among a group of anti-monastic thanes based in the influential kingdom of Mercia. In their disaffection for Edward, they had a dedicated ally in Elfrida who, since Edgar's death, had sought to install her own son Ethelred – though he was barely ten years of age – on the throne of England.

It is the historian monk William of Malmesbury who provides us with the most detailed

EDWARD THE MARTYR KING OF WESSEX TREACHEROUSLY STABBED AT THE GATE OF CORFE CASTLE BY HIS STEPMOTHER ELFRIDA 978

Right: Manuscript in Norman notation of three hymns to Edward written by Eadmer. Above: The first hymn normalised

Hec dies presiderida. in qua supna curia. congaudet & dignissimam.

Regi deo dat gloriam. Mira dei bonitas. mira potentia.

que bona cuncta creans ordinat omnia. equo moderamine.

Regni dei clarissime concurs & rex anglie. prestans tuoz gloria

laus & corona splendida. VERSVS DE SCO EDVVARDO REGE 7 MARTIR.
Hec dies presiderida. in qua supna curia congaudet & dignissimam.
Regi deo dar glam. Vir namq; seclo preperens. & scepra regni
possidens. Iam nc poloz gaudet Admiratus; heret angelis. Edwar
dus hic uocamine. clara satus ppagine. cui manus os pectora. Sibi
parariunt sidera. Hinc inuidoz pessima fraus. & nouerca subdo
la. neci beatum subdidit. viuiq; celis intulit. Edwarde rex suauis
sime. decus tuoz nobile. coniunct en archangelis. tuis adesto seruu
lis. Summo patri cu filio. Et sctu paraclito. Sit laus. potestas gla. p cun
cta semp scla. Amen. Item. Mira di bonitas. mira potentia. a ue
bona cuncta creans ordinat omnia. equo moderamine. & dierus
hic solium contulit inclitu Edwardo. qm rex fuit anglie. Iustus pius.
optimus. Dunstani patris hunc os docuit sacru. Inq; dei stabile ex
hibuit uia. a ue dixer eu do. Ld phat esse ratu celitus emicans eius
in examines corporis artus lumen uenerabile. Hinc honor amq;
decus ingenito patri. Singenito q; patris pneumate cu sacro. p
scla pennia. Amen. Item. Regni di clarissime concuris &
rex anglie. prestans tuoz gla. laus & corona splendida. Edwaz

89

account of Edward's eventual assassination. In March 979 Edward had been on a hunting trip in what is now Dorset. Weary of the chase and determined to visit his young step-brother, for whom he entertained a great affection, he approached Elfrida's castle at Corfe. Apprised of his imminent arrival, Elfrida rode out with a party of servants to greet the king and, seeing that he was alone, embarked on an impromptu plan that would result in his death. Feigning pleasure at his unexpected arrival, Elfrida called for refreshment for her step-son; while he supped from the cup, one of the servants "pierced him through" with a dagger. Although Edward spurred his horse to make an escape, he slipped from the saddle and with one foot caught in the stirrup was dragged along, "his blood leaving a trail", until he died.

William of Malmesbury relates that Elfrida ordered the king's body to be thrown into a bog that it might not be discovered, but a miraculous pillar of light marked the spot and the corpse was taken up for burial in the church at Wareham. In 980, Dunstan had the relics removed to Shaftesbury Abbey [see panel below].

In 1001, Ethelred (called 'Unraed' or The Unready) signed a charter by which his late step-brother was dignified "Saint and Martyr"; in 1008 he further ordered the observance of an annual feast of St Edward Martyr King.

As for Elfrida, overwhelmed by remorse she expiated her sin by becoming a nun and founding the monasteries of Amesbury and Wherwell, at which latter she died.

Edward the Martyr's bones to be moved

April 26, 1988: The bones of St Edward, Martyr King, are once again the subject of contention. Murdered in 979 by retainers of his step-brother Ethelred, Edward was canonised after his burial at Wareham; later his relics were removed to Shaftesbury Abbey where they were guarded by nuns until the Dissolution, when they were buried.

The new dispute over the relics – now little more than a skull and some fragments of bone – has arisen between Mr John Claridge, who excavated them in 1931, and his niece, Mrs Georgina Smith, daughter of his brother Geoffrey who died in 1986. In 1943, the brothers inherited the family property at Shaftesbury, which included the ruins of the abbey.

The disagreement is over Mr Claridge's wish to present Edward's bones to the

Russian Orthodox Church in exile at Brookwood, near Woking. Mrs Smith, acting as executrix for her father, insists that the relics should remain the property of the Shaftesbury estate. Ironically the bones, said to possess miraculous powers, are at present in the vault of the Midland Bank, Woking.

The decision of the court yesterday was that the relics should go to the Russian Orthodox Church at Brookwood so long as there was adequate security. This ruling was given pending a further trial contesting the ownership and final resting place of St Edward's remains.

Mr Claridge decided to make his gift to the Russian Orthodox community after both the Church of England and the Roman Catholic Church had failed to meet his strict security demands.

The Petit Treason* of Mary Channel
The Murder of Mr JAMES CHANNEL
by his Wife MARY
at a village near Dorchester
and her Execution in April 1703

Mary Channel was the daughter of one Mr Woods, a person of good repute, who resided in a little village near Dorchester, in the county of Dorset. He was a person of known wealth and good credit, who, by his industry and diligence, daily increased his riches. Perceiving his daughter to be of a promising disposition, and amiable both in body and mind, he gave her a liberal education, to improve and refine those good qualifications by art and study wherewith she was liberally endowed by the bounty of nature. She made so speedy a progress in her learning that she soon outvied her schoolfellows; and the strong imagination, polite behaviour and majestic graces in her carriage so lively displayed themselves that she became the mirror and discourse of all who knew her. Though her birth gave place to those of the highest rank and quality, yet her education was not inferior to them; and her incomparable wit, united with her beautiful presence, rendered her so agreeable that she was to be preferred even to many of a superior rank.

Her charms did not consist in adorning and dressing herself in magnificent and gay attire, decked with pearls and diamonds, which gives a false gloss of beauty to persons whose natures are opposite, and only serve to brighten the lustre of their pretended fine qualities. In a word, she was generally esteemed the most celebrated wit and accomplished beauty of her age.

Being now in the flower of her youth and bloom of her beauty, she had several suitors of good repute, who all became captives to her beauty and hardly did they find themselves ensnared but they had the boldness to flatter themselves with the hopes of one day possessing such a charming object. Amongst the rest, one Mr Channel, a wealthy grocer of Dorchester, came to pay his respects to her, who, for the great riches

* See *Murder Club Guide No.1* for a note on Petit Treason.

he enjoyed, was gratefully accepted by her parents, though by her altogether contemned and slighted. He had nothing to recommend him but his wealth, which was as much superior to the rest of her suitors as his person was inferior to them: his limbs and body were in some measure ill proportioned and his features in no wise agreeable; but what rendered him the more detestable and ridiculous in her sight was his splay-foot, which did not in the least concur with her sublime and lofty temper. Her father, evidently perceiving the addresses of Mr Channel were received and accepted by her with scorn and reproofs, entreated her to receive him with less disdain and listen to his respectful addresses. Being weary, however, of his fond familiarities, she determined to abandon herself from him, and never more admit him into her presence or society. She had no sooner put her design into execution but it reached her father's ears, who kept a more strict guard and watchful eye over her behaviour and conduct, and forthwith continued his absurd and unreasonable expostulations and imprudent menaces to enforce and augment her love. She in vain endeavoured to excuse herself, by disputing the most solid and rational arguments; but how much the more she

persisted, by so much the more her parents' resolution was incensed and irritated, pressing her to consent to a speedy marriage, and telling her she would discharge the duty under which she was obligated to them by assenting to and complying with their commands. At length, being continually fatigued and importuned by her parents to have the marriage solemnized, she consented, though with the greatest reluctance. And on the day appointed the ceremony was ordained.

Having now gratified her parents' desire, and yielded to their compulsions, by putting the finishing stroke to her marriage, she still continued her slights and contempts towards her husband, and he became the entire object of her scorn. Soon after the solemnization of the marriage she began to plot and contrive new scenes of tragedies, and her thoughts were chiefly employed and taken up in studying what measures to take to get rid of her husband, and set herself at liberty. Nothing would satisfy her enormous desires but his death, which she determined to bring about by poison. And, in order thereto, she sent her maid to the apothecary's for some white mercury, telling her it was to kill rats and mice; though it is certain her design was reverse, which she intended to fulfil as soon as opportunity would give reins to her vicious inclinations. A little after she gave orders for rice milk to be made for breakfast. That morning, particularly, she was observed to demonstrate a seeming diligence in procuring everyone their proper messes; and no one was permitted to serve her husband but herself. Accordngly she prepared and gave him the poisonous draught, mixed and infused with the mercury, which she had reserved for this desperate use, and which proved his fatal dish. After he had eaten somewhat liberally he discovered an ill savour

in his milk, and said it tasted amiss. Hereupon he offered his wife's brother (a youth who boarded with him) to taste it; but she would by no means permit her brother to comply with this reasonable request, which caused a strong suspicion throughout the family. Then Mr Channel required the maid to taste it; but she had no sooner taken it into her hands than her mistress in a violent passion caught it from her, and forthwith conveyed it away. It was now too late to recall what had passed, or to seek for refuge; for his body presently began to swell vehemently, perceiving which, the domestics immediately sent for a doctor. But the infused mercury had so great an effect upon him that no remedy could expel it, and he expired before the physicians came to his assistance. Having thus resigned his breath, and there being visible proofs of his being poisoned, it was not without reason she was suspected to be the principal and only actress and procurer thereof. Thereupon she was immediately seized and conveyed before a justice, before whom she entirely denied the fact; nevertheless, on her servants' information, he committed her to Dorchester Jail.

At the assizes ensuing at Dorchester the defence she made (whether it was real or pretended) was so full of wit and ingenuity, and uttered with such an extraordinary courage and humility, that it caused admiration in the judges, and pity and compassion in all who heard her trial. But this availed nothing; for the evidences appearing plain against her, and the friends of her deceased husband being very substantial people, she received sentence to be burned at the stake till she was dead.

The day whereon she was to suffer being come, she was guarded by proper officers to the place of execution, with her hood veiled over her face. After she had uttered some private ejaculations she pulled off her gown and white silk hood and delivered them to her maid – who accompanied her to the stake – and then suffered death, according to the sentence before pronounced against her, declaring her faith in Christ; and to the last continued to exclaim against her parents' constraints, which had been the sole cause of her torturing death. Thus at a small distance from the town of Dorchester she yielded her breath, in or about the month of April, Anno Domini 1703, in the eighteenth year of her age, being greatly bewailed and lamented, though the sentence was acknowledged to be just and lawful.

Sad and Wicked, Cruel Wretch

The Murder of her own Child
by EMMA PITT
at Park Horner, Hampreston, near Wimborne

BARBAROUS
MURDER OF A CHILD
BY A
SCHOOLMISTRESS.

A child murder has been committed at Park Horner, in the parish of Hampreston, under circumstances of the most shocking barbarity. At the Coroner's inquest it was given in evidence that the child had been beaten on the head with a heavy flint stone, and its tongue cut completely out at the root. It was found wrapped up in another part of a drawer where the body was discovered. The inquiry lasted four hours and a-half, and resulted, in the first instance, in a verdict, "That the child was born alive and murdered by someone." The Coroner pointed out that the evidence was conclusive against Emma Pitt, the national schoolmistress, who was the mother of the child; and he expressed his surprise that such a verdict should have been returned. The Jury after reconsidering their previous finding, returned a verdict of "Wilful murder against Emma Pitt."

We have read of sad and dreadful deeds
 Of mothers cruel and unkind,
But in the annals of history
 Such as this we seldom find;
In the parish of Hampreston,
 This deed was done we hear,
Near to the town of Wimborne,
 In the county of Dorsetshire.

This Emma Pitt was a schoolmistress,
 Her child she killed we see,
Oh mothers, did you ever hear,
 Of such barbarity.

With a large flint stone she beat its head
 When such cruelty she'd done,
From the tender roof of the infant's mouth
 She cut away it's tongue;
Sad and wicked, cruel wretch,
 Hard was her flinty heart,
The infant's tongue from the body was
 Wrapped in another part.

The murderess placed in a drawer,
 And it there, alas! was found,
The news of this dreadful murder,
 Soon spread for miles around;
And first upon the inquest,
 She expected to get free,

Although she was the author
 Of this dreadful tragedy.

A schoolmistress too, how sad to tell,
 Well known for miles around,
Who had many children under care,
 In and near to Wimborne town.
Oh, what a sad example,
 To children she did set,
There was never such a cruel wretch,
 As the barbarous Emma Pitt.

She committed is for murder,
 Soon her trial will take place,
And if she is found guilty,
 How sad will be her case.
If she has a woman's feelings,
 She surely will go wild,
She in such a barbarous manner killed
 Her tender infant child.

The hour is approaching,
 The moments near at hand,
When before a Judge and Jury,
 This monster soon must stand;
And if she is found guilty,
 She her deserts will get,
And mother's, miles round Wimborne,
 Will remember Emma Pitt.

H. Disley, Printer, 57, High Street, St. Giles.

SOMERSET

1 Curry Mallet ●

2 Ilchester ●

Somerset

Keeping it in the Family
The Murder of DORIS WINIFRED BREWER
by FREDERICK MORSE
on the 23rd or 24th of February 1933
at Curry Mallet

SOMERSET RIVER TRAGEDY

Uncle Charged with Murdering his Niece

VOLUNTARY STATEMENT

Fred Morse, aged 34, a labourer, of West Hatch, was taken by car from Taunton police station to Ilminster, Somerset, a distance of 12 miles, on Wednesday night, and was there charged before two local magistrates with the murder of his niece Dorothy [sic] Winifred Brewer, aged 12 years 9 months, by drowning her in a river at Curry Mallet between 10.30am on February 23rd and 10.30am on February 24th.

Inspector Carter, of Taunton, stated that he charged Morse at Taunton police station, and he replied: "I have nothing to say. I put it all in a statement to Det-Insp Bennett".

In reply to the Chairman (Mr L. Hepworth), Inspector Carter said it was a voluntary statement.

A certificate for legal aid was issued, and a remand was granted until March 10. Later in the evening Morse was taken to Exeter Prison.

FUNERAL POSTPONED

The funeral of Dorothy Brewer was to have taken place at West Hatch on Wednesday afternoon, but an instruction rescinding the burial order issued by the Coroner was received by the girl's parents, and the body was again removed to the mortuary at Taunton.

During the morning, Chief Inspector Bennett and Detective-Sergeant Salisbury had an interview with Lieut-Col Metcalfe, Chief Constable of Somerset.

A second visit was paid to the scene of the tragedy, but no further dragging operations in the water were carried out. The detectives returned to Taunton in order to meet Sir Bernard Spilsbury, the famous pathologist, whose assistance had been obtained by the police, who had been in telegraphic communication with him the previous night.

Sir Bernard arrived from London at 1.30, accompanied by his assistant. He was met by Dr Godfrey Carter the hon. pathologist to the Taunton and Somerset Hospital, who made the original post-

mortem examination. The doctors motored to the mortuary where the remains were lying. The pathologists and detectives remained in the mortuary for about two hours. Sir Bernard Spilsbury afterwards returned to London.

THE INQUEST

When the inquest on the deceased girl was opened at Curry Mallet on Monday, the Coroner caused a stir in the crowded court by inquiring: "Is Fred Morse legally represented?"

A man without a collar and tie, and wearing a blue mackintosh, stood up and informed the Coroner that he had no solicitor present on his behalf.

The Coroner addressing the jury, said it would not be possible to complete the investigation that day. "I think it will be a quite difficult case for you," he proceeded. "There are certain further investigations that will have to be made."

NOT QUITE THIRTEEN

"In the first place, you must put entirely away from your minds any local rumours you may have heard."

The girl, he said, was 12 years 9 months old, but of exceptional physique for her age. He thought it correct to say that she could easily have been mistaken for a girl of 16 or 17.

A post-mortem examination revealed an advanced state of pregnancy. She was living with her grandmother and was attending the village school.

To enable the jury to understand the case, it was essential he should refer to a man named Fred Morse, who was, in fact, the dead girl's uncle. According to a voluntary statement Morse made to the police, he went to work in a quarry on the day in question and had breakfast, which took him ten minutes. He then left and met Dorothy Brewer at the cross-roads about 200 yards from a lime kiln. He had apparently made a previous appointment.

CALL AT AN INN

According to his version he wanted her to go to school, but she started to cry and said she didn't want to. They had some further conversation, and he told her he was going to Curry Mallet to pick up some wires and [rabbit] traps. It was arranged that she should go with him.

96

At Curry Mallet the man called at the *Bell Inn* and purchased two pints of beer and half a pint of rum. The couple afterwards went across some fields where the man left the girl, telling her to go to a galvanised shed, and that he would join her later.

According to Morse, he went to the shed three-quarters of an hour later and found that Dorothy had disappeared. He searched for her and found footprints on the river bank and he fell into the water himself.

LIVED WITH HER GRANDMOTHER

It was only fair, added the Coroner, to say that Morse volunteered his statement to the police, and he denied being in any way responsible for the girl's condition or the fact that her body was found in the river.

He (the Coroner) did not propose to call Morse to give evidence that day.

It was stated in evidence that the girl was one of a large family, and had lived with her grandmother for five and a half years. The grandmother, Mrs Alice Morse, who was in a very distracted state, said she questioned the girl as to her condition, and a visit was made to the village nurse.

Three sons lived at home, but one came only for week-ends.

On Wednesday night she went to bed about 9 o'clock and left Fred Morse downstairs playing with Dorothy's hair as was his usual custom.

Mrs Lily Brewer, of Lillesdon, North Curry, the girl's mother, said Dorothy visited her a fortnight before she disappeared. "My suspicions," said Mrs Brewer, "were aroused as to her condition."

In reply to Inspector Carter, of Taunton, she said that on a previous occasion she asked her brother Fred Morse whether anything was the matter with Dorothy, and he replied: "No".

Winifred Annie Crossman, daughter of the licensee of the *Bell Inn*, Curry Mallet, recalled seeing a man she identified as Morse calling at the house at 10.30am on the previous Thursday.

Among other things he asked for 7 shillings worth of rum, which was unusual: "I noticed he was shaking as he gave me the money," she observed.

ARM-IN-ARM

Albert Sansom, labourer, of Curry Mallet, said he was looking through the window of his cottage when he noticed a strange man and a girl in the road. They were walking arm-in-arm, the man pushing a bicycle.

Several times they stopped, and the girl seemed to want to go back in the opposite direction. The girl was looking very strange. She was a very nice looking girl, he added.

Dr Godfrey Carter, pathologist at Taunton General Hospital, stated that there were no marks of violence on the body, but slight bruises were on the face. In reply to the Coroner, Dr Carter said that without analysis he could not say whether there was anything to show the presence of rum in the body.

The Coroner said it was imperative that further analysis should be made, and the police would make further investigations.

He therefore adjourned the inquiry till Tuesday, March 14th, and advised Fred Morse to be legally represented on that occasion.

(*The Somerset Guardian*, Friday, March 3, 1933)

Drowned Schoolgirl Disclosures

Accused Uncle's Alleged Account of Suicide Pact

RIVER BANK SCENE

"I Held Her Hand and Together We Jumped"

SOMERSET VILLAGE DRAMA

A dramatic story of life and death in a remote Somerset village was unfolded in the tiny police court at Ilminster on Friday, when Fred Morse appeared in the dock charged with the wilful murder of his niece Doris Winifred Brewer by drowning her in the River Rag at Curry Mallet.

Crown counsel alleged Morse had been carrying on an intrigue with the girl, the results of which could not much longer have been concealed from public knowledge.

Doris was taken to a doctor, and the result of his examination was communicated to her on February 22nd.

Next day the girl disappeared after having, it is alleged, met her uncle instead of going to school. That afternoon Morse was seen coming away from the river wet through, shivering and crying. The girl's body was recovered from the water the next day.

A statement alleged to have been made to the police by the accused man was read. In this he is said to have admitted his relations with the girl – who was known to him as "Mary" – and narrated how they agreed to drown themselves: "I held Mary's right hand with my left, and together we jumped into the backwash. In the water she clung to my arm and I got her on to the bank; she slipped in again, and I fell in after her. I crawled onto the bank. I was too weak to help Mary".

Statement Admitted after Solicitor's Protest

Morse was arrested at Taunton, and taken by car to Colinston where he was charged before the magistrates; a certificate for legal aid was then granted, and Morse was remanded after evidence of arrest only.

Great public interest was manifested in Friday's proceedings, and there was room under the tiny raftered court for only a handful of people, the majority of them being women.

Mr G. R. Paling represented the Director of Public Prosecutions, and Morse was defended by Mr R. W. Young, solicitor.

Mr Paling said that one of the dead girl's names was Doris, and not Dorothy, as had been stated. She was born in March 1920.

A Visit to the Doctor

When Doris was seven she went to live with her grandparents, the father and mother of Morse, at Slough Green, West Hatch. Morse lived in the same house, and worked at some lime-kilns near by.

At the beginning of last February Mrs Brewer had reason to believe that her daughter had been interfered with, and she sent her to a district nurse to be examined. The nurse was not satisfied with the girl's condition and told a doctor. When the doctor examined Doris on February the 21st, he found that she was in an advanced state of pregnancy.

"The Prosecution suggest", said Mr Paling, "that the prisoner was the person responsible for the girl's condition."

Arm-in-Arm

On February 23rd, at about 10am, a girl and a man pushing a bicycle were seen walking arm-in-arm on the higher road at Curry Mallet, going away from West Hatch towards a public house known as the *Rock House Inn*.

It appeared as if the girl was reluctant to go that way because she kept turning round, while the man pulled her by the arm.

At about 10.20 the couple called at the *Bell Inn* at Curry Mallet, where Morse drank some beer and bought some rum to take away with him which was put in a whisky bottle; he also bought a packet of potato crisps.

Mr Paling held up an empty whisky bottle, and said: "at a farm near the *Bell Inn* is a small stream and its tributary; at 4.00pm the same day Morse was seen crossing a meadow towards the road and away from the river".

At 4.15, his brother Harold met him. Morse's clothes were wet and he was shivering and crying. He told his brother that he had lost Doris; he said he had left her in a shed beside the river while he collected rabbit traps, and when he returned she was missing. The shed was near the river and Morse said he had searched the bank and fallen into the stream. He said he met Doris on the way to school, she said she did not want to go, and he took her with him to collect traps. This is the story he told his friends and relatives when he got home.

The search for the dead girl ended on February the 24th when her body was found in the tributary, fully clothed, and lying downwards. In the hedge near the shed, the girl's attache case was found, and an empty potato crisp packet was found in the shed. A blue-black case which had contained a wristlet watch given to Doris by Morse on her birthday was discovered between the wall and the roof of the shed.

Drank Rum Before Death

Later a whisky bottle containing a small amount of rum was found in bushes overhanging the stream fifty yards from the body. A post-mortem examination showed that death was due to drowning, that shortly before death the girl had drunk some rum – a considerable quantity for a girl of twelve.

When Mr Paling referred to a statement that Morse is alleged to have made to the police, Mr Young asked that its contents should not be disclosed at the moment, and added: "As to the second statement made, I object to that being given at all, because I understand that it was taken under circumstances which made it impossible to call it voluntary." He suggested that phrases in the statement which had been mentioned proved that they had been suggested by persons of greater education than Morse. The magistrates decided that the statement was admissible.

Suicide Pact?

Counsel's Submission After Reading Alleged Statement

Mr Paling read the statement alleged to have been made by Morse to Inspector Carter. In this Morse said he met Doris on her way to school, but when they arrived there she refused to go in. He and the girl then went to the *Rock House Inn* and the *Bell Inn* before going to the road near the river. He directed her to the shed and told her to stay there.

0The statement continued: "I gave her the bag of chips and the watch. When I got to the shed after collecting the traps I could not see her but I could see her footprints going through a gap in the hedge". A description of how Morse searched for the girl without success followed.

0Mr Paling went on to read from Morse's other alleged statement, this time to Chief Detective Inspector Bennett, in which he said that he had seduced his niece.

We Are Better Dead

Reading from one of Morse's alleged statements, Mr Paling said: "On the night after the doctor's examination I was plaiting Mary's hair, and I said 'You know what the doctor said? He said you have got to have a child in six weeks.' She commenced to laugh and then she became serious, and started to pull long faces and said: 'I am not going to school tomorow, I am going to the quarry with you.' I made up my mind to go to Curry Mallet with her and jump in the river to end it all."

Morse had said to her: "What are we going to do?"; she said: "Let's get out of it all." He took her to mean that they should "do away" with themselves, and this he agreed to do.

Mr Paling then addressed the Bench: "It is quite possible that he induced this girl to go to the stream with him. He might have pretended to commit suicide having no intention of doing so, and so induce this poor girl to go to her death. Nobody knows exactly what happened beside that lonely little stream, it might even be possible he pushed her in. The story of the rabbit traps was obviously a lie because he had not got any there."

Morse was remanded for a week.

(*The Somerset Guardian*, Friday, March 24, 1933)

MORSE SENT FOR TRIAL ON MURDER CHARGE

The tragic story of Doris Brewer, was continued before the Ilminster Magistrates, when Fred Morse made his fourth appearance before the bench. He was committed for trial. A crowd of women waited for more than an hour for the courts to open, but only a handful were allowed into the tiny court-room.

Sir Bernard Spilsbury was an early arrival, and in his evidence stated that a small bruise on the left thigh and teeth marks on the tongue were the only signs of outside injury; cause of death, he confirmed, was drowning.

Frederick Morse was put on trial at the Wells Assizes on June the 8th, 1933. The proceedings and evidence were a virtual repeat of the magistrates hearing, and Morse emphatically denied that he had either interfered sexually with his niece or, on February 23rd or 24th, murdered her by drowning. Any statements that he had made to the police giving a contrary impression were, claimed Morse's counsel made as the result of police bullying and badgering.

The prisoner was the only witness in his defence, and from the box gave his own "true" account of what happened on the day Doris died:

I heard rumours about her condition, and then her mother spoke to me about it. I said I didn't know anything, nor of anything wrong . . . [on the morning of the 23rd, Doris refused to go to school] . . . I met her and she said she would not go to school; we had a bit of an argument about it and then walked up the hill. She said: "Where you are going, I am going." I could not take her to the quarry so I thought if I went to get my rabbit traps for half a day it would pass over. I bought rum because I had a cold; when we were walking along Mary said she felt thirsty and said: "Let me have some of that brandy." That's what she called it. I said: "You would not like it", but she had about a tablespoon of it. I told her to walk towards a shed while I got my traps; she said: "Cheerio, don't be long". She did not seem to be depressed at all. When I returned to the shed, she was not there; I called out several times, but there was no answer. I saw her footprints opposite the shed, they went through a gap in the hedge, round the field, and back again. I searched all around, but could find no trace of her. I searched among the trees for two and a half hours, and then under some bushes I found the body of Doris Brewer. She was lying on her back just covered with water. I tried to pick her up, but couldn't move her. I began to get worried; I thought the girl was in my charge, and I could not get her to the bank. I got up onto it myself and drank a lot of the rum. There was no doubt that the girl was dead, so I started to go home; down by the barbed wire I fell head first into the water. I did not know quite what to do. I would have told my mother, but my sister-in-law was with her, and she goes around the parish telling everything. I thought I had better not tell the police, I was feeling very upset and could not eat.

Morse was, nevertheless, found guilty of murder and sentenced to death. On the 24th of July, 1933, he was hanged at Horfield Prison by executioner Pierrepoint, and Phillips, his assistant.

A Very Unpopular Pair

The Murder of JANE BUTTERSWORTH
by ELIZABETH BRANCH and her Daughter MARY
in March 1740

and their Execution at Ilchester on the 3rd May 1740

These cruel women were born at Philips Norton, in Somersetshire. The mother was distinguished from her childhood by the cruelty of her disposition. She married a farmer, named Branch, but the husband soon found what an unfortunate choice he had made; for his wife no sooner came into possession of her matrimonial power than she began to exercise her tyranny on her servants, whom she treated with undeserved and unaccountable cruelty, frequently denying them the common necessaries of life, and sometimes turning them out of doors at night in the midst of winter; but their wages in these cases were sent them by Mr Branch, who was as remarkable for his humanity and justice as his wife for the opposite qualities. Mary Branch, the daughter, was an exact resemblance of her mother in her diabolical temper.

Mr Branch dying, and leaving an estate of about three hundred pounds a year, he was no sooner buried than all the servants quitted the family, determined not to live with so tyrannical a mistress; and her character became so notorious that she could obtain no servants but poor creatures who were put out by the parish, or casual vagrants who strolled the country.

It is needless to mention the particulars of the cruelties of this inhuman mother and daughter to their other servants, at whom they used to throw plates, knives and forks on any offence, real or supposed; we shall therefore proceed to an account of their trial and execution for the murder of Jane Buttersworth, a poor girl, who had been placed with them by the parish officers.

At the assizes held at Taunton, in Somersetshire, in March, 1740, Elizabeth Branch and Mary, her daughter, were indicted for the wilful murder of Jane Buttersworth; the principal evidence against them was a substance as follows:

Ann Somers, the dairymaid, deposed that the deceased, having been sent for some yeast, and staying longer than was necessary, excused herself to her old mistress on her return by telling a lie; on which the daughter struck her violently on the head with her fist, and pinched her ears. Then both of them threw her on the ground, and the daughter knelt on her neck, while the mother whipped her with twigs till the blood ran on the ground, and the daughter, taking off one of the girl's shoes, beat her with it in a cruel manner. The deceased cried for mercy, and after some struggle ran into the parlour, where they followed her, and beat her with broomsticks till she fell down senseless; after which the daughter threw a pail of water on her, and used her with other circumstances of cruelty too gross to mention.

Somers now went out to milk her cows, and on her return, at the expiration of half-an-hour, found her mistress sitting by the fire and the girl lying dead on the floor; but she observed that a clean cap had been put on her head since she went out, and that the blood had run through it. At night the body was buried.

This transaction, added to the character of the mistress, having raised a suspicion in the neighbourhood, a warrant was issued by the coroner to take up the body, and an inquest being made into the cause of the girl's death, Mr Salmon, a surgeon, declared that she had received several wounds, almost any one of which would have proved mortal. The jury found both prisoners guilty, and they were sentenced to die.

As the country people were violently enraged against them, they were conducted to the place of execution between three and four in the morning, attended only by the jailer and about a half-a-dozen people, lest they should have been torn in pieces.

When they came to the spot, it was found that the gibbet had been cut down; on which a carpenter was sent for, who immediately put up another, and mother and daughter were executed before six o'clock, to the disappointment of thousands of people who came too late from all parts of the country to witness the death of two such unworthy and vilified wretches.

WILTSHIRE

● Trowbridge 2, 3

● Westbury 4

● Stourton 1

Wiltshire

The Lords Who Lay You Low*

The Murder of WILLIAM HARTGILL Esq, and his Son JOHN by LORD STOURTON and Four of his Servants

on the Monday after Twelfth Day 1556 near Stourton, Wiltshire

On the 28th of February, 1556, Lord Stourton was arraigned at Westminster Hall, before the judges and several of the council. It was long before he would answer to the charge laid against him, till at last the Lord Chief Justice declared to him that he must be pressed to death, according to the laws of the land, if he would not answer;** after which he made answer, and was convicted, and condemned to be hanged, together with his four men, for the following murders.

In the reign of Edward VI, William Lord Stourton, having charge of one of the King's places near Boulogne, died; and shortly after his death, Charles Lord Stourton, his son and heir, went to Kilmington, to the house of William Hartgill, Esq., where Dame Elizabeth, late wife to Lord William and mother to the said Charles Lord Stourton, sojourned, and earnestly persuaded William Hartgill to be a means that Dame Elizabeth should enter into a bond to him, in a great sum of money, that she should not marry; which the said William Hartgill refused, unless Lord Stourton would assign some yearly portion for his mother to live upon.

In discoursing on this matter Lord Stourton quarrelled with William Hartgill; and on Whitsunday, in the morning, he went to Kilmington church with several men, with bows and arrows, and guns; and when he arrived at the church door, John Hartgill, son of William, being told of the said Lord Stourton's coming, went out of the church, drew his sword, and ran to his father's house adjoining the churchyard side. Several arrows were shot at him in passing, but he was not hurt. His father and mother were forced to go up into the tower of the church with two or three of their servants for safety. When John Hartgill arrived at his father's house he took his long-bow and arrow, bent a cross-bow, charged a gun, and caused a woman to bring the cross-bow and gun after him, and he with his long-bow came forth and drove away the said Lord Charles and his men from the house, and from about the church, except half-a-score that had entered the church, among whom one was hurt in the shoulder with a hail shot. His father advised him to take his horse and ride up to the court, and tell the council how he had been used. On Monday, towards evening, he reported to the honourable council how his father had been dealt with, whereupon they sent down Sir Thomas Speak, the High Sheriff of Somerset, not only to deliver the captives, but to bring with him the said Charles Lord Stourton, who, when he came, was committed to the Fleet, where he remained but for a short time.

It appeared that as soon as John Hartgill had set off towards London, Lord Stourton's men returned to the church of Kilmington, and about Mr Hartgill's house, and continued about there till the arrival of the sheriff, which was on Wednesday; during which time William Hartgill's wife was permitted to go home on Whitsunday, towards night. But in the meantime Lord Stourton's men went to the pasture of William Hartgill, took his riding gelding, and carried him to Stourton Park pales and shot him with a cross-bow, reporting that Hartgill had been hunting in his park upon the gelding. Thus Lord Stourton continued his malice throughout

* Men of England, wherefore plough
  For the lords who lay you low?
    (Shelley, Song to the Men of England)
** See Murder Club Guide No.1 for a note on Pressing to Death.

King Edward's reign, and with violence took from William Hartgill all his corn, cattle, etc.

On the death of King Edward, William Hartgill and his son petitioned Queen Mary and her council for redress, her Majesty being then at Basing End, in Hampshire. The council called Lord Stourton and Wiliam Hartgill before them, and Lord Stourton promised that if William Hartgill and his son would come to his house, and desire his good will, they should not only have it, but also be restored to their goods and cattle; where upon his promise, made in such presence, they took John Dackcombe, Esq., with them to witness their submission. When they came near Stourton House, in a lane half-a-dozen of Lord Stourton's men rushed forth, and letting Mr Dackcombe and William Hartgill pass them, they stepped before John Hartgill, and when he turned his horse to ride away, six others of the said lord's men beset him before and behind; and, before he could draw his sword and get from his horse, wounded him in three or four places, and left him for dead. Nevertheless, in half-an-hour, he recovered himself, got upon his horse, and took refuge in the house of Richard Mumpesson, of Maiden Bradley.

This at last became a subject of Star Chamber inquiry, and Lord Stourton was fined in a certain sum to be paid to the Hartgills, and imprisoned in the Fleet, whence he obtained licence, upon some pretence, to retire to his house in the country, and took an opportunity to murder both the Hartgills.

Within three or four days after his arrival at Stourton Caundle he sent advice to the Hartgills that he was ready to pay them the sums of money as ordered by the Star Chamber, and to end all disputes between them.

They agreed to meet him at Kilmington church on Monday after Twelfth Day, at ten o'clock; and Lord Stourton came accordingly to Kilmington, accompanied by fifteen or sixteen of his servants, sundry tenants, and some gentlemen and justices, to the number of sixty. He went to the church house and sent word to the Hartgills, who were in the church, that the church was no place to talk of worldly matters, and that he thought the church house a fitter place. The Hartgills came out of the church; but fearing ill, refused to enter into any covered place, the church excepted; whereupon it was proposed that a table should be set upon the open green, which was done accordingly.

Lord Stourton laid thereupon a cap-case and a purse, as though he intended to

make payment, and calling the two Hart-gills, said that the council had ordered him to pay them a certain sum of money, every penny of which they should have. Marry, he would first know them to be true men; and then laid hands upon them, saying, "I arrest you of felony"; on which his men, to the number of ten or twelve, by violence thrust them into the church house, where, with his own hand, the lord took from them their purses. Then having in readiness two cords, he delivered them to his man to bind the Hartgills; and to the younger of the Hart-gills, when bound, he gave a blow in his face, and coming out of the house with his sword, and finding at the door young Hartgill's wife, he kicked at her, and gave her such a stroke with his sword between her neck and head, that she fell to the ground nearly dead. From hence he caused the two Hartgills to be conveyed to the parsonage of Kilmington, where they were kept with their arms bound behind them, and without meat or drink. About one o'clock in the morning they were conveyed to a house called Bonham, near Stourton; and arriving on Tuesday about three in the morning, they were laid, fast bound, in separate places, without meat, drink, or fire, or anything to lie upon.

About ten o'clock Lord Stourton sent to Bonham, William Farree, Roger Gough, John Welshman and Macute Jacob, com-manding them to convey the Hartgills to a place appointed, and warning them, that in case they should make any noise, to kill them at once. These four brought them into a close adjoining Stourton, and knocked them on the head with two clubs, till the murderers thought they had been dead (his lordship in the meantime standing at the gallery door, which was but a small distance from the place). This done, they wrapped themselves in their own gowns, and carried the bodies through a garden into his lordship's gal-lery, and from thence into a place at the end, his lordship bearing the candle be-fore them. Being not quite dead, they groaned much, especially old Hartgill. When William Farree, one of the murderers, swearing by God's blood they were not yet dead, his lordship himself ordered their throats to be cut, lest a French priest, lying near to the place, might hear them; and William Farree took out his knife and cut both their throats, Lord Stourton standing by with the candle in his hand. One of the murderers then said: "Ah! my lord, this is a pitiful sight. Had I thought what I now think before the thing was done, your whole land should not have won me to consent to such an act." His lordship answered: "What a faint-hearted knave is this: is it any more than ridding us of two knaves that, living, were troublesome both to God's love and man's? There is

no more account to be made of them than the killing of two sheep." Then their bodies were tumbled into a dungeon; and after Henry Sims and Roger Gough had been let down with cords, for there were no steps, they dug a pit and buried them together; Lord Stourton often calling to them from above to make speed.

The bodies were afterwards taken up by Sir Anthony Hungerford, and were found in the same apparel that they were taken in, buried very deep, covered first with earth, then two courses of thick paving, and finally with chips and shavings of timber, above the quantity of two cart-loads.

In the examination of the atrocities of Lord Stourton it appeared that he had caused, not long before, a barn of one Thomas Chaffin to be set on fire by three of his servants; and then against Chaffin, for saying it was not done without the knowledge of the said Lord Stourton, or some of his servants, he brought an action, and recovering a hundred pounds damage, he took for the payment out of his pasture by force twelve hundred sheep, with the wool upon their backs, and all the oxen, kine, horses and mares that he could find. On another occasion, from one Willoughby he caused to be taken, for his pleasure, a whole team of oxen, whereof two were found fatting in the stall of his house when he was apprehended.

On the 2nd of March Lord Stourton and four of his servants rode from the Tower with Sir Robert Oxenbridge, the lieutenant, with certain of the guards, through London towards Salisbury. The first night they lay at Hounslow, the next day they went to Staines, thence to Basingstoke, and to Salisbury.

Lord Stourton was accordingly executed on the 6th of March, in the market-place at Salisbury, and his four men in the country near the place where the murder was committed; and previous to his death he made great lamentation for his wilful and impious deeds.

The Killing at Road

The Murder of FRANCIS SAVILE KENT
on Friday the 29th of June 1860
at Road Hill House, Nr. Trowbridge
and the Trial and Conviction of CONSTANCE KENT
for the Crime

Constance was born in 1844, ninth of ten children, to Samuel Savile Kent, a factories inspector, and Maryanne, his wife.

Of the previous eight, three children had survived – two daughters, and a son named Edward. In the following year a further son, Edward, arrived, though Maryanne finally succumbed to a steadily worsening mental complaint for which her husband, to avoid the stigma of 'insanity in the family', had not wished to have her certified. She died in 1852.

During Mrs Kent's 'illness', the family governess, a Miss Mary Pratt, had taken every opportunity to enveigle herself into the family, and into Samuel Kent's affections in particular; so successful was she that in 1853 she was fully prepared to become the second Mrs Kent. Between them, Samuel and Mary produced a second set of offspring – two girls and a boy, Francis Savile. Of her stepchildren, Mary had never been fond, and when not engaged in active abuse, ignored and neglected them; a characteristic seemingly borrowed from their father.

On the night of June 29th, 1860, in the family home at Road Hill House, Wiltshire, Mary Kent's four-year-old son Francis was taken from his cot, probably asphyxiated, and then had his throat savagely cut through to the vertebra. His body was found the following morning where it had been crudely hidden in an unused outside privy.

The killing seemed as inexplicable as it had been brutal. There had been no other observable disturbance to the house, and nothing had been stolen; and for these reasons the finger of suspicion pointed inevitably at a member of the Kent household. Most notably, it was at the nursemaid Elizabeth Gough and the 16-year-old Constance that that finger was directed. There seemed little tangible evidence to support a case in either instance, indeed, the only tangible evidence – a blood-stained nightdress recovered from the boiler flue by another servant – had already been carelessly lost by the police. The coroner's jury returned an open verdict.

The unfortunate Constance was hastily packed off to France, where she was cloistered in a convent at Dunat. Two months later Elizabeth Gough was re-arrested, and once again released.

By the time Constance returned to England, to join St. Mary's, a convent in Brighton, the tragic fate of Francis Savile Kent had been all but forgotten. And might have continued so had it not been for the strength of Constance's religious faith, and the zeal of her Mother Superior and the founder of the 'retreat', the Rev. Arthur Wagner. By a process of persuasion (with the promise of her confirmation as spiritual 'bait') Wagner extorted out of Constance a confession to the murder of her little step-brother which he promptly communicated to *The Times* newspaper of August 30th 1865 in the form of a letter:

A few days before the crime she obtained possession of a razor from a green case in her father's wardrobe and secreted it. This was the sole instrument she used... Soon after midnight she went downstairs and opened the drawing room door and shutters... She took the child from his bed and carried him downstairs through the drawing room... Having the child on one arm, she raised the drawing-room sash with the other hand, went round the house and into the closet, lighted the candle and placed it on the seat of the closet, the child being wrapped in the blanket and still sleeping. While the child was in this position, she inflicted the wound in the throat. She said she thought the blood would never come... so she thrust the razor into the left side and put the body with the blanket round it into the vault... She went back to her room, examined her dress and found only two spots of blood on it... She thought the blood stains had been effectively washed out... but afterwards she found the stains were still visible... She eventually burned it (the dress) in her bedroom... As regards the motive for her crime, it seems that although she entertained at one time a great regard for the present Mrs Kent, yet if any remark was at any time made which in her opinion was disparaging to any member of the first family, she treasured it up and determined to revenge it. She had no ill will against the little boy except as one of the children of her stepmother. She declared that her father and her stepmother had always been kind to her personally.

Subsequent upon her additional confession to the police (again prompted by the Rev. Mr Wagner), and her brief trial at Salisbury Assizes on July 21st, sentence of death was passed on Constance; a sentence later commuted to life imprisonment. For Constance, the sentence ended twenty years later, in 1885. It is said that she changed her name and emigrated to Canada to become a nurse, and died there in 1944. But for this fact, as with so much else in the case, it is not possible to find any evidence. As in many of the classic murder mysteries, there will always remain a question mark over the identity of the murderer.

What is certain is that for the whole of her life, Constance Kent was a sad victim of the times in which she was unfortunate enough to grow to womanhood.

Constance Kent

TRIAL AND SENTENCE
OF
CONSTANCE KENT.

On Friday, July 21st, Miss Constance E. Kent was placed at the Bar of the Salisbury Assize Court, charged with the murder of her brother, Francis Saville Kent.

The Clerk of the Assize, addressing the prisoner, said: How say you, are you guilty or not guilty? The prisoner in a voice scarcely audible, said—Guilty.

A profound silence then ensued in court, which was broken by Mr Coleridge, the prisoner's counsel, standing up and saying, I desire to say three things before your Lordship pronounces sentence. First, solemnly before Almighty God, she wishes me to say that the guilt is her own alone, and that her father and others, who have so long suffered most unjust and cruel suspicions, are wholly and absolutely innocent; and secondly, that she was not driven to this act by unkind treatment at home, as she met with nothing there but tender and forbearing love, and I may add that it gives me a melancholy pleasure to be the organ of these statements for her, because, on my honour, I believe them to be true.

The Judge, with much emotion, then said—Constance Kent, it is my duty to receive the plea which you have deliberately put forward. I can entertain no doubt that the murder was committed under great deliberation and cruelty. You appear to have allowed your feelings and anger to have worked in your breast, until at last they assumed over you the influence and power of the Evil One. It remains for me to pass the sentence which the law adjudges. The learned Judge then passed upon her the usual Sentence of Death. During the passing of the sentence, prisoner burst into a violent flood of tears, sobbing aloud.

Oh, give attention, you maidens dear,
My dying moments are drawing near,
When I am sentenc'd alas to die,
Upon a gallows gloomy and high.
　Oh what s sight it will be to see,
　A maiden die on the fatal tree.

I am a maiden in youth and bloom,
I a wretched murderer to die am doom'd,
And in the city of Salisbury,
My days must end on a dismal tree.

My little brother, a darling sweet,
That fatal morning did soundly sleep,
I was perplexed. I invented strife,
Fully determined to take his life.

To the dirty closet I did him take,
The deed I done caus'd my heart to ache,
Into the soil I did him thrust down,
Where asleep in death he was quickly found.

My own dear father they did suspect,
That he would suffer they did expect,
I was apprehended, but I got clear,
Tho' I was the murderess of my brother dear.

Long, long I pined in deep distress,
At length the murder I did confess,
The vile Road murder, as you may see,
Committed was no one but me.

Farewell my father, my father dear,
I know for me you will shed a tear,
Yes, your wicked daughter in shame must die,
For that cruel murder on a gallows high.

How many maidens will flock to see,
A female die upon Salisbury's tree.
Constance Emily Kent is my dreadful name,
Who in youth and beauty dies a death of shame.

I must go to my silent grave,
Father. is there no one your child to save,
Oh the awful moments are drawing near,
Father, forgive your daughter dear.

Oh, God in heaven, look down on me,
As I stand on the dreadful tree,
Forgive the crime, I, alas, have done,
Wash me with the blood of thy blessed son.

I must not live, I am bound to go,
I must be hurried to the shadows below,
My guilty heart long did quake with fear,
Why did I kill my little brother dear.

I see the hangman before me stand,
Ready to seize me by the law's command,
When my life is ended on the fatal tree,
Then will be clear'd up all mystery.

Disley, Printer, High street, St. Giles, London.

A contemporary broadsheet announcing the fate of
Constance Kent

Like a Dog to his Vomit*

The Murder of Mr LANCELOT WILMOT, Esq, his Wife, and his Daughter
by PATRICK O'BRYAN
near Trowbridge, in the County of Wiltshire
and his Hanging (for the second time) on the 30th of April 1689

The parents of Patrick O'Bryan were very poor; they lived at Loughrea, a market-town in the county of Galway and province of Connaught in Ireland. Patrick came over to England in the reign of King Charles II and listed himself into his Majesty's Coldstream Regiment of Guards, so called from their being first raised at a place in Scotland which bears that name. But the small allowance of a private sentinel was far too little for him. The first thing he did was to run into debt at all the public-houses and shops that would trust him; and when his credit would maintain him no longer, he had recourse to borrowing of all he knew, being pretty well furnished with the common defence of his countrymen – a front that would brazen out anything, and even laugh at the persons whom he had imposed on to their very faces. By such means as these he subsisted for some time.

* As a dog returneth to his vomit, so a fool returneth to his folly, (*Proverbs*, xxvi, 2.)

At last, when he found fraud would no longer support him, he went out upon the footpad. Dr Clewer, the parson of Croydon, was one of those whom he stopped. This man had in his youth been tried at the Old Bailey and burnt in the hand for stealing a silver cup. Patrick knew him very well and greeted him upon their lucky meeting; telling him that he could not refuse lending a little assistance to one of his old profession. The doctor assured him that he had not made a word if he had had any money about him, but he had not so much as a single farthing. "Then," says Patrick, "I must have your gown, sir." "If you can win it," quoth the doctor, "so you shall; but let me have the chance of a game at cards." To this O'Bryan consented and the reverend gentleman pulled out a pack of devil's books; with which they fairly played at all-fours, to decide who should have the black robe. Patrick had the fortune to win and the other went home very contentedly, as he had lost his divinity in such an equitable manner.

There was in Patrick's time a famous posture master in Pall Mall; his name was Clark. Our adventurer met him one day on Primrose Hill and saluted him with "Stand and deliver." But he was mightily disappointed, for the nimble harlequin jumped over his head and instead of reviving his heart with a few guineas, made it sink into his breeches for fear, he imagining the devil was come to be merry with him before his time, for no human creature, he thought, could do the like. This belief was a little mortification to him at first; but he soon saw the truth of the story in the public prints, where Mr Clark's friends took care to put it, and then our Teague's qualm of conscience was changed into a vow of revenge if ever he met with his tumblership again; which, however, he never did.

O'Bryan at last entirely deserted from his regiment, and got a horse, on which he robbed on the highway a long time. One day in particular he met Nell Gwyn in her coach on the road to Winchester, and addressed himself to her in the following

Nell Gwyn and her two sons by Charles II

manner: "Madam, I am a gentleman, and, as you may see, a very able one. I have done a great many signal services to the fair sex, and have in return been all my life long maintained by them. Now, as I know you are a charitable w---e, and have a great value for men of my abilities, I make bold to ask you for a little money, though I never have had the honour of serving you in particular. However, if an opportunity should ever fall in my way, you may depend upon it I will exert myself to the uttermost, for I scorn to be ungrateful." Nell seemed very well pleased with what he had said, and made him a present of ten guineas. However, whether she wished for the opportunity he spoke of, or no, cannot be determined, because she did not explain herself; but if a person may guess from her general character, she never was afraid of a man in her life.

When Patrick robbed on the highway he perverted several young men to the same bad course of life. One Claudius Wilt in particular was hanged at Worcester for a robbery committed in his company, though it was the first he was ever concerned in. Several others came to the same end through his seducements; and he himself was at last executed at Gloucester for a fact committed within two miles of that city. When he had hung the usual time, his body was cut down and delivered to his acquaintances, that they might bury him as they pleased. But being carried home to one of their houses, somebody imagined they perceived life in him; whereupon an able surgeon was privately procured to bleed him, who by that and other means which he used brought him again to his senses. The thing was kept an entire secret from the world, and it was hoped by his friends that he would spend the remainder of his forfeited life, which he had so surprisingly retrieved, to a much better purpose than he had employed the former part of it.

These friends offered to contribute in any manner he should desire towards his living privately and honestly. He promised them very fairly, and for some time kept within due bounds, while the sense of what he had escaped remained fresh in his mind; but the time was not long before, in spite of all the admonitions and assistance he received, he returned again to his villainies like a dog to his vomit, leaving his kind benefactors, stealing a fresh horse, and taking once more to the highway, where he grew as audacious as ever.

It was not above a year after his former execution before he met with the gentleman again who had convicted him before, and attacked him in the same manner. The poor gentleman was not so much surprised at being stopped on the road as he was at seeing the person who did it, being certain it was the very man whom he had seen executed. This consternation was so great that he could not help discovering it, by saying: "How comes this to pass? I thought you had been hanged a twelvemonth ago." "So I was," says Patrick, "and therefore you ought to imagine that what you see now is only my ghost. However, lest you should be so uncivil as to hang my ghost too, I think it my best way to secure you." Upon this he discharged a pistol through the gentleman's head; and, not content with that, dismounting from his horse, he drew out a sharp hanger from his side and cut the dead carcass into several pieces.

This piece of barbarity was followed by another, which was rather more horrible yet. Patrick, with four more as bad as himself, having intelligence that Lancelot Wilmot, Esq., of Wiltshire, had a great deal of money and plate in his house, which stood in a lonely place about a mile and a half from Trowbridge, they beset it one night and got in. When they were entered they tied and gagged the three servants, and then proceeded to the old gentleman's room, where he was in bed with his lady. They served both these in the same manner, and then went into the daughter's chamber. This young lady they severally forced one after another to their brutal pleasure, and when they had done, most inhumanly stabbed her, because she endeavoured to get from their arms. They next acted the same tragedy on the father and mother, which, they told them, was because they did not breed up their daughter to better manners. Then they rifled the house of everything valuable which they could find in it that was fit to be carried off, to the value in all of two thousand five hundred pounds. After which

they set the building on fire, and left it to consume, with the unhappy servants who were in it.

Patrick continued above two years after this before he was apprehended, and possibly might never have been suspected of this fact if one of his bloody accomplices had not been hanged for another crime at Bedford. This wretch at the gallows confessed all the particulars, and discovered the persons concerned with him; a little while after which, O'Bryan was seized at his lodging in Little Suffolk Street, near the Haymarket, and committed to Newgate; from whence before the next assizes he was conveyed to Salisbury, where he owned the fact himself, and all the other particulars of his wicked actions that have been here related. He was now a second time executed, and great care was taken to do it effectually. There was not, indeed, much danger of his recovering any more, because his body was immediately hung in chains* near the place where the barbarous deed was perpetrated. He was in the thirty-first year of his age at the time of his execution, which was on Tuesday, the 30th of April, in the year 1689.

---

*See *Murder Club Guide No.2* for a note on Hanging in Chains.

[*See also Appendix One to this volume*]

The Price of Friendship
The Murder of JEANNE SUTCLIFFE and her Daughter HEIDI by HEATHER ARNOLD
on Wednesday April the 30th 1986 at their home in Westbury

Teacher denies axe killings

April 1, 1987: A jury at Bristol Crown Court was told yesterday how teacher Paul Sutcliffe arrived home with two of his children on the evening of April 30 last year to discover the dead bodies of his wife Jeanne and baby daughter Heidi lying side by side in the sewing room of their house in Westbury, Wiltshire.

In the dock accused of the murders was a colleague of Mr Sutcliffe's, 50-year-old mathematics teacher Heather Arnold. Divorcee Mrs Arnold, of Orchard Road, Westbury, has pleaded not guilty to both counts of murder.

Mr David Elfer QC, for the prosecution, told the court: "The killer probably told Mrs Sutcliffe that she wanted to buy some dress-making cotton or thread [Mrs Sutcliffe ran a small dressmaking business from home], and was clearly let into the house. As Mrs Sutcliffe bent down to get whatever it was, the killer hit her on the back of the head." She then turned her attention to the baby, and it too was fatally attacked. The two bodies were then laid side by side. Mr Elfer said

Mrs Heather Arnold

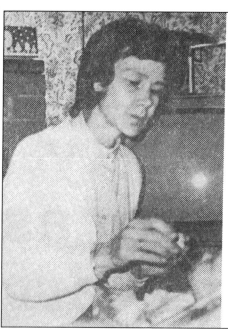 

Left: Mrs Jeanne Sutcliffe; right: Baby Heidi, aged six months

that a household axe, which had at one time been painted red, was used in the attack, and forensic evidence had linked the murder weapon with an axe-head in Mrs Arnold's possession; the accused had washed the axe and tried to burn it, but fragments of red paint were found both on Mrs Sutcliffe's body and in Arnold's car.

Mother's blood on baby

April 2, 1987: Continuing the prosecution case today, Mr Bill Kennard, a Home Office pathologist, detailed part of the forensic reconstruction of the murders of 39-year-old Jeanne Sutcliffe and her eight-month-old baby Heidi. He told the court that the cause of Mrs Sutcliffe's death was haemorrhage due to a cut throat; there were thirteen injuries to her head and face, all of them caused by a blunt instrument. Mrs Sutcliffe's skull had been extensively fractured and pushed into the brain, the cut to her throat went through to the spinal cord. The victim had been anorexic and weighed only about six stone and stood just over 5ft. tall. Stunned before she knew what was happening, Mrs Sutcliffe was able to put up little resistance, though injuries to the backs of her hands were consistent with having tried to protect herself. Blood on the knee of baby Heidi's romper suit was of the same group as

Mrs Sutcliffe's, and indicated that the child had crawled into its mother's blood before she too had had her throat cut. The bodies had then been laid side by side, a tea-towel covering the baby's neck wound.

Axe-head hidden in skirt

April 6th, 1987: From the witness stand of Bristol Crown Court, Mrs Caroline Buckley, the solicitor daughter of Mrs Heather Arnold, told how her mother had come to stay at her home over the May Bank Holiday [1986], and towards evening broke into tears and told her that she had found a small axe in her garage. She admitted chopping up the handle of the axe and burning the pieces before disposing of them. Mrs Arnold then produced the axe head, wrapped in blue tissue, from the top of her skirt. Mrs Buckley said her mother was obviously very frightened, but told her: "I didn't do it."

Detective Constable Bob Richards told the jury that for a week after the murders a team of four detectives had worked under cover with council refuse collectors. Wiltshire CID had played the imaginative hunch that the killer would sooner or later try to dispose of the murder weapon along with household rubbish. DC Richards had seen Mrs Arnold walking out of her front door with a white carrier bag and said to her: "All right love, I'll take that, it will save your legs." The carrier bag was later found to contain the three charred pieces of an axe handle.

Court told of 'confessions'

April 7, 1987: In the case against Mrs Heather Arnold today, the jury was told by Detective Constable Caroline Enright that Mrs Arnold broke down in the back of a police car and confessed to killing Mrs Jeanne Sutcliffe and her baby daughter. The confession was made as Mrs Arnold was being driven to Wiltshire police headquarters after her arrest.

The court then heard that Mrs Arnold had signed the notes taken down of this alleged confession, but on the advice of her solicitor had subsequently denied going to the Sutcliffe house on the day of the murders.

Court told of panic

April 8, 1987: Mrs Heather Arnold went into the witness box to give evidence in her own defence today. She told the murder trial that when she found a household axe that she did not recognize in her garage she panicked. Mrs Arnold said she felt some "inexplicable" need to get rid of the axe, and later cut the head from the handle, cut the handle in three pieces, and disposed of it with the household rubbish. She could not remember anything about the axe head until she "rediscovered" it in her handbag on the evening of her visit to her daughter. Explaining her panic, the prisoner said: "I just felt I was already under suspicion, why I did not know. This thing [the axe] was going to make the situation even worse and I felt some inexplicable need to get rid of it."

Murder jury retires

April 14, 1987: The jury in the Heather Arnold trial will finally be sent out today to make their decision. The judge's summing-up was delayed because one of the jurors injured his back at the weekend and was unable to attend court. With the agreement of defence and Crown counsel, Mr Justice Henry formally discharged the man from further duty and proceeded with an 11-member jury.

Teacher gets life for double murder

April 15, 1987: The jury retired on Tuesday to consider their verdict, but after a six-hour

deliberation were unable to agree. Mr Justice Henry sent them to a hotel for the night. Today, after a further 90-minute retirement, the jury returned to the court to present their unanimous verdict. Mrs Arnold broke down and wept as the forewoman gave a verdict of "guilty" on the first count; she collapsed in the dock when a second "guilty" verdict was announced, and had to be supported by two women prison officers.

Sentencing Mrs Arnold to life imprisonment, Mr Justice Henry told her: "The jury has rightly convicted you of these two terri-

Mr Paul Sutcliffe

ble murders, murders which have shocked and horrified the community. That community is now left to mourn the quality of these two innocent lives you took."

At a press conference after the sentence had been passed, Mr Paul Sutcliffe, the victims' husband and father, spoke about the innocent friendship that had brought tragedy to his family. Mr Sutcliffe and Mrs Arnold had been colleagues at Kingsdown Comprehensive school in Warminster, and when Mrs Arnold was going through a difficult divorce from her husband, both he and his wife had been very supportive. Mr Sutcliffe suggested: "I think there must have been some form of envy. I have a feeling that Mrs Arnold had a rather empty existence. I had a fairly chaotic family existence which I clearly enjoyed." Mrs Arnold may have been jealous of Jeanne Sutcliffe's happy marriage, and when new baby Heidi was born felt that the Sutcliffes were about to build a life in which she would have no place.

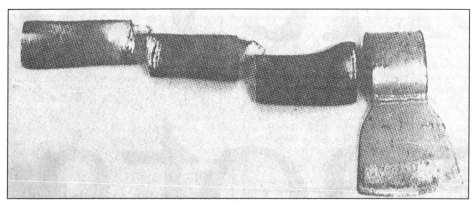

The murder weapon, showing Mrs Arnold's attempt to dispose of it

---

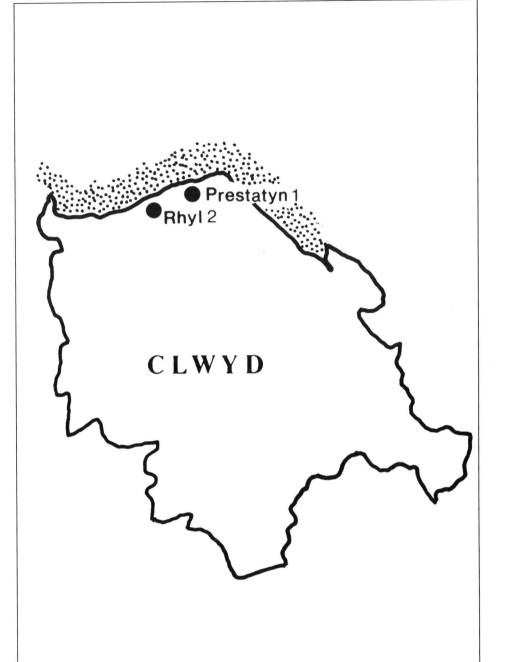

Clwyd

The 'Reginald Perrin' Murders
The Murder of GREEBA HEALEY
and her Daughter MARIE WALKER
by ROBERT HEALEY
on Tuesday July the 29th 1986
at their home in Longmead Avenue, Stockport

Police plea to 'Perrin' man

Tuesday, August 5th 1986: Further to the apparent suicide last Wednesday of Mr Robert Healey, police are now fearful that his missing wife Greeba, aged 40, and thirteen-year-old stepdaughter Marie Walker are dead. Healey, a thirty-seven-year-old self-employed driving instructor, has not been seen since driving away from his home at Longmead Avenue, Hazel Grove, Stockport, last Tuesday; his metallic silver Vauxhall Chevette (registration TEH199R) was left in a multi-storey car park in Park Street, Birmingham, on Thursday, and police are anxious to talk to anyone who saw it being parked.

On the previous day a suicide note addressed to Mr Healey's mother had been found with a pile of men's clothing on the beach at Prestatyn, in North Wales. The note stated that Mr Healey felt his marriage was breaking up, and that life was no longer worth while. A subsequent police check of the Healey home revealed that Mrs Healey and Marie were also missing; forensic experts found traces of blood in the bedroom.

The discovery of video tapes of the television series 'The Fall and Rise of Reginald Perrin' have aroused grave doubts about the 'suicide' of Mr Healey. Perrin, the central character, is seen at the beginning of each episode undressing and putting his clothes into a pile on the beach to persuade the police that he has drowned himself, and then going off to start a new life.

Detective Chief Superintendent Clive Atkinson, who is leading the inquiry, said: "I am making a personal appeal to Robert Healey to come forward and speak to me, or to any police officer, to relieve the anguish of his parents, his wife's friends and his stepdaughter's father."

Bloodstains link with wife and daughter

Wednesday, August 6th 1986: Forensic tests on the bloodstains found at the Healey home in Stockport revealed that they match the group of missing Mrs Greeba Healey and her daughter Marie: they were last seen at lunchtime last Monday. Police now believe that Robert Healey's suicide was faked, and Det Chief Supt Atkinson said: "I am now treating this case as a murder hunt, and I am very anxious to trace Mr Healey."

Quilt clue to murder

Saturday, August 9th 1986: Police officers leading the Healey murder investigation revealed yesterday that bloodstains on a quilt found in a ditch off the A5117 near Chester match in group those found at the Healey home earlier this week. These in turn matched the group shared by Mrs Healey and her daughter. Matching stains were also found in the car abandoned by Mr Robert Healey in a Birmingham car park. An RAF helicopter search using heat seeking equipment has failed to trace either bodies or recently disturbed ground.

Bodies found

Man charged in 'Perrin' case

Monday, August 18th 1986: Mr Robert Healey, who it is understood has been living under a false name in the Harrow Road area of West London, was last night charged with the murder of his wife and stepdaughter at their home in Stockport.

Mr Healey, who presented himself at New Scotland Yard on Saturday night, will appear before Stockport magistrates today. Police have issued a bulletin in which it is stated that Mrs Greeba Healey died of multiple skull fractures, while her daughter had been suffocated. Their naked bodies were

Robert Healey, his wife Greeba, and stepdaughter Marie

found in a shallow grave in a wood at Caerwys, in North Wales, on Friday night.

Tuesday, August 19th 1986: Magistrates at Stockport yesterday remanded Robert Healey in custody until August 26th. During the three-minute hearing, Mr Healey stood silent as the charges were read to him.

'Reginald Perrin' Trial Opens

Tuesday, March 24th 1987: The trial began at Liverpool Crown Court yesterday of Mr Robert Healey, accused of the murder of his wife and stepdaughter. Mr Healey denied the charges.

Mr Brian Leveson, QC, opening for the prosecution said that after the bodies of Mrs Healey and her daughter Marie were found in a shallow grave in North Wales last August, Healey had given himself up to the police. While in custody he had produced a notebook filled with what appeared to be a rationale for the killings. According to the handwritten entries, after being taunted by his wife over his sexual prowess, Healey had "as if in a dream" battered her to death with a rolling pin as she lay in bed. His step-daughter, attracted by the noise, had come into the room, and Healey claims he gripped her by the throat to prevent her struggling.

Mr Leveson then told the jury that a rather different story would emerge from the evi-

dence; that both Mrs Healey and Marie had had sexual intercourse just before their deaths; that Mr Healey, after bludgeoning his wife, had carefully cleaned and replaced the rolling pin in a kitchen drawer, washed down the blood-spattered kitchen walls, and changed the stained bed linen. He then wrote a note cancelling the milk and news-papers, and put the bodies into his wife's car. Shortly afterwards, Healey applied for a passport giving the name of his brother-in-law. On the morning of the following day, a pile of men's clothing was found on the beach at Prestatyn, and in the coat pocket was Mr Healey's wallet containing a note to his mother ending: "I might as well die now."

Wednesday, March 25th 1987: The jury at Liverpool Crown Court heard yesterday how seventy-two-year-old William Douglas had been walking in a wood at Caerwys, North Wales, when he kicked aside a pile of leaves and earth to be confronted with a human hand and foot protruding from a shallow grave. Police later removed the bodies of Mrs Greeba Healey and her daughter from 12 inches of soil.

In his evidence to the court, pathologist Dr Donald Wayte said that the injuries to Healey's stepdaughter Marie resembled those that he had seen on victims crushed to death in road accidents. Healey sat in the dock covering his ears as Dr Wayte esti-mated that it could have taken as long as five agonised minutes for Marie to die.

Healey in witness box

Thursday, March 26th 1987: In the witness box yesterday, Mr Robert Healey, who pleads not guilty to two charges of murder, spoke of his failing marriage. He had met his wife Greeba through a lonely hearts advertisement in the local newspaper, and after their marriage: "She started to become obsessive towards me. I must be there constantly, all the time." He said that often after sex his wife would storm off into the garden and refuse to come in, shouting: "You don't want me, you don't love me!"

Asked if he had been engaging in sexual intercourse with his stepdaughter Marie, and whether he had killed her to prevent her exposing him, Healey replied: "Nothing of the sort."

Friday, March 27th 1987: Continuing his evidence, Robert Healey described the killing of his wife and stepdaughter as "like a film. I was watching myself on television." He said that on July the 29th of last year his wife had once again criticised his lovemaking, and that: "I felt like screaming. I felt frustrated." He walked down to the kitchen: "I stared at things, objects. There was a rolling pin. I picked it up. I didn't know what I was doing... I went upstairs to our bedroom. I walked round the bed. I hit her with the rolling pin on the head. She jumped up; she didn't say anything; she didn't scream, she just moaned. I hit her again; I don't know how many times. Even-

tually she was down on the floor. Marie came in and I told her to get out. My hand caught her face. She went out and came straight back in again. I didn't want her to see her mother on the floor. I grabbed her by the throat and pushed her up against the wall. The next thing I remember she was down on the floor. I don't know how long it was before I realised they were both dead."

Healey then staged the fake suicide at Prestatyn before burying the two bodies and returning to London to adopt a new identity.

Suggesting that he derived the inspiration for his charade from the Reginald Perrin television series, Mr Leveson for the Prosecution, asked him: "Does not the Perrin character walk into the sea, then start a new life with a new name and a beard? You did all these things." Mr Healey: "Yes, but I didn't get the ideas from the programme." He said that he had fully intended to go ahead with the suicide.

In closing, Mr Leveson maintained that Robert Healey had intended to kill his wife and then, after intercourse with her, Marie; the proper verdicts would be guilty.

Judge's summing-up

Saturday, March 28th 1987: Concluding for the defence yesterday at Liverpool Crown Court, Mr John Hugell, QC, on behalf of the prisoner, invited the jury to consider the following questions: Why should Healey have made such a frenzied attack on the two

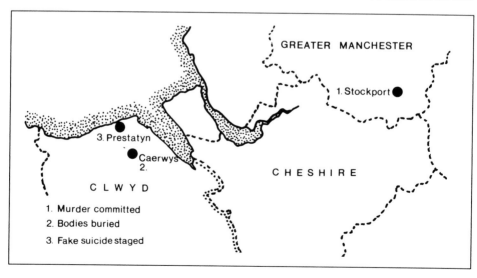

1. Murder committed
2. Bodies buried
3. Fake suicide staged

Robert Healey in custody in Stockport

Guilty verdict in 'Perrin' case

Tuesday, March 31st 1987: After a retirement of three hours yesterday, the jury returned unanimous verdicts of guilty of murder in the case of Robert Healey. As the verdict was announced, Healey turned away, his hands trembling violently, and burst into tears.

Sentencing the prisoner, Mr Justice McNeill told him: "You know there is only one sentence. The sentence fixed by law upon conviction for murder is that on each count, to be served concurrently, you will go to prison for life."

The Healeys' home in Stockport

women? And why should he then, after killing them, fake his own suicide? He continued: "The case is upsetting for many reasons. One is the sheer ordinariness of everyone concerned... it is all so ordinary. You may think you have seen a tortured soul before you. He is a man in considerable distress, and rightly so because, in any view, he has committed a dreadful crime."

The judge, Mr Justice McNeill, in his summing-up advised the jury of seven women and five men that if they decided that Mr Healey had not committed murder, then it must return a verdict of guilty of manslaughter: "It is not in dispute here that in the case of each killing it was the defendant who caused death by direct and unlawful violence." He said that they must consider whether Mrs Healey had given provocation: "Would a reasonable man take a rolling pin and rain blows down on her head so as to kill her?" There was no suggestion of provocation on the part of Marie Walker.

Motive

At no time during the trial was any motive for the murders disclosed. Police, however, are convinced that it was Healey's illegal relationship with his stepdaughter that was the key. Detectives are now able to reveal that Healey was put on two years' probation four years ago for inciting a young girl to an act of gross indecency. If Marie Walker had threatened to expose him for his current acts of indecency, it was not beyond the bounds of reason that Healey might kill rather than face the inevitable prison sentence consequent upon a second conviction for interfering with a child.

The Rhyl Mummy Case
The Death of Mrs FRANCES KNIGHT
on a date in April 1940
at 35 Kinmel Street, Rhyl
and the Trial of SARAH JANE HARVEY for her Murder

Number thirty-five Kinmel Street in the coastal resort town of Rhyl, North Wales, had been home to Leslie Harvey for most of his childhood and youth; his mother, Sarah Jane Harvey, still lived there, and since the death of her husband Alfred in January 1938 she had shared the modest two-storey terrace house with a succession of paying guests. Now at the age of sixty-five, Mrs Harvey was beginning to feel the consequences of a long life, and in April 1960 she was taken into hospital for observation.

Though Leslie was married now, and living in nearby Abergele, the filial affection remained as strong as ever; and it was as a token of this affection that he and his wife stood on the threshold of the family home in Kinmel Street on the afternoon of May the 5th 1960. Leslie had decided to take advantage of his mother's confinement in order to decorate the house for her. After making their way to the top of the stairs taking mental notes of jobs to be done, clutter to clear, musty corners to air, Leslie and his wife found themselves in front of the large wooden cupboard on the first-floor landing. In Leslie's recollection the cupboard had always been locked, and strictly out-of-bounds. The only explanation ever given to the inquisitive small boy was that it contained some belongings of a long-since departed lodger named Frances Knight.

With a renewed curiosity Leslie Harvey prised open the double doors with a screwdriver, prepared at worst for the task of clearing out some dusty old suitcases. With understandable horror, he stood speechless as the contents of the cupboard were revealed by the invading light. These were not somebody's possessions – it was *somebody*; a body that had obviously been there for a very long time.

By late evening the usually quiet street had become busy with policemen, and inside No.35 Flint's chief constable, Reginald Atkins, and coroner Dr Rhys Llewellyn Jones peered closely at the grim bundle that had so recently occupied the landing cupboard. The body was in a doubled-up position, and clothed in a now-faded and cobweb encrusted nightdress and dressing gown; the skin was shrunken and leathery, what flesh remained was hard as stone. The whole corpse had been mummified – not by art, as was the custom in ancient Egypt, but by the natural process of warm, dry air rising and circulating around the cupboard tomb, slowly desiccating the body tissues. An atmospheric freak which had made it possible to conceal a corpse for many years without the tell-tale stench of putrefaction.

Mrs Sarah Jane Harvey

126

No. 35 Kinmel Street in 1940

Despite the hideous appearance of the face, Leslie Harvey observed that the mummy bore some resemblance to the former lodger Mrs Knight, whose 'possessions' were supposed to have been deposited behind the locked doors of the cupboard. Mrs Knight, he recalled, had been a divorcee living on a small weekly maintenance payment from her former husband; but she had left in 1940. Could her dead body possibly have lain where it was found for twenty years? And who on earth would have wanted to keep it there? Who had hung a fly-paper over the corpse with the obvious intention of dealing with the infestation of insects that prey on dead flesh? It was clear that Mrs Sarah Harvey would have a lot of questions to answer.

With the discovery of a body in mysterious circumstances – and there could be few more mysterious circumstances than those surrounding the Rhyl mummy – the well-oiled machinery of a major police investigation is set in motion. Teams of investigating officers and scientists, each with their well-defined areas of expertise combine resources to track down and bring to justice a killer.

First, a minute examination of the human remains attempts to answer the three seminal questions – who, how, and when? In this instance it was the job of Dr Gerald Evans,

pathologist to the Home Office, to undertake the post-mortem; an examination that had to be delayed until the body had soaked long enough in a tank of glycerine solution to become pliable enough to examine. It was then that Dr Evans found the remains of what appeared to be a knotted ligature, and a groove in the neck consistent with strangulation by that ligature. While Dr Evans was cautious enough not to be positive about his suspicions, the police were now treating the case as one of murder; an opinion endorsed by the extraordinary findings of Detective Inspector Hugh Williams and Detective-Sergeant William Evans. Williams and Evans had been trying to confirm a link between Mrs Frances Knight and the mummified body, and had routinely visited the registrar's office at St Asaph, where there was no record of a death certificate being issued for the woman in question. When the two officers transferred their inquiries to the Rhyl municipal offices, the mystery deepened. Yes, they knew Mrs Knight, she was an elderly lady who had resided for many years in Kinmel Street; she lived with a Mrs Harvey who had been collecting her housebound lodger's maintenance cheque for the past twenty years! What came to light next was beyond the belief even of Hugh Williams. Investigation showed that no less than seven further detahs had occurred among the occupants of 35 Kimmel Street during the past twenty-five years:

1926, May 30: Thomas Evans, aged 57, died of a malignant disease.
1928, February 16: Ellen Evans, 60, encephalitis lethargica and exhaustion.
1928, March 11: Jane Jones (Sarah Harvey's mother), 64, cerebral edema.
1938, January 28: Alfred James Harvey (Sarah's husband), 67, cerebral embolism and exhaustion.
1940, December 1: Jonathan Mould, 67, enteritis and chronic cardiac disease.
1940, December 23: Edith Mould (Jonathan's sister), 69, senile decay, anaemia, and sarcoma of the uterus.
1941, September 4: Herbert Lomas, 74, myocardial degeneration.

Misfortune? They were, after all, elderly people; and with the flow of residents passing through a lodging house there must be a greater percentage of deaths. At any rate the

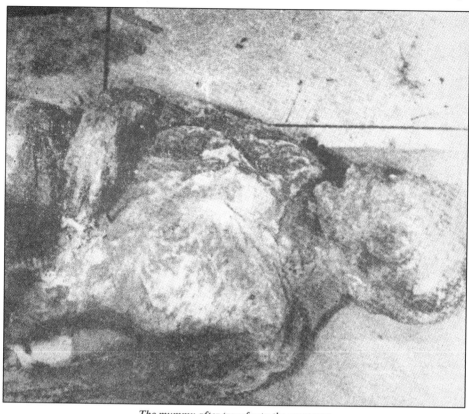

The mummy after transfer to the mortuary

police decided to pursue only one case. The case of Mrs Frances Knight.

On June the 9th 1960, at six o'clock in the morning, Sarah Jane Harvey was arrested on a charge of murder.

By comparison, the trial was an anti-climax. On June the 30th at the Town Hall in Rhyl, the prosecution advanced the proposition that Sarah Harvey had strangled her lodger, on some date during 1940, in order to avail herself of Mrs Knight's weekly £2 maintenance money. In her defence, Mrs Harvey claimed that the victim had died of natural causes and that she had panicked and hidden the body in the cupboard (though one might have thought she was more accustomed than most to having people dying in her house).

As to the stocking found knotted around Frances Knight's neck, the somewhat unlikely explanation was offered that an old folk-cure for sore throats was to tie an unwashed stocking or sock around the sufferer's neck – perhaps Mrs Knight had accidently strangled herself.

In what must be seen as an act of compassion towards an elderly, sick woman accused of a twenty-year-old crime that could not even be unquestionably proved, the trial was stopped after three days. Sarah Jane Harvey was found guilty, on her own admission, only of the lesser charge of fraudulently obtaining money, and sentenced to fifteen months imprisonment.

[For two other cases of mummification see *Murder Club Guide No.3*, pages 24-26 and 99-102]

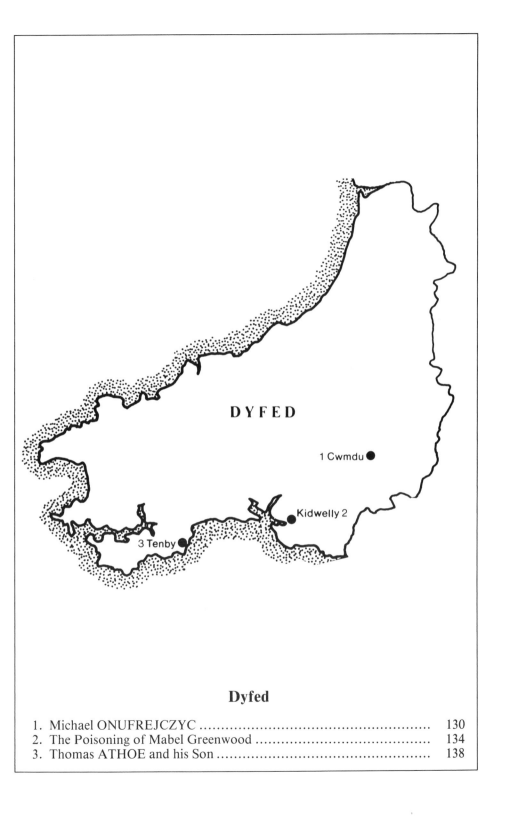

D Y F E D

1 Cwmdu ●

● Kidwelly 2

3 Tenby ●

Dyfed

The Case of the Missing Corpse

The Murder of STANISLAW SYKUT
by MICHAEL ONUFREJCZYC
at Cefn Hendre farm, Cwmdu
on Monday December the 14th 1953

Michael Onufrejczyc had served as a warrant officer with the Polish Army during the hostilities of 1939-1945, his conspicuous gallantry earning him nine medals. At the end of the war Onufrejczyc had settled in Britain, and in 1949, with money borrowed from Polish Army funds, he realised the dream of a lifetime; at the age of fifty-eight, Michael Onufrejczyc bought a farm. Or rather, he bought what was left after years of neglect and exposure to the elements had rendered it virtually derelict. A bleak, inhospitable patch of land with its ruined farm buildings, Cefn Hendre was situated about a mile from the village of Cwmdu, in what was once Carmarthenshire and now lies in the county of Dyfed. Here Onufrejczyc, himself a withdrawn man, came face to face with the natural reserve of the Welsh. While not openly hostile, the local community had an inborn mistrust of this foreigner, and he a dismissive, almost arrogant approach to his neighbours.

The land at Cefn Hendre soon proved to be as barren as it was bleak, and after years of stubborn effort, Michael Onufrejczyc, veteran campaigner in some of Europe's bloodiest theatres of war, found himself engaged in a battle he could not hope to win; the farm bordered on bankruptcy. In a final effort to salvage his future, Onufrejczyc took on a partner in the person of Stanislaw Sykut. There had been two previous attempts at a partnership, each of which ended disastrously following Onufrejczyc's violent outbursts of temper. But this time it might be different. Sykut, like Onufrejczyc, was a Pole, a former military man, and the same age as his prospective partner. In temperament, however, they were at opposite extremes, Sykut being a quiet, meditative man. Thus it was, that only a short time after the partnership commenced in March 1953, Sykut was obliged to report to the

local police that Onufrejczyc had physically attacked him. Onufrejczyc bluffed his way out of any serious trouble with the law over the matter, but things had clearly gone too far for Stanislaw Sykut. In the second week of June, 1953, he instructed a solicitor to serve a termination order dissolving the partnership as of November the 14th, and adding that if the £600 that his client had invested in the business was not refunded by that date, then the farm would be auctioned to raise the necessary reimbursement.

Surprisingly, given the general atmosphere of acrimony that had developed over the previous months, Stanislaw Sykut continued in residence at Cefn Hendre. More surprising still, November the 14th came and passed with Onufrejczyc still refusing to refund his partner a single penny of his money, and Sykut still remained.

On December the 14th, Sykut visited the village blacksmith, whose forge was at the end of the lane leading to Cefn Hendre, and had the work-horse shod. Then the smith watched as he returned along the lane to the

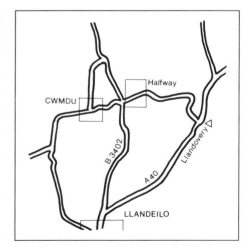

farm. It was the last time that Stanislaw Sykut was seen – to this day there has been no trace of him, alive or dead.

That a man is not seen around for a couple of days, particularly a man as reclusive as Sykut, would have attracted no particular attention locally even if the villagers were interested – which they weren't. And when an officer of the Sheriff paid a visit to Cefn Hendre on December the 16th, there was no suggestion of a mystery. This man, through a Polish interpreter, spoke briefly to Onufrejczyc who, when asked Sykut's whereabouts, replied that he had taken a trip to Llandeilo to visit his doctor. It was only later that this was proved to be untrue. Slight suspicion was generated, however, by Onufrejczyc's refusal to conduct this conversation in the shelter of the farmhouse. It was a freezing day with a biting wind blowing down from the hills, and despite his visitors' obvious discomfort, and several suggestions that it might be warmer inside, Onufrejczyc resolutely insisted on conducting the business *al fresco*.

It was on December the 30th that official attention was again focussed on the Onufrejczyc farm. This time it was a visit by police sergeant Phillips on a routine check on aliens in the district. In reply to his question, Phillips was told that Stanislaw Sykut had gone to London for a fortnight.

By this time gossip was beginning to spread around the neighbourhood, emanating from that mecca of local tittle-tattle, the village post-office. It had been Stanislaw Sykut's daily routine to visit the Cwmdu office in order to set his watch by their clock, and to pick up his mail. He had not been since December 14 and his letters were piling up.

By January 1954, rumours and suspicions had reached the ears of the police, and on the 13th of that month a detective from Llandeilo, accompanied by a Polish interpreter, once again approached the surly owner of Cefn Hendre on the matter of his partner's whereabouts.

At the end of a particularly frustrating interview, in which Onufrejczyc made extravagant play of his poor command of English and refused even to comprehend questions in his own tongue, the officer was convinced that the farmer was trying to hide something. As a result, Mr T. H. Lewis, chief constable of Carmarthenshire and Cardiganshire, requested a magistrate's warrant to search the farm-house. But despite the most thorough search, police officers were still no nearer finding the missing alien. The farmland, a considerable amount of which was unproductive bog, was combed by police with tracker dogs, men and animals often wading thigh deep in the mud and slime. However, as far as locating Stanislaw Sykut, the search proved negative.

Detectives, now convinced that Sykut had been murdered, but having no shred of evidence on which to proceed, interviewed their chief 'suspect' again. This time, for no very good reason, Onufrejczyc changed his earlier story. Whereas before he had claimed that his partner had gone to the doctor in Llandeilo the previous December, he now maintained that Sykut had gone to London. Onufrejczyc then produced a paper purporting to have been signed by Stanislaw Sykut transferring his interest in the farm to Onufrejczyc for the sum of £600, £450 paid already, the balance in May 1954. Anticipating the obvious question, Onufrejczyc volunteered the information that he had borrowed the money from his niece, a Mrs Pokora.

When Mrs Pokora was traced to London and interviewed by officers of the Metropolitan Police force, she made a full and very intriguing statement. For a start, she had most certainly not lent Onufrejczyc any money. The bizarre truth was, that he had asked her to pretend to lend him the money by sending two packets by registered post that looked the size and shape of £450 in one-pound notes. Wisely, she had refused. At the same time, the police learned that it was Mrs Pokora who had written the transfer paper in Stanislaw Sykut's name returning ownership of the farm to Onufrejczyc; furthermore, she had written several letters for Onufrejczyc purporting to come from Sykut – written on the assurance that her uncle would get his partner's signature. Examining these documents later, the South Wales and Monmouthshire Forensic Science Laboratory was able to state categorically that the scrawl at the foot of the pages was not Sykut's signature. Predictably, when confronted with this new evidence, Onufrejczyc flew into one of his violent tempers and branded Mrs Pokora a liar.

Confident of the case they were building up against farmer Onufrejczyc, the police carried out a further search of Cefn Hendre in collaboration with the Forensic Science Laboratory. This time the investigating team identified more than two thousand tiny dark stains on the walls of the kitchen and hallway, and a large dark stain of a familiar shape on the surface of the kitchen dresser. On one of the plaster-board walls a reversed double impression of Stanislaw Sykut's signature was found, as though the wall had been used as a blotter. Partly covering one of these images was a bloodstain; the implication was clear – the blood had been splashed on the wall *after* Sykut's arrival at the farm.

Onufrejczyc's reluctant explanation was that he had been killing and cleaning rabbits in the kitchen. A story that was quickly changed when the Laboratory identified the stains as being blood of human origin; the mark on the dresser, a bloody handprint. The Pole's subsequent version was that Sykut had cut his hand and shaken the blood from his injury so that it splattered the wall. Improbable though the story was, it was unshakeable.

By August the 19th, and not without hesitation, the Director of Public Prosecutions decided that a charge of murder could be brought against Michael Onufrejczyc. After a lengthy hearing in the magistrates' court, the prisoner was committed for trial at Glamorgan Assizes.

Dispelling a widely held, and quite erroneous, belief that still persists – that a charge of murder cannot be brought without a body – the judge, Mr Justice Oliver, told the jury: "At the trial of a person charged with murder the fact of death is provable by circumstantial evidence, notwithstanding that neither the body nor any trace of the body has been found, and that the accused has made no confession of any participation in the crime. Before he can be convicted, the fact of death should be proved by such circumstances as render the commission of the crime morally certain and leave no ground for reasonable doubt. The circumstantial evidence should be so cogent and compelling as to convince a jury that upon no rational hypothesis other than murder can the facts be discounted".

The jury clearly felt that the evidence *was* both 'cogent' and 'compelling', and within three hours had returned a verdict of guilty. At the time of the trial there was only one sentence that a judge could pass on a person found guilty of murder – the ultimate sentence of Death.

Onufrejczyc, though, was still fighting, and when, on January the 11th 1955, his appeal was dismissed by the Court of Criminal Appeal, his solicitors immediately applied for leave to appeal to the House of Lords. The application was, in the end, refused; but on January 24th, Onufrejczyc's sentence was commuted to life imprisonment.

In 1965 the Pole was released from prison, still protesting his innocence, and still apparently determined to prove it. His first action was to return to the Cwmdu area to ask if Stanislaw Sykut had reappeared while he had been away! A year later, Onufrejczyc was killed in a traffic accident in Bradford, and with him the true story of Cefn Hendre was buried for ever.

––––––––––––

So what *could* have happened to Stanislaw Sykut's body? That he was killed is certain; that Michael Onufrejczyc was responsible for his death is equally certain. How, then, did he dispose of the corpse? In his own account of 'The Butcher of Cwmdu', ex-Detective Superintendent David Thomas – himself involved in the case – makes this suggestion:

> My own opinion, which I put forward at the time of the investigation and which I still hold to, is that the chopped-up pieces of Sykut's body were probably fed to a herd of ravenous pigs which roamed the farm. It would have been a simple matter for Onufrejczyc to have boiled the parts of the dismembered body with the pigs' mash in the days immediately following December 14, and before Sykut was missed... Onufrejczyc always seemed confident the body would never be found. What better confidence did he need than to know his pigs had eaten the evidence.

(Seek Out The Guilty, see Bibliography)

FED TO THE PIGS

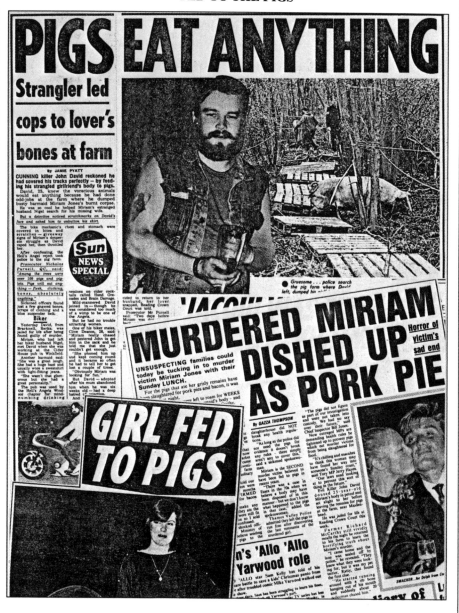

In 1988, when John David raped and murdered barmaid Miriam Jones, he thought he had found the perfect means to dispose of the body. Although he had never heard of the 'Onufrejczyc solution', the twenty-five-year-old biker from Bracknell knew that pigs would eat anything. When police searched the pig farm where Miriam Jones had been dumped after her killer had tried to burn the corpse, all they found were a few chewed bones and parts of her underwear.

At the trial at which David was sentenced to life imprisonment, Crown Prosecutor, Nicholas Purnell QC, told the jury: "Pigs will eat anything – flesh, clothing, bones, absolutely anything."

The Kidwelly Poison Case

The Death by Poisoning of Mrs MABEL GREENWOOD on Monday the 16th of June 1919 at her home in Kidwelly

and the Trial and Acquittal of her Husband HAROLD for the Crime

"'Morning Mrs Williams; District Nurse been to see your Evan has she?"

"Yes indeed Mrs Hughes. Had a nice cuppa tea afterwards we did; very interesting little chat too. Wonder if you'd know what about now?"

"Well yes, I was just talking to Mrs Phillips the other day, and she told me Nurse had something on her mind. About that terrible Harold Greenwood man isn't it? Scandalous I call it, and him a high and mighty solicitor himself. Mind you, never been much of a hand at it if you ask me – nothing but Jews and money lenders hanging round him. All the money for that flashy house and their fanciness come from her you know – Mabel Greenwood. Still, he didn't get a penny from the will; everything to the children – and he knew it beforehand, so it wasn't that!"

"No – it was another woman, Mrs Williams, that it was. Fed up to the back teeth with Mabel he was – always messin' around with some other woman behind her back – horrible I call it, gives me the creeps. And then, after he'd done whatever it was to her and she was lying, dying in dreadful pain, what was he doing? Messin' round with that Miss Griffiths, the doctor's sister, in her own front parlour; there's been something going on there for years I reckon. Miss Griffiths isn't letting on of course, but I heard she told Miss Phillips that Harold Greenwood was very jolly that evening; told her he didn't think Mabel would get over it this time, and smiling all the while. There's shocking – he should know too, shouldn't he?"

"Well, Mrs Hughes, I heard the Nurse say she never seen a case like it in all her twenty-three years' nursing. Wished she'd asked for a post-mortem she told Miss Phillips. She ought to go straight to the police, I said; he could end up murdering us all!"

"She wouldn't do that now, would she? Open up too many awkward questions if the police got into it wouldn't it? For instance, why didn't she insist on having Dr Griffiths back during all those hours the poor woman was in her death agonies? And him only living opposite. No, she's got too much on her conscience to call on the police. Bit sweet on Greenwood herself if you ask me. Probably canoodlin' and cuddlin' with him over the corpse of that poor woman before it was even dead."

"There's horrible..."

The village of Kidwelly in South Wales was having the time of its life. Never in its whole history had there been such a rich and

Harold Greenwood

134

fascinating vein of gossip; and the locals mined that vein for all it was worth. In the pubs, on doorsteps, over tea, after chapel, the whispers whistled up a wind of suspicion surrounding the death of Mrs Mabel Greenwood and the strange 'goings-on' of her husband Harold.

It was not long before the rumours of foul-play reached the ears of the police; and it is an unwise country copper who does not cock at least half an ear in the direction of village tittle-tattle. By March 1920 – almost nine months after Mrs Greenwood's death – the matter had risen as high as the chief constable of Carmarthenshire, and on the 9th of the month Mr Picton Phillips sent a report to both the coroner and the Home Secretary summarising such evidence as the police had so far gleaned in the matter of the death at Kidwelly.

It could not be denied that the demise of Mrs Greenwood was surrounded by some very suspicious circumstances. She had been visited by Dr Thomas Griffiths at about six o'clock on the evening of Sunday June the 15th 1919; it should be mentioned that Griffiths was the only doctor in the village, and not renowned for the accuracy of his diagnoses. He treated Mabel Greenwood for biliousness – laying the blame squarely on the gooseberry tart that she had eaten with lunch; Mabel was confined to bed on a temporary diet of milk and soda, barley water, and sips of brandy. Afterwards, Griffiths and Harold Greenwood strolled in the garden where they played a game of clock golf. Later the doctor sent over a bottle of bismuth for his patient.

By 7.30 pm, Mrs Greenwood's condition had deteriorated. Her friend Miss Phillips, who had been invited for supper, sent for the district nurse, who arrived some fifteen minutes later.

The nurse sent Greenwood to summon the doctor at around 8 pm, and she and the Greenwoods' daughter Irene sat by the sick-bed of a patient who was by now very ill. Dr Griffiths lived directly opposite the Greenwood home, and when an hour had passed and neither Harold Greenwood nor the doctor had returned to the house, Irene went to fetch her father. To her embarrassment she found Greenwood and the doctor's sister, between whom gossip had already spread rumours of a flirtation, happily closetted in the drawing-room. It was left to Irene Greenwood to alert Dr Griffiths to the needs of his patient.

Griffiths returned to Mabel Greenwood's bed-side, gave her a cursory examination, and handed the nurse a couple of pills, one to be taken immediately, the other in an hour or so. It was 10.30 pm before Harold Greenwood got home, and when he did so, dismissed the nurse and his daughter from the room and sat for the next four hours watching his wife getting steadily weaker, suffering increasing pain and discomfort, never once did he summon professional help. At 3 am, the nurse, checking on her patient, insisted that Dr Griffiths be brought in immediately; unhappily for Mabel Greenwood it was too late; within the hour she was dead.

It was almost a year before police enquiries justified any interference in the life of Harold Greenwood. In the meantime Greenwood, seemingly impervious to mounting gossip, had remarried four months after the death of his first wife to Gladys Jones. It was a Superintendent Jones who broke the news: "...having regard to the rumours which are around, the matter being so much talked about, I am afraid we shall have to exhume Mrs Greenwood's body."

"Just the very thing. I am quite agreeable," Greenwood replied affably.

"Have you heard the latest, Mrs Williams?"

"What's that, Mrs Hughes?"

"They're digging up Mabel Greenwood!"

"No! Poor soul! and she in the ground these ten months past. Horrible sight that'll be – terrible!"

In fact the body had suffered such putrefaction as to make unreliable any conclusions from the examination. However, forensic experts were able to identify convincing traces of arsenic in the organs.

Statements subsequently taken from Greenwood and the visiting nurse differed not only from each other, but also from the recollections of Dr Griffiths. As the result of the coroner's inquest – which neither Harold

Irene Greenwood

Greenwood nor his daughter, Irene, attended – Greenwood was arrested on a charge of murdering his wife.

"Mrs Hughes, are you going to Carmarthen for the trial?"

"Of course; I wouldn't miss it for the world. November the 2nd isn't it?"

"That's right. Mind you, we'll have to go early, my cousin Willy says every hotel in the area's booked out, and there'll be standing room only in the Guildhall. Exciting, isn't it?"

"Yes. And I'll tell you another thing – between you and me, Mrs Williams, there'll be some trouble in Carmarthen. Some of the men are bound on showing that nasty little monster that good Welshmen don't go around poisoning their women. There'll be some fun – you see if there isn't!"

Greenwood had to be escorted by police guards through the hostile crowds massed along the route to the packed Guildhall courtroom.

He was a cool and confident prisoner, listening without emotion to the evidence of the foreman of the company that had sent him the parcel containing their arsenic-based weed-killer 'Eureka' less than a month before the death of his wife; the statement of the caretaker at his office who had found a half-burnt letter dated the day before the death. The letter, in the hand of Gladys Jones, read: "It will be nice when I am your wife"; the testimony of his own maid who remembered seeing Greenwood in the pantry for the first time ever on the morning of the day Mrs Greenwood was taken ill. "He had been doing something in the pantry and went straight from there to the dining-room."

From the medical evidence, there was no doubt that Mabel Greenwood had been poisoned with arsenic – but by whose hand, and by what means? The prosecution built up its case around the Burgundy wine which Mrs Greenwood always took with her lunch, and which, on the day of her illness, she had complained tasted "bitter". It would, of

Harold Greenwood and his second wife, Gladys

course, be the perfect vehicle for the poison – one half of a teaspoonful in the bottle would provide a fatal dose in each glass!

The dramatic focus of the prosecution on the bottle of Burgundy was as suddenly to be defused. Like a rabbit from a conjuror's hat, the defence pulled Irene Greenwood. She too had drunk from this poisoned bottle. Had Irene been called as a witness at the inquest, the Crown might have had time to cope with this evidence; at this eleventh hour they were left with no more wind in their sails; the ship was sunk. The jury could do nothing but find a verdict of "Not guilty".

Harold Greenwood had been in jail for four-and-a-half months before the trial; on his release, his career and reputation shattered, he changed his name to Pilkington and lived quietly in Ross until his death.

For all it may have mattered to him, the trial swung public sympathy much in Harold Greenwood's favour. As Mrs Williams might have said: "...Poor man, we'll never know for sure whether he did it or not – but he's certainly paid for it in any case!"

['*The Kidwelly Poison Case*' was written by *Susan Dunkley*]

Harold Greenwood after his release from court

THE MARSH TEST FOR ARSENIC

Although the identification of arsenic by analytical means had been pioneered as early as the 1770s – notably by the Swedish chemist Karl Wilhelm Sheele – it was not until much later that a test was developed which was held to be reliable enough for its results to be accepted as evidence in a court of law. In 1836 James Marsh, an Englishman, published a paper detailing a method for coverting arsenic traces in body tissue and body fluids into arsine gas, which itself was recovered as a metallic 'mirror' on a piece of porcelain. So sensitive was the test, that amounts of arsenic as small as one fiftieth of a milligram could be identified. The principles of the Marsh Test are still used, though improvements and developments of Marsh's equipment make the Reinsch and Gutzeit Tests more reliable and easier to conduct.

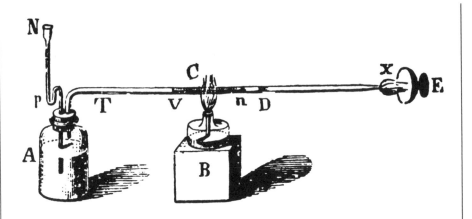

Above: A diagam of James Marsh's first test for the presence of arsenic
Below: The elctrolytic Marsh-test apparatus designed by Professor Thorpe

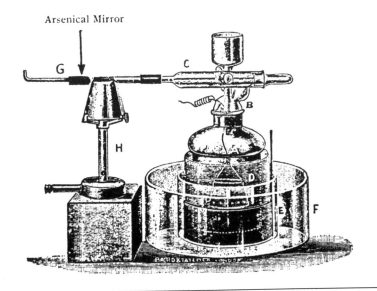

Conduct Unbefitting
The Murder of GEORGE MERCHANT
by THOMAS ATHOE and his Son
on the 23rd of November 1722
outside the town of Tenby

THOMAS ATHOE the elder, Mayor of Tenby, in Pembrokeshire, and Thomas Athoe the younger, his son, for Murder, June, 1723.

AT the assizes held at Hereford, March 19, 1722-3, Thomas Athoe the elder, and Thomas Athoe the younger, who by a Habeas Corpus were brought thither from Pembrokeshire, were indicted for the murder of George Merchant, by beating and kicking him on the head, face, breast, and privy members, and thereby giving him several mortal wounds and bruises, on the 23d of November, 1722, of which he died the same day.

They were a second time indicted on the coroner's inquisition for the said murder.

The principal witness against the prisoners was Thomas Merchant, the deceased's brother. They had used him in so barbarous a manner, that at the time of the trial, though it was four months afterwards, he was in so weak a condition that he could not stand, and therefore the court permitted him to give his evidence sitting.

The Evidence against the prisoners was to this Effect.

On the 23d of November, 1722, a fair being that day kept at Tenby, in Pembrokeshire, the prisoners came thither to sell some cattle, and there they met with the deceased, George Merchant, and his brother Thomas Merchant. A quarrel arising, young Athoe and the deceased fell to fighting ; but the deceased had the advantage, and beat young Athoe. Upon this, old Athoe was advised by some pettifogger to bring an action against the deceased ; but he answered, No, no, we will not take the law, but we will pay them in their own coin.

The fair breaking up between ten and eleven at night, the deceased and his brother left the town. The prisoners went to the inn, where the two brothers had taken horse, and enquired which way they were gone. The ostler giving them the best information he could, they mounted and followed them directly. The brothers stopped on the road, at a place called Holloway's-Water, to let their horses drink. Presently they heard a trampling of other horses behind them ; and turning about, saw two men on horseback at a little distance, but the night was so dark, that they could not discern who they

they were; though they were not long in doubt, for they
heard old Athoe's voice. This put them under ftrong appre-
henfions that fome mifchief was intended; for old Athoe,
when he was at the fair, had threatened a fevere revenge,
and therefore, to prevent it, they endeavoured to conceal
themfelves behind the bridge, but the fplafhing of their
horfes difcovered them. The prifoners coming up with
great fticks, I owe thee a pafs, and now thou fhalt have it,
faid young Athoe to the deceafed, and knocked him off
his horfe. Thomas Merchant was ferved in the like manner by old Athoe, who at the fame time cried out, Kill
the dogs! kill the dogs! the brothers begged them for
God's fake to fpare their lives; but the prifoners had no regard to their cries. Old Athoe fell upon Thomas Merchant,
beating him in a terrible manner, and taking faft hold of his
privities, pulled and fqueezed him to fuch a violent degree,
that had he continued fo doing a few minutes longer, it had
been impoffible for the poor man to have furvived it. The
pain he fuffered is paft expreffion, and yet it fell fhort
of what his brother endured. Young Athoe, when he had
tired himfelf with beating him, feized him by the privy members, and tore out one of his tefticles; and calling to his father, faid, Now I have done George Merchant's bufinefs!—
This horrible action occafioned a vaft effufion of blood:
but young Athoe's revenge was not yet glutted, for catching
hold of the deceafed's nofe with his teeth, he bit it quite off,
and afterwards tied a handkerchief fo tight about his neck,
that the flefh almoft covered it. The laft words the deceafed
was heard to fay were, Don't bite my nofe off. He lived
a few hours in the moft grievous agony imaginable, and then
expired.

When his body was examined by the furgeons, they declared, that by the bruifes they found upon him, they believed the blows he received were alone fufficient to have
killed fix or feven men. He had twenty-two bruifes on
his back, three great ones on his head, and two on his
breaft.

The prifoners in their defence faid, that they were affaulted upon the road by the brothers, who had long borne
them a grudge; and that what they did was in their own defence.

The jury found a fpecial verdict, upon which the cafe was
referred to the determination of the whole bench of judges;
and the prifoners were brought up to London, and committed
to the King's-Bench prifon in Southwark, where they lay till
Saturday,

140

Saturday, June 22, 1723, and then were carried up to the court of King's-Bench in Weftminfter-Hall.

In their motion for an arreft of judgment at the King's-Bench-Bar, the point of law debated was, Whether a man can be tried for a fact in a county in which the fact was not committed. The queftion was decided on producing the act of parliament, which enacts, That all murders and robberies, committed in, on, or about the borders of Wales, fhall be triable in any county in England, where the criminal fhall be taken.

Young Athoe made fome trifling excufes in behalf of his father.

Then the court proceeded to judgment, and both the prifoners received fentence of *Death*. After which they were carried back to the King's-Bench prifon.

An Account of THOMAS ATHOE *the Father, and* THOMAS ATHOE *the Son.*

Thomas Athoe the elder was born at Carew, about three miles from Mannerbeer, in the county of Pembroke, in the principality of Wales. Mannerbeer was the place of his laft habitation, before the murder was committed. —————
He rented there upwards of a hundred a year, and lived, as he faid, in good repute for the fpace of twenty-four years. In the year 1721, and part of the year 1722, he ferved the office of mayor in the corporation of Tenby, which town is two miles from Mannerbeer, and fix from Pembroke, and is joined with Pembroke in the privilege of electing one burgefs to ferve in parliament.

His family confifted of a wife and two children. His fecond child was Thomas Athoe the younger, who was born in the parifh of Mannerbeer. He always lived with his father, who had brought him up to hufbandry and grazing. In the time of the old man's mayoralty, this fon of his ferved as bailiff of Tenby.

George Merchant, the murdered perfon, and Thomas Merchant his brother, were nephews, by the moth r's fide, to Athoe the elder; for their father, John Merchant, a hufbandman in the fame parifh of Mannerbeer, married old Athoe's fifter.

After the murder was committed young Athoe was fent to Ireland: but, thofe who were concerned in fending him were foon obliged to ufe their utmoft endeavours to get him back again; and by good management they fucceeded.

'As

As to the behaviour of the father and son in the King's-Bench prison, and at the place of execution, take it in the words of Mr. Thomas Dyche, the chaplain of that prison.

" I pressed them both very earnestly to make an open and full confession of the crimes whereof they stood convicted.

" In all my visitings of the prisoners, I found the spirit of devotion always upon them : they behaved themselves with that temper, gravity and tenderness, which became them, and employed their time very much in reading of such books as were suitable to their melancholy circumstances.

" They expressed abundance of seeming penitence, praying earnestly, and declaring that they were in charity with all the world.

" However, they pretended that they had been injured by the Merchants :

" First, In their detaining an estate from them.

" Secondly, That they, the Merchants, had bought some cattle out of their hands at Weston fair, October 28, 1721.

" Thirdly, That the Merchants had opposed their elections: and,

" Fourthly, That Mr. George Merchant, the murdered person, had married a sweet-heart of young Athoe's.

" Now, admitting all these pleas of the Athoes to be true, will they justify the crying sin of murder, when the Almighty has declared, that, He that sheddeth man's blood, by man shall his blood be shed ?

" Thus, therefore, prompted by jealousy and revenge, these criminals committed this horrid fact, for which they have deservedly suffered the justice of the law.

" In the whole course of the proceedings against them, all the favours they desired were granted ; notwithstanding which the county of Pembrokeshire, upon what grounds are unknown, took their part, as not believing the facts so bad as they were proved to be upon the strongest evidence.

" They buoyed up each other with hopes of life, till the rule of court came down for their execution. After this they began to shew some signs of prevarication ; for, I was assured at the prison, by the testimonies of several persons, they denied some circumstances which they had before owned:

particularly

particularly the time of Mr. George Merchant's deceafe, which was clofe put to them by a Divine, the very morning of their execution.

"Mr. Chapman, the turnkey, alfo affured me, that on Thurfday night they offered him a very confiderable reward to be permitted to make their efcape; but finding they could not prevail with him to break his truft, they earneftly defired him to attend them to the place of execution: and that he would take care their bodies might not hang longer expofed to public view, than the time the law prefcribed.

"When they were tied up by the executioner, old Athoe covered his face firft, and after he was turned off, he bled very much at the nofe.

"On Friday the 5th of July, 1723, about 11 o'clock in the morning, they were conveyed in a cart to the place of execution. When they came to the fatal tree, they behaved themfelves in a very decent manner, embracing each other in the moft tender and affectionate manner; and indeed the fon's hiding his face bedewed with tears, in his father's bofom, was, notwithftanding the barbarous action they had committed, a very moving fpectacle.

"When our devotions were finifhed, the father declared, That he was innocent of the crime laid to his charge, and that he had not lifted up his hand againft George Merchant, the deceafed.

"The fon declared, That he had no premeditated malice againft George Merchant, the deceafed; but that being affaulted, what he did was in his own defence; that the deceafed having no hair upon his head to get hold of, the damage he received muft be by his handkerchief, which was tied about his neck in two knots. And he fhewed the fpectators, by pointing to his own neck, in what manner he throttled him.

"On Friday, June 28, the prifoners received the facrament with great reverence and devotion; and early in the morning before their execution they did the fame.

"They begged of all good people to take warning by their ignominious death. They had fome time allowed to their private devotions, and then the cart drew away, they all the while crying out, Lord have mercy upon us!

"There were two other divines with me to affift upon this occafion. The two Athoes were brought from the place of execution in two hearfes to the Falcon-Inn in Southwark, in order, as was faid, to be buried in St. George's churchyard."

Old

Old Athoe was about 58 years of age, and his fon wanted but one day of being 24 years old at the time of their deaths.

They were executed at a place called St. Thomas's-Watering, a little beyond Kent-Street in Surry.

Facsimile from the *Newgate Calendar* of 1776

Early view over Tenby

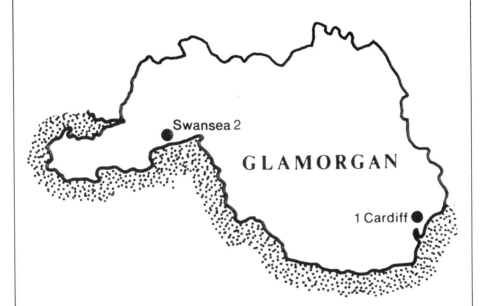

Glamorgan

The Cardiff Race-track Gang

The Murder of DAI LEWIS
by Members of the ROWLANDS GANG
on Thursday the 29th of September 1927
in St Mary Street, Cardiff

In any pursuit where it is possible to make a few dishonest pennies, there will be gangsters to make them. Men – for the female of the species is rare – who will use muscle rather than brain to keep a few pounds ahead. Sports have always offered good pickings; gambling on sports even better; horse racing one of the best.

The 1920s, particularly, spawned this sub-culture of race-track gangsters, and as in the twilight world of hoodlums everywhere, the race-course was a jealously guarded territory. At Cardiff, the reigning gang was run by the brothers Rowlands – John, and 'Titch' – his real name was Edward, but probably even he had forgotten. Violent men by nature, even without the 'muscle' with whom they surrounded themselves, the Rowlands brothers would suffer no invasion of their territory without retribution.

Now, on the fringe of any society can be found that character popularly fictionalised as 'the loveable rogue' – a sentiment easier to comprehend with the heart than with the head! Dai Lewis was so described by those who knew him well; Dai Lewis: former athlete, and professional boxer in the welter-weight class. Like many boxers of his day, Lewis had become attracted to the less glamorous elements of that rather unglamorous sport, and had turned his bulk and pugilistic skills to the 'defence' of others. More accurately, he was a one-man protection racket. Lewis's trade was to hire out to bookmakers on the course small items like stools, chalk, and buckets of water to clean their boards. Those who availed themselves of this service had insured against 'accidents' which might befall them – such as having their stands tipped over, or worse, being attacked and robbed.

Dai's permanent 'office' was Monmouth race-track, and in this precarious way of business he may have grubbed along at a leisurely pace, on just the right side both of the law and of his clients.

But in September 1927, Lewis made a grave error of business judgement; an error that would cost him not only his livelihood, but his life. On the 28th of that month, Dai Lewis expanded his activities to Cardiff; to the race-course 'owned' by John and Titch Rowlands.

Even before the meeting was over on that Wednesday afternoon, Lewis had received threats against his life; threats that with his customary braggadocio he had scorned and dismissed. Even so, he took the precaution of avoiding his home in Ethel Street, Cardiff, that night, and booked into a hotel in St Mary Street.

On the following morning, the 29th of September, Dai Lewis was up early and on his way to Monmouth to offer his 'services' on the track. But his want of etiquette on the previous afternoon had not been forgotten, and when Lewis returned to St Mary Street and the *Blue Anchor* pub, he found himself drinking in the company of a sizeable number of the Rowlands gang – including John and Titch themselves.

Apparently unconcerned, Dai Lewis continued to drink and make merry until closing time, unaware that several of the Rowlands' cronies had detached themselves from the company and moved across to the cafe opposite the *Blue Anchor*.

Outside on the pavement, Lewis, befuddled by drink, stood looking about him. What he saw was John Rowlands and a man named William Price coming towards him from the gloom of the ill-lit street, followed by less defined human forms. What he did not see were the men creeping up behind his back. In the most unevenly matched fight of his life, Dai Lewis struck out with powerful, desperate blows; but within seconds he was grounded, and from the mêlée of arms and legs that struck out at him came the momentary flash of the knife blade that was to rob Dai Lewis of his life. He cried out just once as his assailants scuttled off in all directions; then he was still, blood pouring from a deep gash in his throat.

As the ambulance arrived to rush him to the Cardiff Royal Infirmary, Dai Lewis was still breathing, and with a tenacity born of years in the ring, he clung on to his life. And with a stubbornness born of years on the edge of gangsterdom, he refused absolutely to name his assailants. Neither the police, in the person of Detective Chief Inspector Tom Hodges, nor his wife Annie, could budge his determination to prove that there was 'honour among thieves'.

In another part of the Infirmary, a quick-thinking night-nurse on duty in the reception office was taking a telephone call:

"Can you tell me how Dai Lewis is?"
"Who is speaking, please?"

The only reply was the click of a receiver being replaced.

In the early hours of the morning the same nurse answered the same telephone to hear the same rasping voice:

"Can you tell me how Dai Lewis is?"
"Who is that speaking, please?"
Click.

This time the nurse alerted police officers to the reluctant caller, and arrangements were made with the local telephone exchange to trace any further calls. Another hour passed, and while Dai Lewis's grip on life weakened, the duty nurse was startled for a third time by the insistent ring of the telephone on her desk. On this occasion she managed to keep the unknown voice talking for long enough for the call to be traced to the notorious Colonial Club in Custom House Street. At the same time, officers at police headquarters were receiving a mystery call of their own; a hastily spoken claim that the Rowlands gang was responsible for the attack on Dai Lewis. At the Colonial Club, John and Titch Rowlands, Daniel Driscoll, John Hughes, and William Price were arrested on

a charge of attempted murder.

When it became clear that Lewis was unlikely to make it through the day, a final desperate attempt was made to cajole him into giving vital information as to the identity of his assailants. A magistrate and his clerk were summoned to the hospital to take the dying man's deposition; the five accused men stood at the foot of Dai Lewis's bed. After informing him that he was near death, the magistrate's clerk told Lewis: "These men are accused of attacking you... take things very slowly, and say what took place."

The boxer opened his eyes, and in a faint, hesitant voice began to speak: "I do not know how I have been injured... I do not remember how it happened... there was no quarrel or fight. Nobody did any harm to me... I did not see anyone use a knife." Inclining his head in Edward Rowlands' direction, he continued: "You had nothing to do with it... we've been the best of friends." To Driscoll: "You had nothing to do with it either; we were talking and laughing together. My dear old pal."

That Lewis was lying was obvious; that he would never alter his story was as pathetically apparent. Later that day he died.

It was several days after Dai Lewis's funeral that John Rowlands, under interrogation, confessed to his involvement in the violence of the night of September the 29th. His story was that it had been Lewis who drew the knife and attacked him first; during a fierce struggle he had wrested the weapon from his opponent's grip, but in the process must have accidentally caused the boxer his fatal injury. And improbable though this account sounded, it was gratefully accepted as direct evidence. Brother Edward and Daniel Driscoll still maintained that they were guiltless onlookers who had made off when they saw Lewis fall to the ground wounded. John Hughes was released for want of reliable evidence, and the remaining four were committed for trial.

The trial opened at the Glamorgan Assizes on November 29th before Mr Justice Wright. The case for the Crown was led by Lord Halsbury, who opened with the words: "This was murder as cruel and beastly as you could possibly imagine, premeditated, and carried out – I might almost say flaunted – in Cardiff's main street." His case, however, was weak from the start; such witnesses as came forward gave hopelessly conflicting accounts of the sequence of events, and even the policemen who arrived on the scene of the crime were in clear disagreement.

The trial lasted for three days, ending for the jury with as confused a picture as that with which they had begun. Nevertheless, on Friday the 2nd of December they returned a verdict of guilty against the Rowlands brothers and Daniel Driscoll, and all three were sentenced to hang. William Price was found not guilty and released from custody.

No sooner had the sentences been passed than public dissatisfaction with the verdicts was mobilised into a solid fighting force. Large sums of money were raised by public subscription to fund an appeal; more than 250,000 signatures were collected demanding a Home Office inquiry, and the case was discussed in the Chamber of the House of Commons. Three doctors who had been present at the post-mortem on Dai Lewis's body claimed that the victim had died not from his wounds, but from a heart attack; and in an unprecedented move, eight members of the trial jury petitioned the Home Secretary, Sir Austen Chamberlain, that: "Sentence of death should be waived as an act of mercy."

Legal opinion, however, was not to be swayed by sentimentality – or by suggestions of a miscarrige of justice for that matter – and at the Appeal Court hearing on January 11th 1928, Lord Hewart the Lord Chief Justice, Mr Justice Avory, and Mr Justice Branson declared that there was no further evidence on which to divert the due process of the law.

On January 27th, at 8 am, Edward Rowlands and Daniel Driscoll stood on the scaffold at Cardiff Gaol. John Rowlands, who had gone berserk in the van on his way to the Appeal Court, and was later certified insane, had already been confined to Broadmoor.

In his autobiography* Detective Superintendent David Thomas added this postscript to the case: "Lewis's killing was to become known, in later years, as the Hoodoo Murder. Within twelve months John Hughes was dead and one of the prostitutes who had given key evidence committed suicide... Price, acquitted at the Assizes, was blinded in one eye with a butcher's hook. A police constable who gave evidence died while still young of tuberculosis; another constable who never ceased saying: 'We are all doomed, we sent an innocent man to the scaffold,' died in his thirties of a mysterious stomach ailment; a detective-sergeant who investigated the case committed suicide; and another sergeant died, while still relatively young, from cancer. Harold Lloyd, the solicitor who represented Price, was sentenced to five years' penal servitude... on charges of converting clients' money to his own use."

---

* *Seek Out The Guilty* [see Bibliography]

'The Abode of Peace'
The Murder of MAMIE STUART
by EVERARD GEORGE SHOTTON
some time in November or early December 1919
at 'Ty-Llanwydd', on the Mumbles, near Swansea

Mamie Stuart: age 26; very attractive appearance; height five feet three or four inches; well-built; profusion of dark brown hair, worn bobbed; dark grey eyes; four faint teeth marks on right cheek, the result of a dog bite when a child.

It will be three years before this description is distributed to every police officer in Britain with a request to be on the look-out for Mamie. She had been a chorus girl but had left the stage, and early in the year 1917 was living with her father – a master mariner – and her mother, in Sunderland.

In July 1917 Mamie met Everard George Shotton, a marine surveyor from Cardiff, then in Sunderland on business. A believable, honest-looking young man, it was not long before George was slipping an engagement ring on to Mamie's finger. On March 25th 1918 they married.

In February 1919, George and Mamie

View across the Mumbles

George Shotton and Mamie Stuart

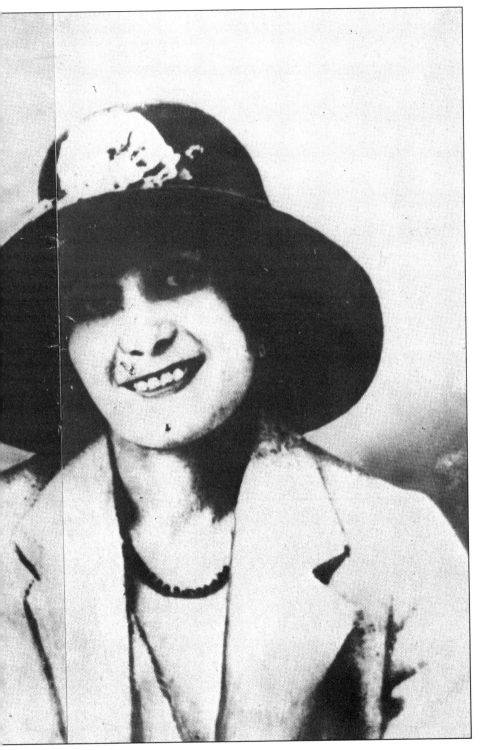

moved home to Swansea where they became paying guests of Mr and Mrs Hearn at 28 Trafalgar Terrace. Within a few months – July 19th to be precise – George Shotton announced that business pressed, and he would have to leave Swansea for a while; a fact which his wife accepted resignedly, after all, if business had not taken him from home on a previous occasion he would not be her husband now. So, making the best of the situation, Mamie departed a few days later to visit her parents.

It was November before Mr and Mrs Shotton resumed normal married life, and this time George had rented a detached villa half a dozen miles from town, overlooking the Swansea Bay. On November the 5th 1919 the couple moved into Ty-Llanwydd – in English 'The Abode of Peace'.

A week later, on November the 12th, Mamie wrote a lettercard home to her parents. Dutifully they replied; their letter was returned marked 'House Closed'. Convinced that there must have been some mistake, Captain Stuart sent a reply-paid telegram to Ty-Llanwydd. This too was returned by the post office: 'House Closed'. Strangely enough, despite their unease, the Stuarts let the matter drop. A few days before Christmas a telegram arrived at the home in Sunderland, apparently from their daughter, wishing the Stuarts "compliments of the season". It was the last they were to hear from her.

In March 1920, the Swansea police were called by the manager of the Grosvenor Hotel to take charge of a large portmanteau which had been left by a guest and had lain unclaimed for several months. Further examination showed the case to contain another, rather battered piece of luggage. This in turn revealed two dresses and a pair of shoes, inexplicably cut to shreds; intact were a Bible, manicure set, and some jewellery. At the bottom of the case was a scrap of paper bearing the Sunderland address of Captain and Mrs Stuart, who subsequently identified the remnants as having been clothes belonging to their daughter.

At the same time another, more sinister discovery was being made. Behind the washstand in a bedroom at Ty-Llanwydd, a cleaning woman preparing the house for new tenants had found a mildewed brown leather handbag; it contained a few pounds in loose change and, significantly, a ration card issued to Mamie Stuart.

It was at this stage that Chief Inspector William Draper was seconded from Scotland Yard to assist the local detectives in their investigation of what was beginning to look increasingly like a case of murder.

Draper's first obvious move was to establish the whereabouts of George Shotton, the elusive husband. In the event, they did not have to look far – Shotton was located at an isolated house in Caswell Bay, named Grey Holme; it was barely two miles from 'The Abode of Peace'. Sharing the house was Shotton's real wife and their small child.

Shotton's story was simple, and in its own way quite believable. Yes, he had lived with Mamie Stuart; no, he hadn't married her; and no, he didn't know where she was now. They had quarrelled in early December, parted company, and gone their separate ways – he back to his wife, she, heaven knows where.

But the investigating officers were beginning to learn a lot more about the man Shotton. For a start, people close to him began to recall incidents from the past, events which showed the ostensibly mild George Shotton as one capable of intense jealousy accompanied by violence, both of word and action. Mrs Hearn, their former landlady, remembered Mamie asking her: "If I am ever missing, do your utmost to find me, won't you?" These fears were elaborated in a letter from Mamie to her parents: "If you don't hear from me, please write to Mrs Hearn and see if she knows anything about me. The man is not all there. I don't think I will live with him very long. I am very much afraid of him. My life is not worth living." But lest the narrative seem one-sided, it must be observed that, while there was no excuse for violence, George Shotton had every reason to be jealous. His 'wife' had, indeed, been seeking and distributing favours outside of her marriage to George, writing to one of her amours: "My old man seems to know quite a lot... but what the eye don't see the heart don't grieve... Just dying to see you and feel your dear arms around me."

Fearing the worst, the police decided to hedge their bets; a description of Mamie Stuart was circulated throughout Britain, and at the same time they made an exhaustive search of Ty-Llanwydd, dug over every inch of its grounds, and combed the countryside around for indications of foul-play.

Still there was no trace of the missing chorus girl.

On May 29th 1920, George Shotton was arrested on a charge of bigamy. At Glamorgan Assizes he advanced the preposterous defence that it was not he, but somebody impersonating him who had married Mamie Stuart. Shotton then went on to offer an explanation of the portmanteau affair. Going back to Ty-Llanwydd after their separation the previous December, he claimed he found a number of Mamie's belongings scattered about which he collected up, put into a case, and dumped during a stay at the Grosvenor Hotel. His bigamy earned George Shotton eighteen months' hard labour.

As for Mamie Stuart, the file was all but closed; within a year, all but forgotten.

It was almost forty years to the day since Mamie Stuart had first entered Ty-Llanwydd as Mrs George Shotton – November the 5th 1961. Graham Jones, John Gerke, and Chris MacNamara, three experienced potholers, descend the air shaft of a disused mine at Brandy Cove on the Gower coast. In a cavern at the base of the shaft, they are about to solve the mystery of Mamie Stuart's disappearance. In front of them, her bleached white bones protruding from a rotting sack; still on her skeletal finger, her wedding and engagement rings.

Subsequent examination of the remains by Home Office pathologist Dr John Griffiths and Dr William James further revealed that after death the body had been cut into three pieces, being sawn through the thighs, spine, and upper arms. Although the age, sex, and build of the skeleton matched the description of Mamie Stuart, and clothing associated with the remains at the foot of the mine shaft were of a style current when Mamie had gone missing, the coroner's court would require much more positive proof of identity than these similarities.

Using a technique which had been so successful in identifying the victims of Dr Buck Ruxton* in 1936, and Harry Dobkin** in 1942, a full-size negative of the skull was superimposed on a life-size enlargement of Mamie's portrait, and showed an incontrovertible correspondence of features.

The verdict of the coroner's inquest at Gowerton on December 14th 1961, was that Mamie Stuart had met her death by the hand of George Shotton some time in November or December 1919.

Where, then, was George Shotton now? The answer to the question was as undramatic as it was final. On April the 30th 1958, the man who had escaped the penalty of the law for thirty-eight years died in Bristol's Southmead Hospital. Penniless at his death, Shotton was buried in an unmarked grave, plot 000405, in Arno's Vale cemetery, Bristol.

---

* For an explanation of the photographic methods used in this case see *Murder Club Guide No.3*: North-West England.
** See *Murder Club Guide No.1*: London.

A Christmas Tale
The Murder of Mr REES MORGAN, his Wife, and Daughter
by EDWARD MORGAN
at Christmas-tide 1756
and his Execution at Glamorgan on the 6th of April 1757

The circumstances which came out on the trial of Edward Morgan, at the assizes of Glamorgan, were these. According to annual custom he had been invited by Mr Rees Morgan, of Lanvabon, his cousin, to spend the Christmas holidays. He had partaken of the first day's festivity, and retired to bed along with a young man, apprentice to Mr Rees Morgan. No sooner had he laid his head upon the pillow, to use his own expression, than the devil whispered to him to get up and murder the whole family, and he determined to obey.

He first made an attempt on the apprentice, his bedfellow, but he struggled so far as to effect his escape and hide himself. The murderer then provided himself with a knife, which he sharpened on a stone as deliberately as the butcher uses his steel.

Thus prepared, he softly crept to the bedchamber of his host and hostess, and cut their throats in their sleep; then he proceeded to the bed of their beautiful daughter, with whom the monster had but an hour before been sporting and playing, and with equal expedition, and by the same means, robbed her of life.

Not, however, satisfied with causing this inundation of blood, he seized a firebrand and proceeded to the barn and outhouses, setting fire to them all; and to complete the sum of his crime he fired the dwelling-house, after plundering it of some articles.

The Gloucester Journal of the year 1757 describes the property consumed by fire on this melancholy occasion to have been "the dwelling-house, a barn full of corn, a beast-house with twelve head of cattle in it; and the farmer, his wife and daughter were either murdered or perished in the flames."

It was at first conjectured that the unfortunate people had perished in the conflagration. Their murdered bodies, it is too true, were consumed to ashes; but the manner of their death was proved partly by what the concealed apprentice overheard, but chiefly from the murderer's own confession. Morgan was executed at Glamorgan, on the 6th of April, 1757 and hung in chains.*

* See *Murder Club Guide No.2* for a note on Hanging in Chains.

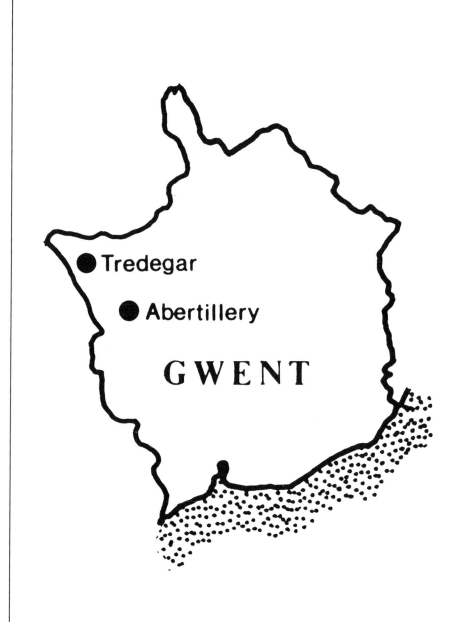

Gwent

Second Time Lucky
The Murder of FREDA BURNELL and FLORENCE IRENE LITTLE
by HAROLD JONES
on the 5th of February 1921 and the 18th of July in the same year, respectively at Abertillery

That juries are fallible is obvious from their very constitution. It would be a miracle if errors of judgement were not made by these twelve ordinary citizens thrown, usually for the first time in their lives, into the bewildering world of criminal law. Generally, these mistakes can be seen as regrettably human; but there are occasions when the consequences reach far beyond the jury box.

On the evening of the 5th of February 1921, eight-year-old Freda Burnell walked into an oil and seed merchant's in Abertillery on an errand for her father. Mr Burnell kept a few chickens in the back yard at home, and it had been Freda's duty and pleasure to shop for the poultry grit. She would never feed the chickens again.

On the morning of the following day, Sunday the 6th, Freda Burnell's body was found in a lane near to the seed shop; the girl's hands and feet had been bound, and some attempt at rape had been made. Death had resulted from partial strangulation and shock, probably occasioned by a savage blow to her forehead.

It was in the shed behind the shop that investigating officers found little Freda's handkerchief – the clue that was to put Harold Jones, shop assistant, and only fifteen years old, into the dock at Monmouth Assizes. Despite strong evidence in favour of a conviction, some spirit of the perverse seemed to infect the seven men and five women that made up the jury. We will never know what debate passed between them in the retiring room on that late June afternoon, but whatever it was produced the astonishing verdict of "Not Guilty".

Now if the jury had seemed perverse, it was left to the general public – not least the good citizens of Abertillery – to add caprice to the case. No sooner had Jones's acquittal been announced, and he had been released by the Court, than he was elevated to that position of popular approbation normally reserved for the return of conquering heroes (or at least a winning football team). After his slow – almost majestic – return to his home town in an open bus decked with bunting, Harold Jones addressed a jubilant crowd from a hotel balcony.

On the 18th of July in the same year, 1921, Florence Irene Little, aged eleven, was found at the end of a trail of blood leading to the attic of the Jones family house. Her throat had been cut with a kitchen knife over the downstairs kitchen sink.

Harold Jones, by the time he had been indicted at Monmouth for the second time in six months on a charge of murder, had confessed not only to the killing of Florence Little, but also to that of Freda Burnell. His reason for such cruelty: "my desire to kill".

In November 1921, Jones was found guilty. That he evaded the sentence of death was due solely to his youth; sentenced just before his sixteenth birthday, Jones was ordered to be detained during His Majesty's pleasure. The final word went to Mr Justice (later Lord) Roche, who observed that the quite undeserved adulation showered on Jones after his previous acquittal almost certainly contributed to his arrogance in killing again.

The Mystery of Cefn Golau
The Mysterious Death of TOM PHILLIPS
on Wednesday the 4th of March 1959
near his home in Tredegar

Farming the inhospitable land of the Welsh mountains is a precarious occupation, and it requires a hardy breed of men to make a living from the harsh, uncompromising landscape in the often uncertain weather of the uplands. Such a family were the Phillipses, headed by thirty-year-old David and his twenty-five-year-old brother Tom.

The weather on the night of March the 4th 1959 was as wild as any that the Phillips family could remember, the lightning storm

and torrential rain had lashed the hillsides for hours, and from the comfort of their home at Half Way House, Tredegar, the two brothers' thoughts returned constantly to the fate of their livestock, the hundreds of sheep and scores of valuable Welsh ponies that would be huddling to what small shelter they could find on the weather-beaten mountain side of Cefn Golau.

As darkness fell, Tom Phillips walked to the window of the farmhouse and took stock of

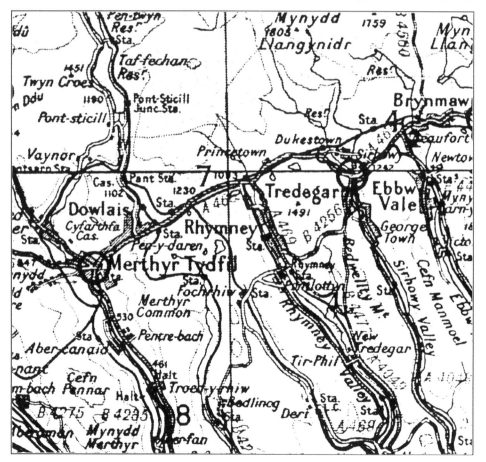

the bleak aspect outside. Characteristically, Tom made his decision with the best interests of the farm foremost in his mind: "I think I'll go out and bring in some of the ponies. The storm looks like getting worse; they'll be safer nearer the house." Without another word, Tom Phillips wrapped his powerful frame in an old raincoat and set his steps for the darkness.

It was several hours before David Phillips began to get anxious; on a night like this rounding up the half-wild hill ponies was going to be no light work. But there were other considerations playing on David's mind: the perilous outcrops of rock made slippery with the downpour, the deep crevices and cracks that scarred the boulder strewn slopes; Tom might have had an accident. With this awful premonition, David Phillips and another brother were soon facing the gale, soaked before they left the farm gates, calling Tom's name only to have their voices lost in the howling of the wind.

Not far from the house, in the hesitant light of their hurricane lamp, the two brothers saw a group of ponies taking what shelter they could from a clump of sparse trees. It was obvious from their position that the ponies had not been driven there under Tom's command, he would have known that there was safer shelter nearer the house; and if the beasts had wandered down from the

mountainside on their own, then where was Tom Phillips? Tormented by the elements, defied by the darkness, the brothers returned to the farmhouse, hardly daring to hope that they would find Tom sitting drying before the fire. And for the rest of the night the family sat, their eyes fastened on the door, waiting, willing the latch to lift.

By morning there was still no sign of Tom, and after reporting his disappearance at the Tredegar police station, David Phillips organised a party to search every foot of the mountain top around Cefn Golau. Eventually the police brought up dogs to try to track the missing man's scent; but at the end of the day Tom Phillips was still a missing person.

Taking the matter increasingly seriously, Divisional Superintendent Leonard James widened the search across the valley and down to the reservoir, which was systematically dragged – still without solving the enigma of Tom Phillips's disappearance. The discovery near the water's edge of the corduroy hat in which Tom took his last walk, put some impetus back into the search, and the banks of the reservoir were patrolled daily in the expectation that the waters would yield up Tom's body. After four weeks it looked as if the file on this missing person was to remain open.

And then on April the 19th, a young man

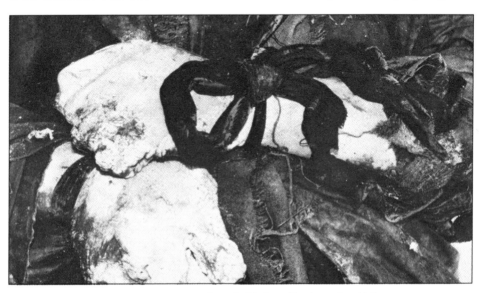

Tom Phillips's wrists, bound with the polka-dot neckerchief

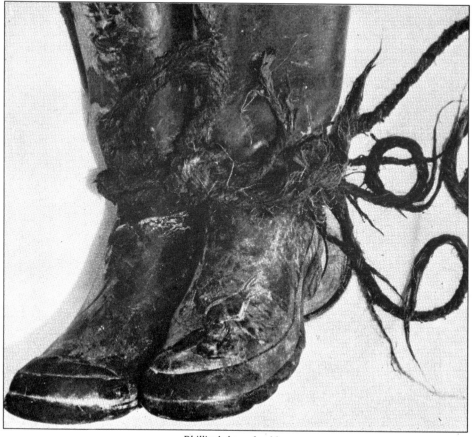

Phillips's bound ankles

out for a stroll noticed a bulky shape at the edge of the reservoir. Tom Phillips was missing no longer; he was dead. The body's ankles had been bound with rope, and the wrists with a polka-dot neckerchief. Local gossip was fanned into a new blaze when David Phillips stated categorically that the neckerchief had not belonged to his brother, and the word "murder" was in every mind if not on every lip.

The police, however, could not afford to jump to so hasty a conclusion; a conclusion that would simply have exchanged an un-solved disappearance for an unsolved homi-cide. There were other possibilities, and however irrational it may seem in retrospect, the police opted for Tom Phillips committing suicide. True, it was demonstrated by offi-cers at the inquest that it was physically *possible* for a man to tie himself up in such a way as that in which the body had been

found and then to hop to the edge of the water and throw himself in. But was it likely? In his evidence to the coroner's court, David Phillips – convinced that mur-der had been committed – stated that his brother was a very "jolly" person, poetically describing his frame of mind on the night of his disappearance as "happy as a bird in springtime". And would even a suicidal man walk several miles from his home in one of the worst storms of the year, go through the elaborate charade of tying himself up, just to jump into the reservoir? There were, after all, plenty of other deep ponds much nearer home. And then, where did the spotted neckerchief come from, and the rope that tied his legs and which the Phillips family had never seen about the farm? Was it credible that Tom's body had been under water for five weeks without having being weighted down? One would normally expect the build-up of gasses generated by putrefaction to re-float the body in around ten days. Despite these weighty doubts, the coroner, Lieutenant-Colonel K.D. Treasure, decided that the only verdict that was worthy of consideration was one of "suicide during a period of mental depression". But there are many people, including some in authority, who feel that the possibility of foul play should not have been dismissed in quite such a cavalier fashion.

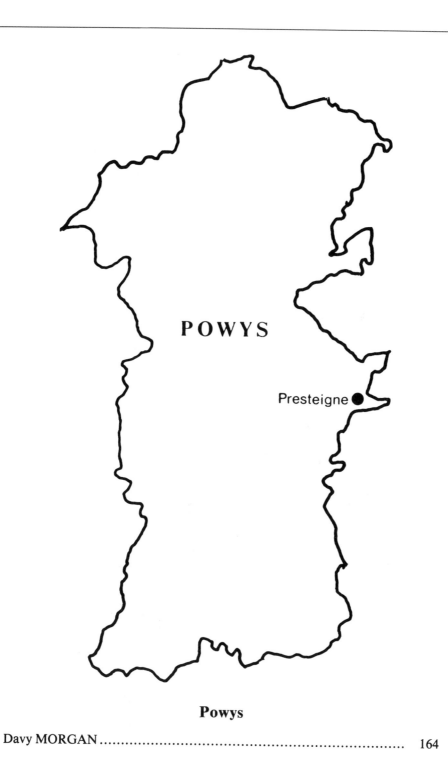

POWYS

Presteigne ●

Powys

"I want money, sir . . ."
The Murder of EDWARD WILLIAMS
by DAVY MORGAN
and his Execution at Presteigne
in April 1712

Davy Morgan was born at Brecknock, the chief town in Brecknockshire, in South Wales, whence he came up to London in the quality of a serving-man to a Welsh knight, when about eighteen years of age; but young as he was, he quickly learned to rob his master of money and clothes, to the value of about ten pounds, and then ran away from his service.

Being now his own master, the company he kept was none of the best, for they were all the greatest housebreakers, pickpockets and shoplifters, both in town and country; by whose conversation becoming as wicked as the best of them, he had not long turned thief before he broke open the house of a Venetian ambassador in Pall Mall and robbed him of about two hundred pounds' worth of plate, for which, being shortly after apprehended, he was committed to the Gatehouse at Westminster.

After he had procured his liberty again he broke, one night, into the house of Doctor Titus Oates*, in Axe Yard, in Westminster, and stood sentinel over that reverend divine whilst his comrades rifled most of the rooms; and then, tying him neck and heels, after the same manner as they do a soldier, with a couple of muskets which they found in the kitchen, Davy very sorely gagged him, saying that if his mouth had been as well crammed but a few years ago, he had not sworn so many men's lives away for pastime.

Another time, getting into a gaming-house frequented much by Bully Dawson, and perceiving he had won a great

---

*See *Murder Club Guide No.1* for a note on Titus Oates, the Popish Plot, and the murder of Sir Edmund Berry Godfrey.

deal of money, he requested the favour of speaking a word or two with him in the next room. Dawson, taking him to be some chub or cully, went along with him, where, shutting the door, Davy pulls out a pistol, and presenting it to his breast, quoth he: "I want money, sir, for a very extraordinary occasion; therefore deliver what you have without any resistance, for if you make but the least noise soever I'll shoot you through the heart, though I were sure to die on the spot." Bully Dawson, being strangely surprised at these words, and dreading what a desperate man might do in his rage, gave him all his money, which was about eighteen guineas. Then, tying him hand and foot, Davy went about his business. By that time the bully thought this bold robber

TITUS OATES. D.D.

A gentleman highwayman in gaol, a drawing on the wall behind shows a felon hanged in chains

was gone, so calling out for help, several sharping gamesters came out of the gaming-room to him and, untying him, asked how that adventure came to pass. Which Dawson relating through several volleys of loud oaths, they fell a-laughing heartily at him, and cried: "Dawson, 'twas a fair nick."

At last Davy Morgan, having committed a great robbery in London, in breaking open a Jew's house in Duke's Place, and taking from thence above two thousand pounds in gold, fled into Wales; and in Presteigne, in Radnorshire, did not only rob the church of its communion plate, but also broke open the house of one Edward Williams, whom he barbarously murdered. But being apprehended at Bristol, and sent to jail in the county where he committed this most barbarous crime, he was executed at Presteigne, in April, 1712, aged forty-three years, and hanged in chains*.

---

* *See Murder Club Guide No.2* for a note on Hanging in Chains

The Ones They Couldn't Hang

Although the extraordinary case of John Lee quoted in an earlier part of this book is a rare one, there were an appreciable number of early executions that failed the first time; in most cases this was due to the incompetence – usually through drink – of the executioner.

The two major causes of error were misjudging the length of drop, so that when the prisoner fell he landed on his feet; and failing to secure the rope to the gallows properly so that the man tumbled to the ground followed by the rope. Not infrequently the rope itself would break, and in one such instance the prisoner had to be carried back up to the scaffold and held under the beam because he had broken his leg in the fall. It must, though, be said that in the vast majority of cases the operation worked successfully the second time.

As it did in the case of Benjamin Renshaw, immortalized in the *Newgate Calendar*. "...After he was turned off, the noose of the rope moved under his chin, and it was deemed proper to put him back in the cart, that the rope might be adjusted afresh, after which he was turned off again. This circumstance occasioned considerable sensation among the spectators, who generally expressed their abhorrence of the executioner, to whose carelessness they attributed the accident."

One of the most ghastly cases of bungling took place at the execution of soldier Private Hales, at Jersey: "He was accompanied to the place of execution [by the Rev G. Du Heaume]. He joined him in prayer, and ascended the scaffold with coolness and composure. At length he was turned off; and, when he had hung about a minute and a half, the executioner, taking hold of his convulsed body, suspended himself on it, and by this additional weight, the rope gave way, in such a manner that the miserable sufferer's feet touched the ground. The executioner then pulled him sideways, with a view to strangling him, and being unable to effect it in this way, and got upon his shoulders. To the great surprise of all who witnessed this dreadful scene, the poor criminal rose straight up on his feet, with the hangman on his shoulders, and immediately loosened the rope from his throat with his fingers. No language can describe the sensations which were excited among the bystanders by this shocking scene. The sheriff ordered another rope to be prepared; but the spectators interfered, and the sheriff agreed that, before proceeding with the execution of the sentence, he would wait till the will of the magistracy should be known... Petitions were prepared by the inhabitants and forwarded to His Majesty, and he was pardoned accordingly."

A further complication that arose in consequence of the crude early method of hanging – which amounted to little more than slow strangling at the end of a rope – was that the time of fatality differed from one person to another. There are more than a few reports from anatomists (to whom the bodies of executed criminals were consigned for the purpose of medical dissection and teaching) of 'corpses' maintaining a heartbeat some several hours after being cut down from the gallows. One or two even made a complete recovery; such a one being resuscitated by Sir William Petty, Professor of Anatomy at Oxford University in 1650. After hanging for half an hour, the woman concerned recovered to live, it is said, for a further nine years during which she married and gave birth to two children. [See *Murder Club Guide No.8* for a note on Revivals after Execution].

THE LIFE, TRIAL, CHARACTER, AND CONFESSION
OF
The Man that was Hanged
IN FRONT OF NEWGATE, AND WHO
IS NOW ALIVE !
WITH FULL PARTICULARS OF THE RESUSCITATED.

"There are but two classes of persons in the world—those who are hanged, and those who are not hanged; and it has been my lot to belong to the former."

THERE are few men, perhaps, who have not a hundred times in the course of their life, felt a curiosity to know what their sensations would be if they were compelled to lay life down. The very impossibility, in all ordinary cases, of obtaining any approach to this knowledge, is an incessant spur pressing on the fancy in its endeavours to arrive at it. Thus poets and painters have ever made the estate of a man condemned to die one of their favourite themes of comment or description. Footboys and 'prentices hang themselves almost every other day, conclusively—missing their arrangement for slipping the knot half way—out of a seeming instinct to try the secrets of that fate, which —less in jest than in earnest—they feel an inward monition may become their own. And thousand of men, in early life, are uneasy until they have mounted a breach, or fought a duel, merely because they wish to know, experimentally, that their nerves are capable of carrying them through that peculiar ordeal.

Now *I* am in a situation to speak from experience, upon that very interesting question—the sensations attendant upon a passage from life to death. I have been HANGED, and am ALIVE—perhaps there are no three other men at this moment, in Europe, who can make the same declaration.

Before this statement meets the public eye, I shall have quitted England for ever; therefore I have no advantage to gain from its publication. And, for the vanity of knowing, when I shall be a sojourner in a far country, that my name—for good or ill—is talked about in this,—snch fame would scarcely do even my pride much good, when I dare not lay claim to its identity. But the cause which excites me to write is this—My greatest pleasure, through life, has been the perusal of any extraordinary narratives of fact. An account of a shipwreck in which hundreds have perished; of a plague which has depopulated towns or cities; anecdotes and inquiries connected with the regulations of prisons, hospitals, or lunatic receptacles; nay, the very police reports of a common newspaper—as relative to matters of reality, have always excited a degree of interest in my mind, which cannot be produced by the best-invented tale of fiction. Because I believe, therefore, that to persons of a temper like my own, the reading of that which I have to relate will afford very high gratification ;—and because I know also, that what I describe can do mischief to no one, while it may prevent the symptoms and details of a very rare consummation from being lost ; for these reasons I am desirous, as far as a very limited education will permit me, to write a plain history of the strange fortunes and miseries to which, during the last twelve months, I have been subjected.

I have stated already, that I have *been* hanged and *am* alive. I can gain nothing now by misrepresentation —I was GUILTY of the act for which I suffered. There are individuals of respectability whom my conduct already has disgraced, and I will not revive their shame and grief by publishing my name. But it stands in the list of capital convictions in the Old Bailey Calendar for the Winter Sessions of 18—

Hodges, Printer (from the late J. Pitt's) Wholesale Toy Warehouse, 31, Dudley Street, 7 Dials.

THOMAS SAVAGE

A Profligate Apprentice who murdered a Fellow-Servant, was executed twice, and finally buried 28th of October, 1668

This unhappy wretch was born of very honest parents in the parish of St Giles's in the Fields, and between fourteen and fifteen years of age bound apprentice to one Mr Collins, a vintner, at the *Ship Tavern* at Ratcliff Cross, with whom he led but a very loose and profligate sort of life for about two years.

Breaking the Sabbath (by his own confession, he having never once heard a whole sermon during that time) was the first inlet to all his other vices, especially whoredom, drunkenness and theft, for he used commonly to pass away the Sabbaths at a bawdy-house in Ratcliff Highway with one Hannah Blay, a vile common strumpet, who was the cause of his ruin, and brought him to a shameful end.

He was carried at first to drink there by an acquaintance, who afterwards went to sea; but having once found the way, he went after that alone, without his companion, and would often carry a bottle or two of wine to junket with her. This, however, not satisfying her wicked desires, she told him frequently that if he would enjoy her company he must bring good store of money with him. To this he always replied that he could bring none but his master's, and that he had never wronged him of twopence in his life. Nevertheless she still continued urging him to rob him privately, but he answered he could not, because the maid was always at home with him. "Hang her, a jade!" said this limb of the devil; "knock her brains out, and I'll receive the money, and go with you beyond sea, to avoid the stroke of justice."

She was often giving him this bad advice and preaching this infernal doctrine, and she repeated it in particular on the very day when he unhappily took her counsel

and perpetrated the murder; for being at her house in the morning, she made him drunk with burnt brandy, and he wanting a groat to pay his reckoning, she again persuaded him to knock the maid's brains out, and bring her what money he could find.

Hereupon he went home, between twelve and one o'clock, and seeing his master standing at the street door did not dare to go in that way, but climbed over a wall, and getting in at the back door went into the room where his fellow-servants were at dinner. "Oh, sirrah," said the maid to him, "you have been now at the bawdy-house; you will never leave it till you are utterly ruined thereby."

These words provoked him highly, and he was so much enraged at her that from that moment the devil took firm possession of him, and he fully resolved, even while he was at dinner, to be her butcher. Accordingly, when his master with the rest of the family were gone to church, leaving only the maid and Tom Savage at home, he went into the bar and fetched a hammer, with which he began to make a great noise, as he sat by the fire, by knocking on the bellows. Hereupon says the maid to him: "Sure the boy is mad! Sirrah, what do you make this noise for?"

To this he made no answer, but going to the kitchen window began to knock and make the same noise there, of which the maid then taking no notice, he, to provoke her, got on the clean dresser, and walked up and down thereon several times with his dirty shoes. This piece of malice exasperating the maid, so that she scolded at him pretty heartily, he threw the hammer at her suddenly with such violence that, hitting her on the head, it felled her to the ground, and she shrieked out. He then went and took up the hammer, intending to repeat the blow, but laid it down again thrice, not being yet hardened enough in cruelty to strike her any more; but at last, taking it up the fourth time, the devil had then gained such an absolute mastery over him that he gave her several strokes with all the force he could, and quickly dispatched her out of the world.

The inhuman wretch, having perpetrated this hellish piece of barbarity, immediately broke open a cupboard in his master's chamber, and taking out a bag, wherein was about sixty pounds, hid it under his coat, and went out at a back door directly away to Hannah Blay again. When he came there, and informed her what he had done, the cunning slut, who was hardened in wickedness, would fain have had the money from him; but he would part with no more than half-a-crown, which having given her, he went away without the least remorse for what he had done.

But he had not gone far, when, meeting with a stile, he sat down thereon to rest himself, and then began to reflect on the horrid deed he had perpetrated, and to cry out to himself, "Lord, what have I done!" wishing that he could have recalled the fatal blows, even at the price of ten thousand worlds, if so many had been in his power. After this he was in so much horror and dread of mind that he stirred not a step but he thought everyone he met came to apprehend him.

That night he reached Greenwich, where he took up his lodging, telling the people of the house he was going to Gravesend; but being got to bed he could not sleep, through the terror of a guilty conscience, but got up again, and walked about the room for several hours. Next morning the mistress of the house, perceiving he had a large quantity of money in a bag not sealed up, began to examine him about it, doubting he came not by it honestly. Hereupon, to avoid her just suspicion, he told her he was carrying it down to Gravesend to his master, who was a wine-cooper, and lived on London Bridge; and that if she would not believe she might send to his mistress, and in the meantime he would leave the money in her hands.

This was agreed upon, and accordingly he wrote a note himself to his pretended mistress, which was to be carried by some people who were then going to London, whilst he went his way, wandering towards Woolwich, where he was in the shipyard much about the time the hue and cry came to Greenwich of a murder committed at Ratcliff Cross by a youth upon a maid, who was his fellow-servant; and that he had also robbed his master of a bag of money.

Upon this news the mistress of the house where he had lain presently concluded that it was the same youth who had lodged there, and that the bag he had left with her was that whereof he had robbed his master. Hereupon she immediately dispatched several men in search of him, who found him asleep in an ale-house, with his head upon a table and a pot of beer by him. Upon this, one of the men, calling him by his name, said: "Tom, did you not live at Ratcliff?" He answered Yes. "And did not you murder your fellow-servant?" he answered likewise in the affirmative. "And you took so much money from your master?" He acknowledged all. "Then," continued he, "you must go along with us." To which he replied: "Yes, with all my heart." Accordingly they went forthwith to Greenwich, to the house where he had lain the night before.

By the time he got thither his master and some friends had arrived there likewise, who exaggerated to him the barbarity of the fact, wherewith he was not much affected at first, though a little after he burst out into tears. From thence he was carried back to Ratcliff, and had before a Justice of Peace, who committed him to Newgate.

Being now in safe custody, he was visited by one Mr Baker, to whom, after some little acquaintance, he gave the foregoing account; and he found him at first but little sensible of the heinousness of the crime he had committed. But the next time, asking him whether he was sorry for the fact, he answered with tears in his eyes, wringing his hands, and striking his breast, "Yes, sir; for it cuts me to the heart to think that I should take away the life of an innocent creature; and that is

*Thomas Savage returning to Hannah Blay's
lodgings*

not all, but for anything I know, I have sent her soul to hell. Oh! how can I think of appearing before God's tribunal, when she shall stand before me and say, 'Lord, this wretch took away my life, and gave me not the least time to consider of the state of my soul, that so I might have repented of my sins, and have turned to Thee; he gave me no warning at all, Lord.' Then, what will become of me?"

He was then visited by Mr Robert Franklyn, Mr Thomas Vincent, Mr Thomas Doolittle and Mr James Janeway, who asked him if he was the person that murdered the maid at Ratcliff. To which he answered Yes. Hereupon they endeavoured to set the sin home upon his conscience, telling him the danger he was in, not only of a temporal but of an eternal death, without true repentance, and a sincere and strong faith.

The day he went down to the sessions his fellow-prisoners gave him something to drink, which very much disordered him; and Hannah Blay, whom he had accused, and who was taken into custody thereupon, was heard to say to him: "Others have made you drunk to-day, but I will make thee drunk to-morrow." He lamented this backsliding grievously, but said that it was not the quantity he had drunk, which was much less than he was able to drink at other times without being in the least disordered, but it was something they had infused into his liquor to intoxicate his senses; which made him ever afterwards very cautious and fearful of drinking in their company.

After he had received sentence of death he was again visited by Mr Baker; and the Saturday before his execution he was again with him, when Savage said to him, taking him by the hand, "Oh, my dear friend, come hither." Then opening his coffin, "Look here," continued he, "this is the ship wherein I must launch out into the ocean of eternity. Is it not a terrible thing to see one's own coffin and burial clothes, when at the same time (as to my bodily health) I am every whit as well as you?"

On the Sunday, expecting to be executed next day, he desired to be alone, and spent it in prayer and other religious duties. Next morning the sheriff's men and cart came for him, but the Sheriff of Middlesex not having notice, it was deferred till Wednesday, when, looking upon his clothes that he had put on to die in, he said: "What! have I got on my dying clothes? Dying clothes, did I say? They are my living clothes, the clothes out of which I shall go into eternal glory. They are the best clothes that ever I put on!"

Being brought to the place of execution at Ratcliff Cross, he made a short speech, wherein he exhorted people, both old and young, to take warning by his untimely end how they offended against the laws of God and man. After which, having said a very pathetic prayer, and breathed forth such pious ejaculations as drew tears from the eyes of the beholders, he was turned off the cart, and struggled for a while, heaving up his body. Which a young man, his friend, perceiving, he struck him several blows upon his breast with all his strength, to put him out of his pain, till no motion could be perceived in him. Wherefore after he had hung a considerable time, and was to all appearace dead, the people moving away, the sheriff ordered him to be cut down, when, being received into the arms of some of his friends, he was conveyed to a house not far from the place of execution. There being laid upon a table, he began, to the astonishment of the beholders, to breathe, and rattle in the throat, so that it was evident life was whole in him. Hereupon he was carried from thence to a bed in the same house, where he breathed more strongly, and opened his eyes and mouth, though his teeth were set before, and he offered to speak, but could not recover the use of his tongue.

However, his reviving being blazoned abroad within an hour, the sheriff's officers came to the house where he was, and carrying him back to the place of execution, hung him up again till he was really dead. After which his body was carried by his mourning friends to Islington, and buried on the 28th of October, 1668, being seventeen years of age.

WILLIAM DUELL

Executed for Murder and came to Life again while being prepared for Dissection in Surgeons' Hall*, 24th of November, 1740

William Duell was convicted of occasioning the death of Sarah Griffin, at Acton, by robbing and ill-treating her. Having suffered, 24th of November, 1740, at Tyburn, with Thomas Clock, William Meers, Margery Stanton and Eleanor Munoman (who had been convicted of several burglaries and felonies), his body was brought to Surgeons' Hall to be anatomized; but after it was stripped and laid on the board, and one of the

servants was washing it, in order to be cut, he perceived life in him, and found his breath to come quicker and quicker, on which a surgeon took some ounces of blood from him; in two hours he was able to sit up in his chair, and in the evening was again committed to Newgate, and his sentence, which might be again inflicted, was changed to transportation.

* See *Murder Club Guide No.1* for a note on Surgeons' Hall.

JOHN M'NAUGHTON, Esq.

*Who was twice executed in Ireland, 15th
of December, 1761,
for the Murder of Miss Knox, whom he
pretended to marry*

John M'Naughton, Esq., was the son of a merchant at Derry, whose father had been an alderman of Dublin. To an outward form which was perfectly engaging he added the most genteel demeanour, so as to promise the very reverse of what was the real disposition of his soul, which was subject to every blast of passion.

He was educated in Trinity College, Dublin. When of age he entered into a landed estate of six hundred pounds a year, in the county of Tyrone, which was left him by Dr M'Naughton, his uncle.

The first vice he fell into was gaming, by which he very soon did great injury to his fortune; and though he continued (as most novices do who play with sharpers) in a constant run of ill-luck, and was soon obliged to mortgage, yet his losses made no visible alteration in his temper. His pride kept him within due bounds there. All was placid with the polite M'Naughton, and he lost his money to the very last with that graceful composure that became the man who had a plentiful fortune to support it. But strong as his passion this way might be, it was not strong enough to secure him against the attacks of love, and falling a victim to the charms of a young lady he very speedily married her.

His very agreeable person and soft polite address assured his success with the ladies; but, as his character was generally known, the young lady's friends took all possible care to secure her effects, and the lover was too eager to gratify his passion, and too rash in his temper, to trouble himself about the disposition of fortune.

The unavoidable expenses of a wife and servants in Dublin (as he pursued his old course of gaming) soon increased his difficulties. A sheriff's writ was taken out against Mr M'Naughton for some large debt; and as he suspected the danger he kept himself as secure at home as possible, by which means the bailiffs could get no admittance. The creditor, or some other persons concerned, hearing this, had influence enough with the High Sheriff to prevail on him to go to Mr M'Naughton's house and take him prisoner.

As the sheriff went in a chair, and appeared like a gentleman, the servants admitted him, and showed him into a parlour, where their master was alone. The sheriff then told him he was his prisoner. On this M'Naughton flew into a rage, and, calling out for pistols, he frightened his poor listening wife to such a degree that (being near her time) she fell in labour, and died in childbed.

The High Sheriff was greatly blamed for this seeming officious behaviour; but this dreadful consequence threw Mr M'Naughton into such distraction that he made several attempts upon his life, and was obliged to be attended and watched for some months after. On his return from the country, after eighteen months' absence, he appeared greatly altered – like a wretch worn out with grief – so very susceptible was that frail man of the excess of every passion. But this fatal accident, which nearly cost him his life, was attended with one good consequence: it immediately cut off all expense; and that long retirement into the country was of some service to his troubled fortunes, and gave him an opportunity, on his return to Dublin, to appear there like himself, in some degree of splendour. There he renewed his old and, no doubt, contracted new friendships, and kept most faithfully to his favourite vice, gaming, which he pursued with great spirit.

He then made his addresses secretly to Miss Knox, daughter of Richard Knox, Esq., of Prohen, in the county of Derry, a gentleman possessed of an estate of about fifteen hundred pounds per annum; and as by the marriage settlement five thousand pounds had been settled on the younger children, Miss Knox, having only one brother and no sister, was entitled to the whole of five thousand pounds, even though she disobliged her parents by marriage. We must add to this bait the beauty, sweetness of temper and other accomplishments of the young lady, which were remarkable. She was then about fifteen.

Mr M'Naughton, who was an intimate friend of her father, and a constant visitor, soon obtained a promise from the young lady to marry him if he could get her father's consent. But Mr Knox not only absolutely refused his consent, and gave his reasons for it, but showed his resentment by forbidding him his house.

Mr M'Naughton then begged Mr Knox would permit him to visit as formerly (as he said it would look strange to the world to be forbidden to visit a family all the neighbours knew he had been so intimate with), and solemnly promised, upon his honour, never more to think of or mention this affair; and added, that as he had not spoken of it to the young lady, Mr Knox need never do it, and so the affair would drop of itself. Thus were the father's eyes and ears once more sealed up by this artful man, who continued his addresses to the daughter, and told her Mr Knox had promised him his consent; but desired, however, that no further mention might be made of the affair for a year or two, till some material business was decided, which he would acquaint him with. Thus he deceived the young lady, who now more freely gave way to his passion, and again promised she would marry him as soon as that consent was obtained. Thus he remained some time, constantly watching his opportunity to complete his design.

One day, being in company with Miss Knox and a young gentleman (a very boy) in a retired room in the house, he pressed her to marry him, protesting he never could be happy till he was sure of her; and, with an air of sprightly raillery, pulling out a Prayer Book, he began to read the marriage service, and insisted on the young lady's making the responses, which she did, but to every one she always added, "provided my father consents".

A short time after this, Miss Knox going to a friend's house on a week's visit, Mr M'Naughton, being also an intimate there, soon followed her. Here he fixed his scene for action; here he claimed her, and, calling her his wife, insisted on consummation, which the young lady absolutely refused. She left the house, and went directly and informed her uncle of the whole affair. On this, Mr Knox wrote a letter to M'Naughton, telling him what a base, dishonourable villain he was, and bade him avoid his sight for ever. Upon the receipt of this letter M'Naughton advertised his marriage in the public newspapers, cautioning every other man not to marry his lawful wife. This was answered by a very spirited and proper advertisement from the father, with an affidavit of the whole affair from the daughter annexed.

Mr Knox then brought an action against him in the Prerogative Court to set aside this pretended marriage, which was found to be only a contract; for the breach of which the party can only be sued at common law, and condemned to pay costs and damages. Besides, it is probable that the young lady being under age rendered this contract void in itself. At this time Mr M'Naughton had absconded from his debts, and therefore could not appeal to the Court of Delegates, where the former decree was confirmed. In consequence of this decree, Judge Scott issued his warrant to apprehend him. When M'Naughton heard this, he wrote a most impudent, threatening letter to the judge, and, it is said, lay in wait to have him murdered, when he was last at the assizes there, but missed him, by the judge's taking another road. Upon this the judge applied to the Lord Chief Justice, who issued out another writ against him, that drove him to England.

Mr M'Naughton returned to Ireland in the summer of 1761, and by constantly hovering round Mr Knox's house obliged the family to be on their guard, and the young lady to live like a recluse. However, about the middle of the summer, she ventured to a place called Swaddling Bar, to drink the mineral waters there for her health: thither this unhappy man followed her, and was seen sometimes in a beggar's habit, sometimes in a sailor's. Thus disguised he was detected, and then swore in the presence of several that he would murder the whole family if he did not get possession of his wife; and yet so infatuated were they as to suffer him to get away once more to England, where he was supposed to be by Mr Knox at the time this fatal event happened. He remained in London till the month of October, and gamed, cheated, and borrowed money from all his acquaintants, and imposed on many by forged letters and false tokens from their friends.

About the 1st of November he was seen skulking in the country of Ireland, and two nights prior to the murder was known to sleep with three of his accomplices at the house of one Mr ———, a hearth-money collector. The morning of the 10th, the day the fact was committed, they all came with a sackful of fire-arms to a little cabin on the roadside, where Mr Knox was to pass in his coach-and-six. From this cabin M'Naughton detached one of them to go to an old woman who lived at some distance on the roadside, under pretence of buying some yarn of her, but really to wait the coming up of Mr Knox's coach, and inquire whose it was. When it appeared in sight he asked that question, and was answered that it was Mr Knox, who, with his family, was going to Dublin. He then made her point to show him how they sat, which she did: Mr Knox, his wife, his daughter and maid-servant. As soon as he had got this information he ran off to inform M'Naughton that the coach was coming, and to make ready; that he had looked into the coach, and that Mr Knox was attended by only one servant and a faithful fellow, a smith, who lived near him, and was foster-father to Miss Knox – one whom M'Naughton could never bribe, though most of the other servants had suffered themselves to be tampered with, and, when discovered, had been discharged. As soon as the coach came near the cabin, two of the accomplices, armed with guns, presented them at the postilion and coachman, which stopped the coach, while M'Naughton fired at the smith with a blunderbuss. Upon this the faithful smith, who luckily escaped the shot, presented his piece, which, unfortunately, missed fire, and gave M'Naughton and one of his comrades an opportunity to fire at the poor fellow, and both

wounded him. Immediately upon this two shots were fired at the coach, one by M'Naughton himself, and another by one of his assistants; and finding that the passengers had drawn up the windows he ran round and fired into the coach obliquely, with a gun loaded with five balls, all which entered the body of the unhappy Miss Knox, who was carried into the cabin, where she expired in about three hours.

The murderer and his accomplices fled; but the country was soon raised in pursuit of them, and amongst others, some of Sir James Caldwell's Light Horse, who were directed to search the house and offices of one Wenslow, a farmer, not far distant from the scene of action. But though some of the family knew he was concealed there they pretended ignorance; so that M'Naughton might have escaped, had not the corporal, after they had searched every place, as they imagined, without success, and were going away, bethought himself of the following stratagem. Seeing a labourer digging potatoes in a piece of ground behind the stables, he said to his comrades in the fellow's hearing: "It is a great pity we cannot find this murderer; it would be a good thing for the discoverer; he would certainly get three hundred pounds." Upon which the fellow pointed to a hayloft. The corporal immediately ran up the ladder and forced open the door; upon which M'Naughton fired at him and missed him. By the flash of the pistol the corporal was directed where to fire his piece, which happily, wounding him, he ran in and, seizing him, dragged him out, when they instantly tied him on a cart, and conducted him to Lifford Jail. Here he remained in the closest confinement, entirely deserted by all his friends and acquaintances, as appeared on the day of his trial, which commenced on the 8th of December, 1761, when he was arraigned, with an accomplice, called Dunlap, before Baron Mountney, Mr Justice Scott and Counsellor Smith, who went down upon a special commission to try them.

M'Naughton was brought into court on a bier, rolled in a blanket, with a greasy woollen night-cap, the shirt in which he was taken being all bloody and dirty, and a long beard, which made a dreadful appearance. In that horrid condition he made a long speech, pointedly and sensibly, and complained in the most pathetic manner of the hard usage he had met with since his confinement. He and Dunlap were both found guilty, and, agreeable to the sentence, they were excecuted on Tuesday, the 15th of December, 1761, near Strabane, in the county of Tyrone.

M'Naughton was dressed in a white flannel waistcoat trimmed with black buttons and holes, a diaper night-cap tied with black ribbon, white stockings, mourning buckles, and crepe tied on his

arm. He desired the executioner to be speedy, and when the fellow pointed to the ladder he mounted with great spirit. The moment he was tied up he jumped from it with such vehemence that the rope snapped, and he fell to the ground, but without dislocating his neck, or doing himself much injury. When they had raised him on his legs again he soon recovered his senses. The executioner then borrowed the rope from Dunlap and fixed it round M'Naughton's neck; he went up the ladder a second time and, tying the rope himself to the gallows, jumped from it again with the same force, and appeared dead in a minute.

Thus died the once universally admired M'Naughton in the thirty-eighth year of his age.

WILLIAM PROUDLOVE and GEORGE GLOVER

Executed at Chester, 28th of May, 1809, for Salt-Stealing, after a First Attempt to hang them had failed

In the county of Cheshire were several salt-works; and these men, it appeared, were connected with a gang of villains, who made a practice of committing depredations on those valuable manufactures, and conveying the salt to Liverpool and Manchester, where they found a ready sale for it.

The works at Odd Rode had been frequently plundered by these men; and when they were detected by an excise officer they fired a pistol at him, in order to facilitate their escape. They, however, missed their aim, were taken, tried, and sentenced to death. They confessed the robbery, but solemnly denied the act of shooting at the exciseman, which they laid to the charge of one Robert Beech, one of the gang not then apprehended.

On the morning of their execution they received the Sacrament with much apparent devotion, in which they were joined by the wife of Proudlove, the mother of Glover, and four more convicts under sentence of death. They were then consigned to the custody of the sheriff, and walked with firm steps to the cart waiting to receive them. After they had passed through the principal streets of the city of Chester they were carried to the place of execution, which was covered with black cloth.

We wish we could here end our painful report of the sad scene which followed the dropping of the platform; but alas, horrid to relate, both ropes snapped a few inches from their necks, and the poor sufferers fell upon the terrace.

The impression and shock upon the feelings of a multitude of spectators at this moment cannot be described. Human sensibility was harrowed to the very soul; and the moans, cries and tears of the people loudly spoke the poignancy of their hearts. Stranger yet to tell, the miserable men appeared to feel little either in body or mind from the shock they had received: they lamented it had happened, and spoke of it as a disappointment in going instantly to heaven.

They were conducted back to the jail, to which they walked with equal coolness, and only requested that the chaplain might come again to them. This was complied with; and, stronger ropes being procured, about three o'clock in the afternoon, having passed the intermediate time in prayer, they were reconducted to the fatal drop; and perfectly resigned to their fate, were launched into eternity.

Some More Cannibals

A GHASTLY MEAL ON HUMAN FLESH

On June the 11th, 1874, the collier *Euxine* set sail from North Shields with a cargo of coal bound for Aden. On August the 1st the *Euxine* encountered a heavy storm which so buffetted the vessel as to shift its cargo; on the 5th of the same month captain Peter Murdock was alerted to the smoke coming from the ventilators, and only a cursory inspection was required to ascertain that the cargo had caught fire. Despite desperate salvage attempts, a gas explosion finally ripped open the ship and the captain and crew were obliged to take to the boats and make for the nearest land, which was St Helena. The second mate, James Archer, had in charge of one of these lifeboats, with Peter Jager, August Muller, Manshus Shutt, Alexander Vermeulen, Wictor Sanstrom, and an Italian, Francis Schufus. After three weeks at sea, it became obvious that the second mate was by no means certain of his whereabouts; To make matters worse, the pitifully small craft got into a trough of the sea and rolled over, drowning Jager and another crewman, and losing the precious last remnants of their meagre supplies. Thus did Francis Shufus become the sailors' substitute diet; a fact that, when it was subsequently reported, prompted one commentator, in a moment of chauvinism, to observe that though the original crew of the *Euxine* had been "principally Britishers", there were amongst them "a few foreigners, and happily (if such a word may be used in connection with the terrible crime) it was they who played the principal part in the tragedy that at the time horrified the civilised world."

HORRIBLE CANNIBALISM!

The New York papers recently [nineteenth century] published a telegram from Kingston, Jamaica, that a Negro woman of highly respectable character in the community has been arrested on a charge of cannibalism.

The accusation alleges that she has killed and eaten no fewer than twenty-six children, whom she had enveigled into her house. On a cursory perusal, the natural impulse would be to consider the story an impudent falsehood. Highly improbable as this shocking intelligence may be, it is just and barely possible.

Is Obeahism quite dead in Jamaica? It has been stated that "Vaudouxism" still lingers among the natives of Louisiana; and as regards Jamaica, a careful search through the Parliamentary Blue Books would reveal many extraordinary cases in which evidence was given of the monstrous orgies of Obeah, at which a calabash filled with rum and human brains was standing on a dish.

It would be worth while to trace the parallelism existing between African Obeah and the ghastly human sacrifices offered by the Mexicans to their gods.

(Illutrated Police News)

THE LEOPARD SOCIETY

'I am a member of the Leopard Society. The object of the Society is to catch a person and slaughter him. The victim would not necessarily be an enemy. The course adopted is that one man procures a victim who is killed and divided amongst the members; then each member who receives a share is bound to supply another victim to be killed and divided amongst the members. The members eat their shares. The person is only killed for the purpose of being eaten. It has been the practice in the country for a long number of years. I entered the Society a year ago`. . . Lamina told me he wanted the Leopard Society to finish in the country as soon as they could catch a woman . . . He wanted to make a medicine with the woman. The medicine was to be made in order to get riches. By mixing the medicine with certain leaves a charm would be created to make a man strong and successful. The medicine is put in a box . . . At certain times the grease formed by the fat of the flesh is rubbed on the medicine. The man does not carry it about with him. Before going to a meeting of the general people either before Chiefs or a Commissioner, the man rubs the medicine on himself. Lamina told me that he had a promise of a girl from another member of the Society and told me to follow him to the owner of the child and to go catch the child . . . He had asked Dama Bunjehun for a child . . . We went to Bunjehun's house. I stood outside behind the kitchen and called Bunjehun by name. Bunjehun said . . . I must wait until it was quite dark and then we will talk . . . After some time . . . I called Bunjehun again . . . "It is quite dark now". Bunjehun said "All right, let me go and see if the girl is in the kitchen" . . . Bunjehun left us and returned after a short time with the child. He came running to us, the child ran alongside him and he held it by the arm . . . The five of us ran away into the bush, Bunjehun carrying the child . . . Lansana and I went on, making a track by pressing back the bush with our hands . . . to try and find the road leading to Jangalo . . . When we returned I saw the child dead. The head had been cut off . . . I asked why the child had been killed and . . . Bunjehun said that he had killed the child because we were away so long . . . Bunjehun then cut up the body . . . He cut the body down the centre and across the middle, so dividing it into four parts . . . Bunjehun took the portion to which the right leg was attached, I took the portion to which the right arm was attached . . . Bunjehun cut all the flesh and skin off the head, he also cut out the eyes. The skull was left on the ground . . . Lansana and I went to Lamina's house . . . and gave him the portion . . . also the flesh and hair from the head. Lamina took the flesh . . . put it into a pot and cooked it for a short time and then took it out and ate it. Lamina cut off a portion of the breat and gave half to me and half to Lansana. Next morning Lansana and I went out on his farm and ate the pieces we had received . . . Lamina was naked . . . he took a bottle out . . . and put some grease out of his hand on it [out of it on his hand?] and rubbed it over his body and face. He told me it was the grease from the fat of the child. When cooking the flesh . . . Lamina shimmed off the grease with a spoon and put it in a bottle . . .' . . .

. . . I was charged . . . about the murder of Mawoni and cannibal affairs and I said I did not know anything about the cannibal affairs but I did about the catching of Mawoni . . . I never took my sister to the bush and wiped her or cleaned her private parts. I never put anything on her mouth to stop her speaking . . . I never said in the native court that there was a certain stick near the Porroh bush . . . where we used to meet to cut people's heads off, nor did I say there was a certain stone covered with a country pot, and when they wanted to catch any body the stone would first have to rise and walk . . . The stuff I saw on your gown was not ordinary dirt. The stuff on your gown was human fat . . . I know that since you were arrested another person has been caught by the human leopards at Bandaha. You sent the leopard knife to Bandaha. I saw you put it in a box, and your boy took it away next morning . . . It is a particular knife . . . has two prongs on it. The handle is a piece of wood, with a hole in it through which the holder puts his hand. The prongs are a little shorter than the length of my hand . . .

(Cannibals and Tongo Players)

STOP PRESS

A Cannibal Feast

While this book was being prepared for press, an astounding news story of mass murder and cannibalism broke in the United States which seemed, alarmingly, to bring this Appendix right up to date. The text is based on contemporary newspaper reports.

It was revealed on April the 12th, 1989, that at least thirteen people had been ritually slaughtered in moonlight ceremonies by Satanist drug-dealers.

Police and customs officers found the butchered remains in mass graves at a remote ranch some twenty miles west of Matamoros. A police officer said that the smugglers kidnapped their victims randomly, and after subjecting them to unspeakable torture, ripped out their hearts and brains and boiled them up in a cauldron to eat in a cannibal feast.

The object of the slaughter appears to have been to appease Satan in return for inviolability from police arrest and so that they would not be harmed by bullets. Whenever a major drug deal was about to go through, a human sacrifice was given.

Three Mexicans and a Texan have been arrested in connection with the killings, but the leaders of the cult – an offshoot of the Cuban/Caribbean religion of Santeria – are still being sought. Sara Maria Aldrete, called 'The Godmother', and Adolfo de Jesus Constanzo, 'The Godfather', are believed to have found refuge with Miami's large Hispanic-Caribbean population, among whom Santeria has become an increasing problem.

Sara Maria Aldrete

Select Bibliography

The following Bibliography makes no claim to completeness, and when one single volume is considered to provide a balanced, reliable account of a crime, this title alone is listed; for example, one in the remarkable Notable British Trials series. Published by William Hodge, the 83 volumes provide an unparalleled panorama of British crime, notably the crime of Murder. It is a matter of regret that the series is now long out of print and only occasional single volumes appear on the second-hand book shelves.

Tribute must also be paid to the publishers of this present series of *Guides* for their consistent, imaginative programme of publishing of true crime titles; the Harrap list is particularly strong in the field of the forensic sciences. Happily, many of these are either in print or periodically reprinted.

For many of the historical cases (for example, that of the Reverend Peter Vine) there are few reliable modern sources. In this event contemporary references (most of them used by the authors in compiling this *Guide*) have been cited, though they are not freely available outside the national archives and book depositories.

As a postscript, this may be an appropriate occasion on which once again to thank the staff of the British Library Reading Room for their unfailing courtesy and expertise. Much of this Series was compiled at desk T9, and it is no exaggeration to say that it would have been far poorer in content were it not for the BL resources.

ALLAWAY, Thomas Henry
Famous Trials No. 9, W. Lloyd Woodland. Geoffrey Bles, London, 1929.
Mr Justice Avory, Stanley Jackson. Gollancz, London, 1935.
Seven Murderers, Christmas Humphreys. Heinemann, London, 1931.
Crime and its Detection, W. Teignmouth Shore. Gresham, London, 1931.

ARNOLD, Heather
[Account derived from contemporary newspaper records].

ATHOE, Thomas and Son
The Newgate Calendar: or, Malfactors Register, London, 1776.

AUSTIN, Thomas
The Newgate Calendar: or, Malfactors Register, London, 1776.

BACKHOUSE, Graham
[Account derived from contemporary newspaper records].

BLACK, Edward Ernest
Scales of Justice, Fenton Bresler. Weidenfeld and Nicholson, London, 1973.
The Detective Physician: The Life and Work of Sir William Willcox, Philip H. A. Willcox. Heinemann Medical, London, 1970.

BRANCH, Elizabeth and Mary
The Complete Newgate Calendar, ed. J. L. Rayner and G. T. Crook. Navarre Society, London, 1926.

BRYANT, Charlotte
Murderess, Patrick Wilson. Michael Joseph, London, 1971.

The Crime Doctors, Robert Jackson. Frederick Muller, London, 1966.

'CASTEL-A-MARE', Haunting of
Devon Mysteries, Judy Chard. Bossiney Books, Bodmin, 1979.
Ghosts I Have Seen, Violet Tweedale. Herbert Jenkins, London, 1920.

CHANNEL, Mary
The Complete Newgate Calendar, ed. J. L. Rayner and G. T. Crook, Navarre Society, London, 1926.

EDWARD, Martyr King of England, Assassination of
Lives of the Saints, ? Butler

FARRANT, Thomas, Death of
The Bristol Mercury, issues December 1867 to January 1868. Bristol.

GIFFARD, Miles
Reprieve: A Study of a System. Fenton Bresler. Harrap, London, 1965.
The Mind of the Murderer, Walter Lindesay Neustatter. Christopher Johnson, London, 1957.
Famous Criminal Cases No. 1, Rupert Furneaux. Allan Wingate, London, 195[0].

GOODERE, Samuel, et al
The Bristol Fratricide... [Bristol], 1741.
Memoirs of the Life and Death of Sir John Dineley Goodere...., Samuel Foote. [London], 1782.
A Genuine and Authentic History of the Life and Character of Samuel Goodere Esq... London, 1741.

GREENWOOD, Harold
Notable British Trials, ed. Winifred Duke, 1930.

Six Trials, Winifred Duke. Gollancz, London, 1934.
The Power of Poison, John Glaister. Christopher Johnson, London, 1954.

HEATH, Neville George Clevely
Notable British Trials, ed. Macdonald Critchley, 1953.
Borstal Boy: The Uncensored Story of Neville Heath, Gerald Byrne. John Hill Productions, London, 1954.
Portrait of a Sadist, Paull Hill. Neville Spearman, London, 1960.
The Mind of the Murderer, Walter Lindesay Neustatter. Christopher Johnson, London, 1957.

HINKS, Reginald Ivor
Criminal Files, John Rowland. Pedigree Books, London, [1957].
Crimes That Made News, Bernard O'Donnell. Burke, London, 1954.

JONES, Harold
Children Who Kill, Patrick Wilson. Michael Joseph, London, 1973.

KENT, Constance
Saint With Red Hands, Yseult Bridges. Jarrolds, London, 1954.
Murder at Smutty Nose, and Other Murders, Edmund Pearson. Heinemann, London, 1927.
Victorian Murderesses, Mary S. Hartman. Robson Books, London, 1977.
The Great Crime of 1860, J. W. Stapleton. London, 1861.

LEE, John 'Babbacombe'
The Prison Cell in its Lights and Shadows, J. Pitkin. Sampson Low, Edinburgh, 1918.
My Experience as an Executioner, James Berry. David and Charles (reprint), Newton Abbott, 1972.
The Reluctant Hangman, Justin Atholl. John Long, London, 1956.

MORGAN, Davy
Criminal Chronology, Baldwin and Knapp. London, 1809.

MORGAN, Edward
The Complete Newgate Calendar, ed. J. L. Rayner and G. T. Crook. Navarre Society, London, 1926.

O'BRYAN, Patrick
The Newgate Calendar: or, Malefactors Register. London, 1773.

ONUFREJCZYC, Michael
Famous Criminal Trials No. 2, Rupert Furneaux. Allan Wingate, London, 19[?].
Great Manhunters of the Yard, Leonard Gribble. John Long, London, 1953.

PHILLIPS, Tom, Death of
Seek Out the Guilty, David Thomas. John Long, London, 1969.

ROGERS, John
Famous Criminal Cases, Rupert Furneaux. Allan Wingate, London, 19[?].

ROWLANDS, John and Edward, *et al*
Seek Out the Guilty, David Thomas. John Long, London, 1969.

SHRIMPTON, Jack (alias PARKER)
The Complete Newgate Calendar, ed. J. L. Rayner and G. T. Crook. Navarre Society, London, 1926.

STOURTON, Lord, *et al*
The Newgate Calendar: or, Malefactors Register. London, 1776.

THOMAS, Annie, Murder of
Six Trials, Winifred Duke. Gollancz, London, 1934.
Criminal Files, John Rowland. Pedigree Books, London, [1957].
Poison Mysteries Unsolved, C. J. S. Thompson. Hutchinson, London, 1937.

THOMAS, Sarah Harriet
Notable British Trials: The Trial of Kate Webster, ed. Elliott O'Donnell, 1925.

VINE, Reverend Peter
A warning piece to all clergymen... Exeter and London, 1743.
Execution of the Rev. Peter Vine... [London, 1811].

GENERAL REFERENCE BOOKS

The Guilty and the Innocent, William Bixley. Souvenir Press, London, 1957.
True Crime Diary, James Bland. Futura, London, 1987.
Sir Bernard Spilsbury: His Life and Cases, Douglas G. Browne and Tom Tullett. Harrap, London, 1951.
Murderers England, Ivan Butler.
Memories of Murder, Tony Fletcher. Weidenfeld and Nicholson, London, 1986.
The Murderers' Who's Who, J. H. H. Gaute and Robin Odell. Harrap, London, 1979.
Murder Whatdunit, J. H. H. Gaute and Robin Odell. Harrap, London, 1982.
Murder Whereabouts, J. H. H. Gaute and Robin Odell. Harrap, London, 1986.
The Pleasures of Murder, ed. Jonathan Goodman. Allison and Busby, London, 1983.
Murders of the Black Museum, Gordon Honeycombe. Hutchinson, London, 1982.
Francis Camps, Robert Jackson. Hart-Davis MacGibbon, London, 1975.
Poisoner in the Dock, John Rowland. Arco, London, 1960.
The Concise Encyclopaedia of Crime and Criminals, Sir Harold Scott. Andre Deutsch, London, 1965.
Forty Years of Murder, Professor Keith Simpson. Harrap, London, 1978.

Select Bibliography

Mostly Murder, Sir Sidney Smith. Harrap, London, 1959.

Cause of Death, Frank Smyth. Orbis, London, 1980.

Companion to Murder, E. Spencer Shew. Cassell, London, 1960.

Clues To Murder, Tom Tullett. Grafton Books, London, 1986.

Strictly Murder, Tom Tullett. Bodley Head, London, 1975. (Republished as *Murder Squad*, Granada, 1981).

The Black Museum, Bill Waddell and Jonathan Goodman, Harrap, London, 1987.

A Casebook of Murder, Colin Wilson. Leslie Frewin, London, 1969.

Encyclopaedia of Murder, Colin Wilson and Patricia Pitman. Arthur Barker, London, 1961.

Encyclopaedia of Modern Murder, Colin Wilson and Donald Seaman. Arthur Barker, London, 1983.

Mammoth Book of True Crime, Colin Wilson, Robinson Publishing, London, 1988.

PICTURE CREDITS

The compilers would like to express their gratitude to the many people who have allowed them access to their collections and given permission for the use of their material in this series of *Guides*. We apologise in advance to any whose copyright we have failed to trace.

Index

Index

Index

An Invitation To Join

THE MURDER CLUB

The publication of this series of *Guides* has been timed to coincide with the Club's Public Membership launch.

Criminology will no longer be the exclusive domain of scientists, lawyers and writers, The Murder Club enables every one of its Members to become an arm-chair detective.

You, the readers, are invited to join in the Club's fascinating research programmes, to contribute your ideas to its publications and entertainments, its 'Notorious Locations' tours and presentations.

Or simply sit back and enjoy the regular packages of intriguing true-life crime material prepared by The Murder Club *exclusively* for its Members, stimulating the imagination with a little fireside detective work.

Membership benefits for 1988–1989 include, among other features:

★ The Murder Club's own unique badge, membership card, and personal Certificate of Membership. (Dispatched with Introductory Membership Pack.)

★ *The Murder Club Bulletin,* a two-monthly magazine devoted to all aspects of real-life crime – new cases, old cases, cases to marvel at, cases to solve. A fully illustrated miscellany of information and entertainment; plus full news of Murder Club activities in Great Britain and abroad. (Dispatched to Members bi-monthly.)

continued overleaf

THE MURDER CLUB

APPLICATION FOR MEMBERSHIP

I enclose the sum of £25*, being the annual Membership Fee of The Murder Club. I understand that this entitles me to all the benefits listed above and outlined in the introductory Membership Pack.

Name _____

Address _____

_____

_____

Signature _____

Please send completed form and remittance to:
The Murder Club
35 North Audley Street, London W1Y 1WG

*Due to high overseas postal rates, a small supplement of £5 will be charged to Members outside the British Isles.

★ *Murder World Wide,* a series of illustrated booklets covering Classics of Murder from around the world. Each issue is complete in itself and a printed slip-case will be presented to contain each series as an annual 'volume'. (Dispatched to Members monthly.)

★ *Cabinet of Crime,* a companion series of monthly publications dealing with immortal cases from the annals of British murder. Specifications as *Murder World Wide.*

★ *The Black Museum,* title of The Murder Club's own mail-order catalogue with a difference. A unique illustrated document covering a wide range of publications, facsimiles, posters, prints, photographs and objects, exclusively produced by the Club to enable its Members to build up their own 'home Black Museum' of thought-provoking conversation pieces. (Published annually with bi-monthly supplements.)

★ The Murder-Book Club. A service offered to Members through our contact with the specialist publishers of popular true-crime books. A two-monthly list of available titles will be issued – many of which are available through the Club at lower than publishers' catalogue prices. (Updated bi-monthly.)

★ Concessionary prices and privileges on a wide range of Murder Club and related products, entertainments, and activities.

For Annual Membership including Introductory Membership Pack and monthly supplements, please complete the form overleaf enclosing the sum of £25.

Or send £2.50 (deductible from Membership) for further information.